A Teachable Spirit

A Teachable Spirit

Recovering the Teaching Office in the Church

Richard Robert Osmer

Westminster/John Knox Press
Louisville, Kentucky

©1990 Richard Robert Osmer

Scripture quotations are from the Revised Standard Version of the Bible, copyrighted 1946, 1952, ©1971, 1973 by the Division of Christian Education of the National Council of the Churches of Christ in the U.S.A., and are used by permission.

Book design by Gene Harris

First edition

Published by Westminster/John Knox Press
Louisville, Kentucky

PRINTED IN THE UNITED STATES OF AMERICA
9   8   7   6   5   4   3   2   1

Library of Congress Cataloging-in-Publication Data

Osmer, Richard Robert, 1950–
    A teachable spirit : recovering the teaching office in the church
/ Richard Robert Osmer. — 1st ed.
        p.   cm.
    Includes bibliographical references and index.
    ISBN 0-664-25079-3

    1. Church—Teaching office.   2. Protestant churches—
Doctrines.
3. Church—Authority.   I. Title.
BT91.075   1990
262'.8—dc20   89-29049
                                                            CIP

To Sally—

friend

colleague

partner in life

and love—

one who has

taught me much

Contents

Preface and Acknowledgments   ix

PART ONE: Seeking a Third Way

1. Mainline Churches in Crisis   3
2. The Perils and Possibilities of Modernization   24
3. A Teachable Spirit   46

PART TWO: Discovering the Teaching Office

4. Structure and Spirit   61
5. *Magisterium:* The Teaching Office
   in the Roman Catholic Tradition   73
6. Martin Luther's Break
   with the Roman Catholic *Magisterium*   84
7. The Teaching Office in the Thought
   and Practice of John Calvin   107

PART THREE: Recovering the Teaching Office

8. Recovering the Teaching Office
   in a New Theological Paradigm   139
9. Centers of Authority in the Teaching Office:
   A Contemporary Proposal   175
10. Congregational Education and the Nurture
    of Practical Theological Reflection:
    A Faith Development Perspective   212

Epilogue   252

Notes   255

Index   295

Preface and Acknowledgments

Noticing what is absent is more difficult than we commonly suppose. If a person grows up in a suburb in which all the trees were leveled when the houses were built, it is highly unlikely that he or she will miss the massive beauty of an old oak or the splendor of a large maple in fall. What is missing remains hidden, for it has never been part of the person's experience.

When items that are crucial to human life are missing, the best clues we often have for their absence are a dull ache or a sense of void. An absence of real parenting, for instance, leaves many children with an abiding, if elusive, hunger for significant relationships that can confirm their sense of worth.

Mainline Protestantism faces the difficult task of noticing the absence of an authentic teaching office in its contemporary life. The fact that this essential ministry of the church has been missing for so long makes it even more difficult to recognize what is not present. Its absence, however, is felt in the increasingly widespread sense of something missing; something of great importance is not present in the church's life.

It is rare for persons in congregations to use the language of scripture and Christian tradition to interpret the events and relationships of which they are a part. Even within the church's own life, pastoral relationships, committee meetings, and church school classes all too often make little use of the symbols and narratives of scripture and doctrine to guide their discussion and help them make decisions.

It is no longer possible for Protestant ministers to assume a firm foundation of biblical and theological understandings among their members. Something of great import is missing, leaving the minister at a tremendous disadvantage. How can scripture be appealed to in a committee meeting, if the members of the committee have not thought seriously about the Bible since childhood? How can the doctrine of justification be used to offer hope to a guilt-ridden adulterer, if that person thinks of God primarily as a moral tally counter? How can a minister in good conscience challenge his or her church to a life of obedience in a Sunday morning sermon, knowing full well that the majority of the congregation will interpret the message moralistically? Ministers ought to be able to assume basic understandings of scripture and church doctrine that can be brought to bear upon some situation or relationship, but these basic understandings are just not there.

This is not to say, however, that the problem rests solely or even primarily with a biblically and theologically unschooled laity. What is missing from mainline Protestantism today is a vital teaching office by which the foundations of Bible and Christian doctrine are taught to the members of most congregations. In the absence of such a teaching office, individuals are left to sort out their own understandings of God and the moral life or to turn to groups offering absolutes to fill the void they are experiencing.

This book is an attempt to reopen the question of the church's teaching office in mainline Protestanism. It is based on a relatively simple premise: The single most important task before the mainline Protestant churches today is the reestablishment of a vital teaching ministry at every level of church life. In order to establish this claim and to chart a course toward its fulfillment, the book is divided into three parts. Part One examines contemporary American culture, focusing especially on the problematic nature of the teaching office in the face of rampant individualism and counter-modern authoritarianism. The argument will be made that mainline churches can represent a third way between these two cultural extremes.

This third way grows out of the Reformation heritage of these churches, the focus of Part Two. In the thought of Luther and Calvin an understanding of the teaching office can be found that recognizes the need for real teaching authority in the church but does not absolutize that authority. Scripture as it witnesses to the gospel always remains the authority of authorities in the Reformation churches. This does not negate a legitimate role for teaching authority, however, and it is the task of this part to discern what shape and form that authority should take.

Part Three attempts to relate the Reformers' thought to our present situation. While there is much to be learned from Luther and Calvin, both men lived and wrote in situations that were quite different from our own and cannot be taken over in an unreconstructed fashion. Our task is to retrieve their thought in the present cultural situation. Accordingly, this final part attempts to recover a broader understanding of the teaching office in which multiple authorities and roles play important parts, giving special attention to congregational education within this broader configuration of teaching authorities.

At its best, this book opens a question that is worthy of reflection and discussion. My hope is not so much to have others agree with all that is written here as to convince them that the issues surrounding the rehabilitation of a stronger teaching office are worth taking seriously. If that takes place, I will deem my work a success.

The research and reflection behind this book have stretched over several years, and many persons have provided assistance along the way. Special thanks go go my former teachers and colleagues at Candler School of Theology, James Fowler and Charles Gerkin. The influence of Fowler's work in faith development theory and Gerkin's in practical theology will be evident throughout this book. Jack Nelson, Jean Bozeman, Charles Melchert, Margaret Krych, and Mary Boys read portions of the manuscript while it was taking shape, and their comments proved helpful. Sara Little, my former colleague at Union Theological Seminary in Virginia, deserves special thanks. Her intellectual acumen and supportive spirit helped me deepen and clarify my thoughts at many crucial points. Two students, Jean Theis and Marnie Miller-Gutsell, were especially helpful in the preparation of this manuscript, as was Sally Hicks, a member of the seminary staff. Appreciation also is offered to President T. Hartley Hall and Dean William Arnold of Union Theological Seminary. Their support has been invaluable; without it this book could not have been written.

A final word of thanks goes to the members of my family. My children, Richard and Sarah, have been a constant source of joy, reminding me that there is more to life than work. My wife, Sally, to whom this book is dedicated, has helped in many different ways, offering support, professional insight, and a gentle reminder that everything need not be said in one book. To my family goes my deepest thanks.

Richmond, Virginia, 1989   R. R. O.

PART ONE

Seeking
a Third Way

1

Mainline Churches in Crisis

Throughout the past decade, the mainline Protestant churches in this country have gone through a period of significant self-doubt and reassessment. Changes of major proportions have been taking place in the landscape of American religious life. Many in the mainline churches have begun to wonder if they are going to be left behind. Congregations and denominations have continued to struggle with the vestiges of the civil rights and antiwar movements, which challenged and divided mainline churches. The children and youth of these churches have been vulnerable to new cults and Eastern religions or have been willing to give up religious commitment altogether and join the growing ranks of the nonaffiliated. Conservative churches have been growing, while mainline churches have been experiencing the most precipitous membership decline in this century.

Mainline Disestablishment?

Many in the mainline churches have begun to ask themselves where they went wrong. Intuitively, thoughtful laypeople sensed what social scientists were beginning to demonstrate on the basis of demographics and cultural analysis: The mainline Protestant churches were being replaced as centers of influence and power in American life. Historians and social scientists began to ask if a "third disestablishment" of mainline Protestantism was taking place in contemporary America.[1] Legally, religion was first disestablished with the framing of the Constitution in the separation of church and state; culturally, the hegemony of Protestantism as *the* culture-shaping force was severely shaken during the 1920s and 1930s, which represents a second disestablishment. Other faiths, especially Judaism and Roman Catholicism, began to make their way into the mainstream of American life. Many have now started to ask if a "third disestablishment" began to take place in the 1960s, involving an intensification of religious pluralism and an accompanying decrease in the mainline churches' influence.

Persons within and without the mainline churches have begun to raise serious questions about whether the mainline churches have lost their ability to articulate a dynamic, person-changing, and culture-transforming vision of religion. History tells of the rise and decline of many movements and institutions. Have the mainline churches entered a period of decline? Is the third disestablishment more than a temporary fad, the product of the media's fascination with "born again" Christianity? Does it go beyond a momentary swing of the pendulum back to "spiritual" religion after the tumultuous years of social protest and change in the 1960s?

This book will argue that the recent changes which have taken place in American religion are of major, long-lasting significance and are likely to affect the mainline Protestant churches for years to come. Clearly, a shift in the role of the mainline churches vis-à-vis the broader culture has begun to take place. The sooner the leaders of these churches understand what is happening and why, the better off they will be. Mainline Protestant churches face today a cultural situation radically different from what they faced in the past, a situation that challenges their very identity as a culture-shaping religious presence.

The leadership of these churches must begin to forge responses that go far beyond those currently present in most congregations and denominations. Ill-conceived, theologically deficient evangelism programs that demand little commitment on the part of new members are hardly an adequate response to sagging membership rolls! Nor does a self-righteous retrenchment in social action attitudes and ministerial styles reminiscent of the 1960s point the way ahead. Mainline churches must begin to form responses to the challenges before them that go far deeper than either of these.

In the present work we will focus attention on only one aspect of the mainline church's response: the revival of a vital teaching office. True, far more than a restoration of an authoritative teaching ministry is necessary in the mainline churches today; of particular importance is the revival of preaching and worship and the theological renewal of pastoral care that has begun to take place in recent years.[2] The restoration of a church that can teach with authority, however, may be *the* pressing issue before the mainline churches today. A strong teaching ministry is especially needed in the face of the modern individualism and counter-modern authoritarianism that are so prevalent in American society.

It is possible that the mainline churches' third disestablishment will afford them the opportunity to make a more authentic Christian witness in American society than was possible when they were ensconced in a position of cultural influence and power. It is equally possible that these churches will move into a period of decline in which they do little more than minister to the personal needs of individuals and families during moments of crisis or life-cycle transition.

Which response the mainline churches make will be determined in large part by the vision, competence, and understanding of the leaders who guide them into the future. It is imperative that the leadership of these churches rediscover and even recover the heritage of the classical teaching office as formulated by Martin Luther and John Calvin.[3] The works of these men give understandings of the teaching office that are surprisingly relevant to the issues confronting mainline churches today: the importance of establishing an authoritative teaching ministry that is not authoritarian; the need to teach the basics of Christian faith in order to provide a strong sense of Christian identity; the role of the church in teaching the broader culture; and the important but limited role of individual conscience in the appropriation of the church's teachings.

The American mainline Protestant churches are at a crossroads. Which path they take may very well rest on whether they can restore the teaching ministry of the church to its rightful place of importance. In order to understand better the social context in which this task will be pursued, we must examine the kinds of changes that have characterized the mainline churches over the past decades.

American Religion in Transition

Three trends in particular are worthy of special attention in attempting to understand the shifting role of the mainline Protestant churches in contemporary America: (1) the decline in their membership, (2) the loss of their role as the dominant force in shaping the values of the broader culture and their newfound status as one of many players in an increasingly pluralistic society, and (3) their recent ambiguous relationship to the traditional civic faith of American life. Each trend has received considerable attention in recent years, often in a manner that castigates the mainline churches for failures on their part. These castigations, however, are overly simplistic. A variety of complex trends, both inside and outside these churches, have contributed to their changing position in American life. Not all these trends, moreover, should be evaluated in a strictly negative fashion.

Declining Membership

The first trend, a decline in the membership of the mainline churches, is a case in point. Frequently, conservative critics point to the rapid growth of evangelical and fundamentalist churches and the sagging membership of the mainline denominations as evidence that the latter are soon to be replaced in the new religious America. The mainline churches, so the argument goes, sold their souls to modernity by way of theological liberalism during the first two decades of this century and are now feeling the aftershocks of liberalism's demise on a broad cultural level. A deeper analysis of this trend among the various families of Protestantism can dispel a variety of falsehoods that are commonly accepted.

Wade Clark Roof and William McKinney have constructed a helpful typology of religious America that divides American Protestants into four different families: liberal, moderate, black, and conservative.[4] In large part, the typology is based on the different theological and cultural traditions that lie behind each denomination, traditions shaped in markedly different ways during the liberal/fundamentalist controversies of the first part of this century. Liberal Protestants include Episcopalians, United Church of Christ, and Presbyterians. Moderate Protestants include United Methodists, Lutherans, Disciples of Christ, Northern Baptists, and Reformed churches. Black Protestants include Methodists, Northern Baptists, and Southern Baptists. Conservative Protestants include Southern Baptists, Churches of Christ, Nazarenes, Pentecostals/Holiness, Assemblies of God, Churches of God, and Adventists.

As Roof and McKinney point out, growth and decline of membership in these families are dependent on two basic factors: their ability to reproduce their own membership and their capacity to hold on to their members.[5] In terms of church life, these two factors are best thought of in terms of birth and death rates and switching, the movement of members from one denomination to another. The demographics of these two factors are quite revealing.

Differences in birthrate between women in the more liberal churches of mainline Protestantism and those in conservative churches go a long way toward explaining the differences in growth rate. These differences have been in existence for several generations. The birthrate for liberal Protestant women over forty-five is 2.27; for moderate Protestant women it is 2.67; and for conservative Protestant women, 3.12.[6]

The same trend is in evidence among women under forty-five, even as the overall birthrates of all groups have declined. In the liberal churches, it is 1.60; in moderate churches, 1.80; and in conservative churches, 2.01.[7] To translate these statistics into more graphic terms, if children were born in the liberal mainline churches at the same rate as conservative churches, it would increase the membership of their churches by more than 2.2 million members annually.

This birthrate differential is all the more important when it is coupled with an equally important fact: There are fewer women in the liberal churches of childbearing age. In large part, this is closely related to the second factor of import in church size: switching. Not only do the mainline churches have lower birth rates, they have done a far poorer job than conservative Protestants of holding on to their members, especially their youth and young adults.

Sometimes referred to as the "circulation of the saints," switching has been a long-standing part of American religious life. In recent years, about 40 percent of all American Protestants have switched denominations at one time or another.[8] In the past, the most important pattern of switching in mainline Protestantism was the tendency of persons to switch to churches of higher status as they moved up the socioeconomic ladder. While this pattern continues, far more diversity characterizes switching in contemporary Protestantism. While older adults still switch from one denomination to another according to an upwardly mobile pattern, young adults are just as likely to move to the nonaffiliated sector or switch churches for ideological and life-style reasons.

Several switching trends are extremely interesting in light of common perceptions of the decline of membership in mainline churches. For one thing, the liberal mainline churches are not experiencing membership declines because of an exodus of their members to conservative churches. They actually gain more members from the moderate and conservative families of Protestantism (34.3 percent) than they lose to them (24.8

percent).[9] There is some evidence that the quality of members they gain, however, is less than the quality of those which they lose, quality being defined here in terms of church involvement.[10] It is the moderate mainline churches that come out the big losers in religious switching, losing more members (20.4 percent) to other religious families than they gain (18.2 percent).[11]

One of the most telling switching patterns is the overall loss of members in both liberal and moderate mainline churches to the nonaffiliated sector of the population. The mainline churches do a far worse job than the conservatives in holding on to their members. This trend has intensified as American society has become more tolerant of nonparticipation in religion. The liberal mainline churches fare the worst in this regard, losing 8 percent to the nonaffiliates while picking up only 2.2 percent from this group.[12] Roof and McKinney point out the significance of this trend: "This leads to the observation, one which goes against popular wisdom, that the challenge to liberal Protestantism comes not so much from the conservative faiths as from the growing secular drift of many of their not-so-highly-committed members."[13]

This observation is of great significance in evaluating the decline of membership in the mainline churches over the past two or three decades. It is not the fact of declining membership in and of itself that threatens the future of the mainline churches; this can be accounted for in terms of the overall reduction in the birthrate. What is truly alarming is the inability of these churches to hold on to their own members, especially their youth and young adults. As Roof and McKinney point out, the lure of secularity, of nonaffiliation, is the real threat. What is going on in these churches that renders their younger members so vulnerable to external cultural forces? Is the vision of the Christian life that is articulated so flaccid that many younger members find no compelling reason to remain affiliated with religion at all? Has modern individualism made such inroads that these churches are unable to foster a sense of communal identity?

Decline in membership in mainline churches is far more complex than is commonly recognized. Sophisticated evangelism programs, advertising campaigns, and television ministries do not really address the more fundamental problems of communal and individual religious identity that lie behind this trend. Even if these churches were to address these issues and begin to hold on to their own members, the fact of lower birthrates means these churches are likely to remain smaller than the more conservative churches in the emerging religious America.

Declining Influence

This brings us to a second trend that characterizes the shifting status of the mainline Protestant churches in American culture: the loss of their role as the dominant force in shaping the values of the broader culture and their newfound status as one of many players in an increasingly pluralistic society. The decline in the size of mainline Protestant denominations is not merely a shift within Protestantism, but is indicative of a decline in the overall size of the Protestant majority. In 1952, Protestantism represented 67 percent of the American population. At the present, it represents 57 percent.[14]

Beginning in the 1920s and 1930s, the Protestant mainline began to adjust to the increased presence of Roman Catholicism and Judaism in American life. This trend has continued throughout this century. Roman Catholics, for example, now represent 28 percent of the total American population.[15] More importantly, they have moved into the mainstream of American life in terms of education, occupation, status, and income. As recently as the election of John F. Kennedy in 1960, many Americans expressed fears about having a Roman Catholic as president. Two decades later, Catholic bishops are now looked to by many in the American population for guidance on the economy, abortion, and nuclear disarmament.

This is indicative of a broader trend in American religious life. The pluralism that began in the 1920s and 1930s has accelerated over the last twenty years. Not only are more religious options available, they are treated with greater tolerance. The nonaffiliated portion of the population is currently 9 percent of the overall population. Genuine pluralism is now a reality in American society. The mainline Protestant churches are only one player among many on the religious scene.

The great temptation in the face of this reality is to view it in totally negative terms, nostalgically yearning for days gone by. It is not clear, however, that the rise of greater pluralism in American society should be evaluated in this fashion. While placing the mainline churches under a great deal of stress during this time of transition, it may well be that the trend toward pluralism could free these churches to discover a new vision of their vocation in American life, one that is less closely linked to the values and beliefs of American culture.

It is possible that as the mainline Protestant churches have less hegemony in the cultural mainstream, they will be less inclined to confuse Christianity with the American way of life. As one force among many on the American religious scene, they are now forced to become self-conscious about the vision of society and public life that grows out of their theological traditions.[16] Their disestablishment might well serve as the occasion for a more self-critical and transforming relationship to American culture, a relationship based on a healthier tension between Christianity and its social context.

Increasing Ambiguities of Civic Faith

This possibility is particularly brought into focus by the third trend that characterizes the American mainline churches today: their increasingly ambiguous relationship to the traditional civic faith of American society. From the very beginning of this country's existence, Protestantism has played an important role in fostering a vision of America as standing in a special relationship to God and being called to play a special role in the world. Religious persons have been confident that loyalty to God and loyalty to country were closely related.

This civic faith has had both positive and negative dimensions. On the positive side, it has provided a common set of symbols and beliefs by which a widely diverse people could be brought together. It has also moderated our culture's emphasis on individual freedom and initiative in helpful ways by articulating a religiously based vision of the common good. On the negative side, this civic faith has frequently been unable to maintain a distinction between love of God and love of country. Often, the latter has been allowed to determine the former. Western-style capitalism, democratic governmental processes, and cultural forms of individualism virtually have been identified with the will of God. In this situation, the civic faith has not been based on a healthy tension between religion and the surrounding culture.

The mainline churches historically have participated in both the best and the worst of American civic faith. At important moments in American history, the churches have appealed to religious values and beliefs to criticize accepted social practices, bringing about significant changes in the culture. The abolitionist movement in the mid-1800s and the civil rights movement in the last three decades were both religiously based. Just as frequently, however, the mainline churches have done little more than legitimize an amalgamation of the American way of life and the Christian way of life. In recent years, this was particularly evident during the 1950s when the mainline denominations seemed to be building a new church on every suburban corner. This overidentification of God and country was seriously called into question by many teenagers and young adults during the 1960s. They rejected outright the kind of civic faith that seemed to give religious sanction to racism and a war many perceived to be unjust.

The debate that ensued in the mainline churches did much to make their relationship to traditional civic faith deeply problematic. Frequently, denominational officials and clergy publicly advocated positions at variance with many in the pews. Not only did this create deep ideological divisions within many congregations, it also gave rise to a hands-off view of civic faith. In the face of real and potential controversy in this area, many in the mainline churches called for their leaders to abandon altogether preaching and teaching about matters of public concern. This has reinforced the privatization of religion, which already had gone a long way toward removing the mainline churches from public life.[17]

The net result has been to make the mainline churches' historic relationship to civic faith deeply problematic. But can we evaluate this situation in exclusively negative terms? Clearly, the theologians and leaders of the mainline churches must begin to articulate a new understanding of the relationship between God and country. It is no longer enough to appeal to an easy identification of Christ and culture. But can we really say that this is bad?

Is it not possible that a new, more critical style of civic faith will emerge out of the mainline churches in the years ahead? For all their recent problems, these churches have been far more supportive of the civil rights of minorities than conservative Protestantism. Indeed, studies have shown that conservative Protestantism actually has the effect of making its members more intolerant of the civil rights of minorities.[18] Perhaps, out of the struggle within mainline churches to discover a new civic faith, a style of religious presence in public life will emerge that can draw out the potential for good that is present in the new cultural pluralism.

Back to Benedict?

There can be little doubt that mainline churches are in the midst of a transition. The decline in membership, the prospects of a more limited role in a genuinely pluralistic society, and the problematic nature of traditional civic faith are indicative of changes in the status and role of mainline Protestantism. It is not clear at this point how these churches will respond to the new situation that confronts them.

During the early part of his career H. Richard Niebuhr wrote a small article titled "Back to Benedict?"[19] In the article, he explored the possibility that contemporary Protestantism might benefit from an appropriation of certain disciplines and attitudes that were found in ancient Benedictine monasticism. The church, he implied, periodically needs times of withdrawal from the surrounding culture in order to sort out the boundaries by which it defines its identity. It especially needs such times when it has lost its bearings through an overaccommodation to the surrounding world. Such periods of withdrawal are not based on a rejection of the world or a lack of commitment to social transformation. Rather, as Niebuhr puts it, "Separating itself from the world it might recover its integrity."[20] The church temporarily stands apart from the world, in order to clarify its mission on the world's behalf.

The use of the image of Benedict by Niebuhr aptly expresses the need of the mainline churches today. In the face of the changes in their role and status in contemporary American life, these churches would do well to focus temporarily on issues of identity and heritage, seeking greater clarity about their role as messengers and servants of the God revealed in Jesus Christ.

This is not to suggest a literal withdrawal of mainline churches from American life into a quietistic privatism or a willful disregard for public affairs. Rather, what is desperately needed is a time apart, a kind of temporary monastic retreat during which these churches can rid themselves of a frantic attempt to recapture the dominant role they once played in American life. They would do well to use this time apart to encounter the classic resources of their faith, listening deeply to the message of scripture and tradition as they search for the way forward.

The boundaries of American religion have shifted in recent years. It is appropriate for mainline churches to focus temporarily on their own boundaries in order to become clearer about who they are and what they have to offer to the new cultural situation in which they will carry out their ministries.

An important item to be clarified in this process is the nature and function of the teaching office in the American Protestant church. Classical Protestantism as found in Luther and Calvin represents a distinctive way of thinking about the teaching authority of the church. It clearly affirms the role of authoritative church teaching without being anti-intellectual or authoritarian. It holds great promise for the determination of a kind of teaching authority that is a middle way between the extremes of individualism and authoritarianism that are so prominent in American culture today. It advocates a real but fallible role for church teachings that are defined and promulgated through a constellation of offices and agencies in the church that engage in an intensive, self-critical dialogue.

Part Two will explore the resources of Protestantism and the broader Christian tradition that could help the contemporary Protestant church begin to think creatively about the form that the teaching office might take today. Whether or not mainline churches emerge from this transition with a new, more authentic Christian witness in American life depends in large part on the recovery of functions and structures of the teaching office that have dissipated in recent years. Can mainline churches find ways of resisting the secular drift of their own members, pointed to by Roof and McKinney, without succumbing to the authoritarian alternative that is so successfully exemplified by many conservative churches today?

The Teaching Office Defined

We have used the term "teaching office" several times already. While the term is not a new one, it has taken on certain specific connotations in current theological thought, especially in the debate over the nature of the *magisterium* in Roman Catholicism. It is necessary now to offer a preliminary definition of the way it is being used here.

The term "office" comes from the Latin *officium*, which was originally used to refer to a wide variety of things: duty, service, function, business, place, and appointment.[21] Of these many meanings, two have been appropriated by theology. First, "office" can be used to refer to the *function* that something carries out. For instance, we might say, "It is the office of the arteries to carry blood from the heart to all parts of the body." Here, the focus is on certain tasks or responsibilities that need to be carried out.[22]

In the second usage, "office" refers to the *position or institutional role* to which such tasks or responsibilities are attached. For example, we might say that the office of the President of the United States carries with it certain executive tasks in relation to the governing of this country. Similarly, we might say that it is the office of a mechanic to fix a person's car and that of a cashier to take a customer's money. Here, emphasis is placed on a role that carries out specific functions.

Throughout this book, the term "office" will refer primarily to the first definition. "Teaching office" points to the *teaching function* of the church. It is one of the church's ministries and is part of its *esse* or being. Without this function, the church would not be the church. It would cease to be. It is impossible, however, to think of the exercise of this function without also considering the different institutional roles and agencies that carry out the church's teaching ministry Function implies structure and process. One cannot exist without the other. This is the value of a phrase as rich as "teaching office " It implies both meanings simultaneously. Across the centuries, a wide range of institutional forms have emerged to carry out the church's teaching ministry. The teaching function has remained a constant part of the church's life, but the structures and processes by which it has been carried out have changed.

If the teaching office refers to a distinctive type of ministerial function in the church, how can we specify further what this function is? What are the distinguishing characteristics of the teaching office, especially in relation to other forms of ministry in the church? A variety of contemporary scholars have attempted to define the teaching ministry by comparing it to preaching or proclamation. C. H. Dodd has been especially influential in this regard.

In many of his writings, Dodd draws a sharp distinction between *kerygma* and *didache* or proclamation and teaching.[23] In his view, proclamation refers to the public preaching of the gospel to the non-Christian world, centering on Jesus' fulfillment of Old Testament prophecy, the saving significance of his death and resurrection, and his future coming as judge. Teaching, in contrast, is directed to those who already have faith and involves moral exhortation and instruction in the basic beliefs of the church in preparation for baptism.

In a similar fashion, James Smart distinguishes teaching from preaching.

> It is the same Jesus Christ who is to be taught and who is to be preached. The content of preaching and of teaching is the same. But preaching essentially is the proclamation of this Word of God to man in his unbelief. . . . Teaching essentially (but not exclusively) addresses itself to the situation of the man who has repented and turned to God and to the situation of children of believers who through the influence of their parents have in

them a measure of faith, even though they also have in them a
large measure of unbelief.[24]

There are many problems with the distinction Dodd and
Smart are attempting to make. Perhaps most importantly, it
cannot be grounded explicitly in Jesus' ministry, as many
scholars have pointed out.[25] As will become clearer at a later
point, it is not easy to distinguish teaching, preaching, and
acts of healing in the Gospels' accounts of Jesus' life and work.
Only as the church began to organize itself did various functions and roles in the church became more sharply distinguished. We must look for a more complex understanding of
the teaching office than Dodd and Smart provide.

The teaching function began to receive clearer definition
with the passing of the original generation of apostles and the
rapid expansion of the church. With the death of the eyewitnesses to Jesus' ministry, an authority vacuum was present in
the church. In the face of diverse doctrines and practices, how
could the church discern which were correct? As early as the
apostle Paul, competing versions of Christianity began to
emerge, raising the specter of heresy. As the church expanded
around the Mediterranean Sea, this threat became an actual-
ity, and the church was faced with the task of determining
how it could maintain continuity with the original message of
Jesus and the apostolic church.

In the face of this situation, the teaching office became especially important in the church, focusing on three central
tasks: (1) the determination of the normative beliefs and practices of the church, (2) the reinterpretation of these beliefs
and practices in shifting cultural and historical contexts, and
(3) the formation and sustenance of educational institutions,
processes, and curricula by which the church's normative beliefs and practices are taught, allowing them to be appropriated meaningfully by each new generation and grasped with
deeper understanding by individuals. The church has found it
necessary to carry out each of these tasks throughout its history, even as it done so through different structures and
forms.

Determining Normative Beliefs and Practices

The first task of the teaching office—the determination of
the church's normative beliefs and practices—focuses on the
activity of setting forth those teachings by which the church
identifies itself as a community. In large part this involves the

transmission and preservation of the core elements of the heritage of a church community, those items upon which its identity is based. On the surface, it seems odd to view this activity as part of the teaching ministry of the church, but further examination shows why this has been the case historically.

By definition, every community is bound together by a complex set of social definitions, norms, and practices by which its members can interpret the world and act in it.[26] These beliefs and practices allow community members to interpret both what the world *is* and what it *ought* to be.[27] As such, they are normative. Frequently, these norms and definitions are transmitted and transformed through processes that are largely unconscious—through socialization, for example, or through ordinary everyday interactions between members of the community.

At certain times, however, communities attempt to lift up and give specification to the normative beliefs and practices that constitute them. One of the most important times this takes place is when the identity of a community is threatened. In the first centuries of the church's life, for example, general councils were convened in the face of widespread disagreement and turmoil in order to define the theological positions that maintained genuine continuity with the message of Jesus and the apostolic church. These councils formulated the official teachings of the church.

Such explicit definition of the normative beliefs and practices of a community, however, does not take place only during times of crisis. It also occurs in conjunction with the projection of the *paideia* informing the educational efforts of a given community. *Paideia* comes from Greek culture and represents the self-conscious ideals of human good and excellence that determine how a society educates its members.[28] Under the impress of its *paideia*, a community decides the substance and the process of its educational activities.

Across the centuries, the church's determination of its normative beliefs and practices has taken place in conjunction with the Christian *paideia* informing its educational activities at any given time. Declaratory creeds, for example, which were used in baptismal services during the first century and formed an important part of catechetical instruction, reflected the community's consensus about the beliefs necessary to a proper cognitive apprehension of the God of Christianity.[29] These creeds functioned as part of the self-conscious ideal or *paideia* by which the church educated its members.

It is not as odd as it might seem at first glance that across the centuries the church has viewed its effort to determine the normative beliefs and practices by which it is maintained as a community in terms of the teaching office. In large measure, it has viewed this part of the teaching function in terms of the transmission of the normative expressions of the past by which the church has identified itself as a community. These are thought to provide continuity with the original message of Jesus and the apostolic church.

Reinterpreting Normative Beliefs and Practices

The determination of the normative beliefs and practices of the church at any given time, however, involves more than simple transmission. The teaching office never merely repeats the past in the present. It uses the inherited tradition as a way of formulating normative statements of faith and moral guidelines for today's church. The tradition is preserved by extending it into the present. This brings us to the second task of the teaching office, the ongoing reinterpretation of the church's normative beliefs and practices in the face of shifting cultural and historical contexts.

It would be wrong to distinguish this second task too sharply from the first one. The transmission of the church's past is always selective, involving an interpretative process. In a sense, the first task is concerned with maintenance of the *integrity* of the original witness in the church. The second task focuses on *intelligibility*, setting forth the faith in ways that are understandable and transformational in vastly different historical settings.[30] For this reason, the task of reinterpretation is important in its own right.

From the beginning, the mainstream of Christianity has attempted to be "catholic," relating its particular faith in Jesus Christ to all races, cultures, and eras and striving to be more than a self-enclosed sect. This has involved the church in a process of ongoing reinterpretation of the faith. It has addressed issues, used language, and formed patterns of life that were not explicitly a part of the original message of Jesus and the apostolic church. As it has attempted to teach and preach the gospel "once delivered," it has recognized that it can only truly do so by taking the risks inherent in addressing the sins and needs of its own day.

For example, with the delay of the parousia and the penetration of the church into the Gentile world, new interpretations of the faith were called for.[31] The Jewish eschatological framework presupposed by Jesus and the early church began to give way to one centered on Christology, focusing on the person and nature of Christ in relation to the Godhead.[32] The church began to develop teachings that were meaningful to persons whose worldview was quite different from that of Christians coming from a Jewish background.

At various points in the church's history, the reinterpretive task of the church's teaching office has stood in tension with its effort to transmit and preserve the normative expressions of the community's faith. Reinterpretation frequently involves stretching the inherited tradition in ways that seem to threaten continuity with the past. Innovation in such things as theological language, worship, and social relationships may appear to deviate from normative expressions of the faith that are important foci of the community's identity. For this reason, it is important to recognize that normative expressions of the community's faith inherited from the past—the official teachings of the church—were originally reinterpretations of the faith, limited by the language they use, the issues they address, and the worldview they assume.

The teaching office of the church must embrace the tension between its transmissive-preservative and reinterpretive functions. Ultimately, the church's normative beliefs and practices at any given time are an outgrowth of the interplay of these two tasks. Frequently, certain offices or agencies focus more attention on one or the other. Theologians, for example, may engage in reinterpretations of the faith that go far beyond what the ordinary believer is ready to accept. Representative bodies or denominational leaders such as bishops, on the other hand, may focus more energy on maintaining continuity with the past. Both are essential to the church's teaching ministry.

Forming the Means of Education

This brings us to the third task of the teaching function: the formation and sustenance of educational institutions, processes, and curricula by which the church's normative beliefs and practices are taught, allowing them to be appropriated meaningfully by each new generation and grasped with deeper understanding by individuals as they move through life. The teaching office of the church includes more than educational institutions and material. For instance, when a representative body of a denomination struggles to formulate moral guidelines on a contemporary social issue, the teaching office is at work. It is incumbent upon the church, however, to formulate special institutions, processes, and materials that are designed specifically to carry out its educational ministry. Across the centuries, it has done so in a wide variety of ways.

It is helpful to distinguish two key terms at this point: "education" and "teaching." While closely related, these terms can be distinguished conceptually. Education focuses on ongoing structures and patterns on the level of a community's life. Teaching focuses on specific occasions within educational structures and processes that attempt to foster learning and deepen understanding.

Here is a more precise definition: Education is a community's systematic and intentional effort to transmit and evoke knowledge, attitudes, values, and skills that are deemed worthwhile.[33] The terms "systematic" and "intentional" distinguish education from socialization or enculturation. Unquestionably, much learning takes place during human interaction, learning that is an unintentional byproduct of experience. Human beings are not instinctually patterned, so they must acquire a wide range of behaviors, attitudes, and communicative skills through unconscious processes of socialization.

As defined here, however, education involves *intentionality* in designing structures and processes by which learning takes place. Such intentionality extends through time; hence, it is *systematic*. A body of complex, interrelated information, skills, and attitudes must be mastered, necessitating an organization of institutions, material, and persons that projects an unfolding course of study over time. This traditionally has been referred to as an educational curriculum.

The intentionality and systemization of the educational curriculum means that education is invariably normative. Only certain knowledge, skills, values, and attitudes are deemed worthwhile and an appropriate focus of the educational curriculum. Should we place emphasis on math and the sciences, as happened in this country in the wake of the Soviet Union's launching of Sputnik? Is it important to focus on individual creativity and development, as progressive education does? Should the imitation of classical rhetoric and writing be primary, as in humanistic education? Intentionality and systemization inevitably mean that certain choices are made as to what should or should not be studied and prized. This is based on the *paideia* of a community, the self-conscious ideals of human good and excellence that determine the selective focus of the subject matter of education. Typically, the intellectuals of a community articulate these ideals in philosophical discourse, allowing debate on the basic premises of the community's education.[34]

Moreover, in choosing to invest its resources in transmitting and evoking certain knowledge, skills, attitudes, and values while ignoring others, a community inevitably participates in a political process. Politics is the means by which a community adjudicates various claims on its resources on the basis of competing understandings of what the community can and should be. This involves certain decisions about who should have power and how it should be wielded. The recent debates in public education over whether or not a "creationism" account of the origin of humanity should be taught in the public schools is a case in point. Different understandings of the public good are competing for power in an attempt to determine the shape of educational material and values.

The church's educational ministry is no different from that of any other community with regard to the selectivity of its curriculum. It focuses on some things and not on others. It may make the mastery of the Bible central to its educational program, for example, or focus on individual religious experiences. It is extremely important that persons with special competence in the church's teaching ministry attempt to articulate a full-scale theoretical justification for this normativity in theological or philosophical terms. It is on the basis of such reflection that a community can best debate the moral vision underlying its education.

Inevitably there are political dimensions to educational ministries.[35] In Protestantism and Roman Catholicism alike, there currently are highly charged debates about the political organization of the church in its determination of the church's normative beliefs and practices and the ongoing, authoritative reinterpretation of these beliefs and practices. While philosophy and theology have an important role to play in this political process, it would be naïve to believe that intellectual discourse alone determines the actual shape of the church's teaching ministry. We must come to grips with the institutional forms and processes by which a given church or denomination determines the central foci of its educational ministry and the appropriate processes for teaching and learning. The voices of some are heard; the voices of others are not.

Education, then, focuses on a community's systematic and intentional effort to transmit and evoke knowledge, attitudes, values, and skills that are deemed worthwhile. This involves ongoing institutional structures and processes that project an educational curriculum. The selectivity and normativity inherent in such a curriculum inevitably mean that education is involved in a political process in which different interpretations of the normative beliefs and practices of a community compete for power. These competing visions ultimately have philosophical and theological presuppositions that can be articulated through intellectual discourse.

Within this broad-ranging definition of education, the concept of teaching has a more limited role. As used here, teaching focuses on those specific occasions through which education takes place. Teaching always involves particular people in specific settings. It is an event, not an ongoing process or structure. Education includes more than teaching; it involves administration, the publication of resources and research, to name a few. Teaching, however, is the central goal.

At the heart of teaching is an increase in *understanding* of the subject matter on the part of the student.[36] Broader educational institutions and agencies may determine what knowledge, values, attitudes, and skills should be at the center of the educational process, but when it comes to the actual event of teaching, these items must be brought to bear in a way that enhances the understanding of the learner. Understanding should not be viewed in a narrow intellectual sense but as the integration of internal and external experience into cognitive processes and content in a manner affording meaning.

Teaching should be distinguished from indoctrination in which certain information and skills are presented in such a way as to assure their adoption by the student without any guarantee that he or she has understood what is being presented. In contrast, teaching focuses on an increase in the student's ability to comprehend and grasp the meaning of what is being learned. The subject matter must interact with the patterns of knowing that the student already possesses, being assimilated into them and expanding them. At the deepest level, teaching is based on respect for the student, respect that takes seriously his or her personal appropriation of the subject matter being taught.[37]

Such an understanding of teaching would seem to render the concept "teaching authority" contradictory. If teaching involves respect for the student's capacity to understand the subject matter, does not this rule out, by definition, all authoritarian imposition? It does indeed. However, the concept "authority" should not be confused with "authoritarianism," which implies the coercive imposition of unwelcome obligations and the arbitrary restriction of personal freedom.

In contrast, authority can refer to the possession of superior knowledge, skill, or wisdom that is looked to for guidance and direction out of freely given respect. When viewed along these lines, teaching authority points to a person's or office's ability to engage others in a learning process, directing their attention to certain ideas, issues, or moral imperatives in ways that deepen or transform their prior understandings.

Teaching authority in this sense can be contrasted with commanding authority.[38] The latter rests on juridical power— the ability to determine and enforce ideas and practices through legal means, using coercion if necessary. Persons with power command those under their influence to subscribe to certain beliefs or practices. Concern for the understanding of those being influenced and respect for their ability to give or withhold assent are eliminated. In contrast, teaching authority is fundamentally *persuasive* in its orientation. The authority of the teacher, especially in religious matters, depends on the perceived truth of the subject matter that he or she is offering to the student.

It is no accident that our examination of teaching and education has led us to a discussion of authority. Further examination of contemporary American culture will reveal the extent to which authority is problematic throughout our society, particularly the church. Clarity about the distinctive orientations and authority of education and teaching may provide a first step in sorting out how the teaching office of the church can reaffirm authoritative teaching without becoming authoritarian.

In its educational tasks, the teaching office invariably is involved in a political process by which the community determines the normative beliefs and practices that will constitute the center of its ongoing educational ministry. The political form and intellectual justification of this process have varied greatly from community to community and age to age. In Part Two we will examine the different institutional forms by which the teaching office has attempted to determine the normative beliefs and practices that are the focus of its educational ministry. As we will see, it is quite possible for the political process to overwhelm the noncoercive authority appropriate to teaching. Understanding gives way to blind obedience; respect for personal appropriation gives way to conformity.

The task facing the teaching office in American Protestantism today is a complex one. On the one hand, it must rehabilitate institutional offices, agencies, and structures through which the knowledge, skills, values, and attitudes that are normative for different ecclesiastical traditions are determined. On the other hand, it must do so in a fashion that does not negate the persuasive, respectful orientation proper to true teaching. The difficulties in achieving this balance are made all the harder by the widespread cultural trends of individualism and authoritarianism. It is to these trends that we now turn.

2

The Perils and Possibilities
of Modernization

The shifting religious landscape described in the first chapter reflects broad changes that have taken place in American religion in this century. In large part, these changes have been brought about in response to modernization, raising real questions about religion's ability to remain a viable force in the contemporary world. It is extremely important to view the challenges facing the mainline churches today in terms of the deeper social forces that modernization has unleashed. At least in part, how these churches respond to the various crises before them has been and will be determined by the stance they take toward modernity and the various ways it has influenced religion's role in the contemporary world.

Modernization Defined

Various theoretical paradigms have emerged by which to understand the process of modernization.[1] The point of view taken here is particularly influenced by the "classical" sociological tradition of Max Weber and, to a lesser extent, Emile Durkheim.[2] This tradition views institutional processes and human consciousness as existing in a reciprocal relationship. Neither is reducible to the other. The symbolic world of culture, including religion, has a life of its own and is not seen as merely the ideological concomitant of underlying socioeconomic relations, as in orthodox Marxism.

Human communities are seen as organized around what might be called social practices. These are patterns of human interaction that structure action and its meaning in socially shared ways. Everyday life is largely governed by the social practices that structure people's behavior, providing them with sets of role expectations allowing them to coordinate their actions with others. Social practices in this sense involve patterns of action grounded in the roles appropriate to different institutional contexts. But they also involve understanding or meaning. Persons are constantly engaged in a process of interpreting the actions of others and the demands of particular contexts and in forming responses that are deemed appropriate.

One of the most important dimensions of this interpretive process is the pattern of moral meaning by which a person judges the rightness and wrongness of his or her actions and those of others. As Clifford Geertz points out, moral meanings provide us models *of* and *for* the patterns that make up everyday life.[3] On the one hand, moral meanings reflect these patterns, helping persons make sense out of the social practices they typically engage in. Unless moral meanings provide models *of* everyday life in this sense, they will lose their power. On the other hand, they must also provide models *for* reality, images of the virtuous path that ought to be traveled as persons make their way through the world.

Historically, religion has played a crucial role in binding moral meanings to everyday life in both these senses. It has done so in two ways.[4] In its worship, teaching, and care it provides interpretive schemes of the ultimate context of existence in relation to which our moral reasoning is carried out. Even individuals and societies that are not explicitly religious seem to construct understandings of the ultimate context in this sense. At the same time, religion has carried out a second task, inducing characteristic motives and moods that provide a sense of commitment and obligation to the moral norms governing the social practices of our lives. Cognitive meanings and affective attitudes and dispositions are conjoined in light of a comprehensive understanding of life.

Important questions have been raised about religion's ability to carry out these two tasks in the contemporary world. Modernization is seen as undercutting religion's capacity to bind moral meanings to social practices in every sphere of life. Why is modernization seen as having this sort of effect upon religion?

In the Weberian sociological tradition, modernization is described as the changes in social structure and human consciousness that have emerged from "technologically induced economic growth."[5] Ongoing scientific research, technological innovation, and functional rationality characterize economic processes in all modern societies. The key to modernization is not the form of property relations per se but the much broader process Max Weber called rationalization, the "infusion of rational controls through all spheres of human experience."[6] The primary institutional carriers of rationalization are modern economic institutions, with their highly segmented and specialized modes of technological production, and the massive bureaucratic organizations that have emerged to administer the economy and the political order.[7]

These institutional structures are to be found in every modern society, be it capitalist or socialist. They have challenged and changed the symbolic structures by which consciousness is given shape in the modern world, and they, in turn, have been shaped by emergent cultural patterns. Of particular importance for our purposes is the effect modernization has exerted on religion. Four dimensions of modernity can be pointed to as central to the challenges facing religion, including the mainline churches: technical rationality, rapid social change, structural pluralism, and cultural pluralism.

Technical Rationality

An important part of modern rationalization is the spread of technical or instrumental reason. Technical reason seeks to guide courses of action through cause-and-effect forms of analysis and the rational calculation of consequences. It involves a stance in which situations are viewed as problems to be solved, calling for the rational investigation of the relevant information, the determination of possible solutions, and the implementation of these solutions through technical means.

In the modern world, technical reason is widespread and is frequently employed by persons in situations having little to do with scientific investigation per se. From styles of parenting to the overcoming of sexual dysfunctions, life is framed as a problem to be solved by rational means. The effect on religion has been twofold. The most obvious effect is what Weber called the "disenchantment of the world."[8] It has become increasingly difficult for persons to maintain a religious worldview that contains supernatural elements. God's general and special providence is confined to the kind of world that technical reaon discloses, one that is largely based on a naturalistic metaphysic and subject to scientific modes of explanation.

Just as importantly, much of religion's authority as a tradition has been undercut by the spread of technical rationality. When cultural and religious norms are subject to constant rational reflection, they no longer can be "assumed": that is, tacitly interwoven into the fabric of daily life. Nor do they enjoy a "presumption of truth," the automatic assumption that they represent the best starting point for the determination of how life should be lived. Cultural and religious norms now must be justified rationally. This kind of justification frequently is made in terms of religion's contribution to life in this world (e.g., how it enhances the individual's psychological well-being or serves an integrative function for the community). God and the authority of religious tradition are viewed in terms of their utility value and justified by the ways they supposedly meet human needs.[9]

Rapid Social Change

The second closely related aspect of modernization that has deeply affected religion is rapid social change. Economies grow through ongoing technological innovation and are constantly giving rise to new inventions and new institutional arrangements that are not easily integrated with the moral patterns and norms being handed down.

Examples abound. Advances in medical technology have raised profound questions about human choice in the face of life and death. Organ transplants, artificial means of reproduction, and genetic research are areas in which human control over life makes available possibilities never before faced by humankind. The pressure this sort of constant technological innovation places on religion is enormous. Established moral norms and religious beliefs frequently cannot speak directly to the life situations confronting modern persons. Existing normative guidelines must come under constant review and revision in order to relate them to circumstances they did not originally address. Religion's ability to provide models *of* and *for* everyday life is undercut.

Structural Pluralism

The third dimension of modernization that has affected the role of religion is structural pluralism, the wide diversity and loosely related character of modern institutions. In traditional societies, the basic institutions that structure life are few and closely related. Hunting and fishing may serve as the primary sources of food; a kinship system, revolving around the uncle, may organize life in the community; religion may offer mythic explanations of social and moral norms. Institutions are few and well integrated.

In contrast, modern societies are characterized by a high

degree of structural pluralism. A highly specialized division of labor, for example, characterizes the work force. Areas of work that have relatively little to do with one another (e.g., the manufacture of cars and the production of children's toys) are important parts of the economy. Specialization differentiates one occupation or field from another.

Moreover, society is characterized by a variety of institutions that structure social practices in ways relatively independent of one another. The workplace, leisure activities, religion, the home, volunteer organizations—all exist side by side with a large amount of autonomy. The role one plays at work, for example, may have little to do with how one behaves and thinks while at church or at play.

The most fundamental division of this sort characterizing structural pluralism in modern societies is the distinction between the public and private spheres of life. The public sphere consists of the massive institutions of the state, the workplace, the bureaucracies of education, health care, the military, and so forth. The private sphere consists of family, friends, leisure-time activity, and volunteer organizations. The major influence that structural pluralism has exerted on religion is its privatization. As we have seen, religion once played an important role in binding moral meanings to social practices in every sphere of life. Under the impact of structural pluralism, this role has dissipated as religious symbols and institutions have been confined to the private sphere, focusing primarily on personal, subjective needs and not on social life as a whole.

Cultural Pluralism

The fourth major influence of modernity on religion is cultural pluralism, the division of society into different groups having distinct cultural traditions. The rise of the modern city placed various ethnic and racial subcultures into close proximity to one another and brought the reality of pluralism into consciousness. The mass media also heightened the awareness of the multiplicity of cultural traditions existing in a given society. The result is the emergence of what Peter Berger calls a "plurality of worldviews": the modern awareness that my worldview is only one of several that are in existence in society at a given time.[10]

The effect of cultural pluralism is twofold: the relativization of all cultural traditions and the maximization of human choice in determining the individual's moral and religious convictions. With regard to the former, most modern persons are extremely sensitive to the fact that their beliefs and values represent only one particular perspective currently present in society. Frequently, this results in an "easy relativism" in which the question of truth is suspended and an affirmation of the relative value of all perspectives posited.

This results in a movement from "fate to choice," the second by-product of cultural pluralism.[11] Aware of multiple worldviews, individuals no longer are "fated" to a particular set of convictions given by birth or social status. They are free to choose those they find the most compelling. The effect on religion has been marked, giving rise to the denominational pattern of religious life as seen in modern America. The religious switching examined in the first chapter is an outgrowth of this trend, something that has intensified in the last two decades, as ethnic and class ties to particular denominations have weakened and nonaffiliation has become more acceptable.[12] Modern Americans truly find themselves in a "spiritual supermarket" in which they are free to choose from the many options that are vying for their attention.

To summarize, four major trends can be said to characterize modernization: technical rationality, rapid social change, structural pluralism, and cultural pluralism. Typically, social scientists have viewed the relationship of these four trends to religion as antagonistic.[13] Secularization theories in particular have posited an inverse relationship between modernization and religious influence: the greater the inroads of secularization, the less the potency of religion.

Increasingly, however, this thesis is being called into question. It is by no means clear that modernization automatically leads to a reduced and weakened role for religion. Secularity is facing its own crisis. Modern life in its various forms generates tensions and discontents. As the ideology of unlimited scientific and technological progress has run aground, modern secular culture has generated few viable resources to help persons deal with questions of theodicy or to inspire personal sacrifice and commitment to the larger community good.[14] The weakened ties of individuals to communities leave many modern people with a recurrent sense of loneliness and anxiety. The segmentation of life into different spheres and roles creates a desire for psychic and social wholeness that modernity in and of itself seems unable to provide.

While it is clear that modernization has exerted enormous pressure on contemporary religion, it is increasingly apparent that there are a variety of possible responses which religion can make to this process. Lying behind the mainline churches' response to the recent decline in membership, loss of cultural power, and problematic relationship to traditional American civic faith is a question of fundamental importance: How will they respond to the pressures of modernization? The recent shifts in the American religious landscape described in the first chapter can lead us to ask this question anew. In large part, the mainline churches' positive relationship to the central values of American culture has made them extremely vulnerable to the pressures modernization has exerted. Should mainline churches take a more critical stance regarding modernization? If so, how and in what areas?

At present, most mainline churches are being pulled in two very different directions in terms of how they respond to the pressures of modernization: (1) a continued accommodation to modernization by the internalization of a new, more extreme form of modern individualism, and (2) a rejection of modernization through the reaffirmation of traditional forms of authority in conservative Protestantism. Each of these cultural traditions is currently attempting to shape the role of mainline Protestantism in the new religious America. Each projects a markedly different understanding of the church and its teaching authority. Which represents the way forward for the mainline church?

Individualism and the Demise of Teaching Authority

One of the most conspicuous features of modernization is the plausibility it lends to more extreme forms of individualism. Structural and cultural pluralism in particular create the social conditions in which individualism can flourish. The separation of life into segmented roles and life spheres leaves the individual with both the freedom and the task of piecing together a coherent life plan.[15] When multiple cultural traditions are seen as equally valid, the individual is free to draw on those that contribute to his or her sense of meaning and well-being.

Since the 1960s, individualism has intensified in the mainline churches.[16] The theme of a relatively autonomous believer who is on a spiritual journey with little real involvement in a religious community has shaped the way that many people view their religious lives in the mainline churches. Faith development, spirituality, and other ways of viewing the self's movement through time have gained great popularity.

It will be virtually impossible to rehabilitate an authoritative teaching office in contemporary Protestantism without first reckoning with the peculiar difficulties posed by modern individualism. In its accommodation to modern individualism, the church is in danger of losing the very foundation of its educational ministry: the affirmation of the community's right and obligation to determine normative beliefs and practices, on the basis of scripture, which have relative priority over the individual.

The rise and ascendancy of modern individualism in American life have been brilliantly portrayed in *Habits of the Heart: Individualism and Commitment in American Life*.[17] The authors rightfully call attention to the central role individualism has played in American life from the very beginning. The guarantee of an individual's legal, political, and religious rights has been central to every tradition of importance in American culture. Individualism constitutes what Bellah and his colleagues call the "first language" of American life.[18]

They argue, however, that the way individuals have been conceived has varied greatly among the three cultural traditions dominant in American history: the biblical, republican, and modern individualist traditions. It is the recent ascendancy of the last that has made individualism such a pernicious force in contemporary America.

In both the biblical and republican traditions, the individual is placed in a larger corporate and moral context. Biblical religion, as practiced by the Puritans, for example, placed the individual's rights and responsibilities within a covenantal framework. Obligations in both the private and public spheres were grounded in a relationship with God that entailed certain roles and responsibilities in communal life.

Similarly, the republican tradition has consistently affirmed the individual, while placing him or her within a larger context of moral and civic obligation. Individual freedom is not defined primarily as freedom from arbitrary external coercion (by the state, for example) but is portrayed as something that is realized and sustained only under certain positive conditions: active participation by an educated populace in a vital, representative, public life.

In both biblical and republican traditions, thus, the individual's rights and responsibilities are defined and given shape within the larger moral framework of the community. The matter is quite different in the third tradition identified by Bellah and his colleagues, modern individualism. What they have in mind here is the kind of individualism that originated in the utilitarian and social contract philosophers of the nineteenth century and was assimilated to the aspirations and values of the emerging middle class. Under the influence of modern individualism, communal ties and authority have become deeply problematic, especially in religion.

In many ways, the political philosopher John Locke models this position.[19] While it would be simplistic to suggest a direct relationship between the thought of an intellectual writing in the seventeenth century and the vicissitudes of popular culture today, it is not inaccurate to argue that Locke represents an intellectual tradition that has gradually spread throughout popular culture. In Locke's social contract theory, the individual is viewed as existing before natural and social relationships. Society is pictured as coming into being only through the voluntary contract of individuals who are trying to protect their own self-interest. The state is described negatively, as protecting individuals' rights from the unfair intrusion of others and as negotiating the inevitable conflicts between individuals in the pursuit of their varying interests. Freedom here is defined formally, as freedom from external constraints and freedom to pursue individual goals and values.

No substantive definition is offered of the sorts of goods that are worthy of individual pursuit and the objective conditions under which individual freedom is realized. A "preferential" understanding of moral and social participation is operative. Individuals are portrayed as free when they can determine and actualize the values and goals they *prefer* without external restraint.

But how do individuals decide what they prefer? It is at this point that popular American culture has drawn upon the utilitarian side of modern individualism. Emerging from the ethical philosophies of Jeremy Bentham and John Stuart Mill, utilitarianism determines the good in a given situation by attempting to discover the consequences that will flow from a given course of action.[20] In the thought of the classical utilitarian philosophers, such consequences were evaluated in terms of their contribution to the greatest good for the largest number of persons.

What was assimilated by popular culture, however, was the utilitarian form of decision making: a cost-benefit mode of calculation. The good that is preferred is determined by an analysis of the sorts of costs and benefits that will flow from different courses of action.[21] This style of moral reasoning especially rang true to the rapidly expanding middle class that was emerging out of the old feudal order. It experienced on a daily basis in the marketplace the need to weigh costs and benefits in deciding on courses of action. Bellah and his colleagues have labeled this form of modern individualism "utilitarian individualism," calling attention to the prominence of the utilitarian calculus that characterizes it.

Interestingly enough, it was out of a cultural tradition that initially defined itself over against the middle class that a variant of modern individualism has emerged, what Bellah and his colleagues call "expressive individualism."[22] One of the most important carriers of this tradition has been modern art, which frequently has rejected outright the calculating, ascetic compulsivity of the middle class and placed emphasis on the individual's expressive nature.[23]

Grounded initially in romanticism, expressive individualism presents the individual as determining the good on the basis of personal feelings and intuitions that are not constrained by accepted social conventions. Much modern art has gone out of its way to caricature middle-class life, romanticizing the ecstatic excesses supposedly necessary to overcome the social inhibitions that the individual has internalized.[24] To feel "truly," one must transgress conventional limits. Expressive individualism began to permeate popular culture with the advent of therapy as a widely accepted way of understanding life's problems and possibilities.[25] The individual was encouraged to turn inward and discover what he or she should do on the basis of personal feelings and needs.

While utilitarian and expressive individualism have been present in American culture for many years, the 1960s marked a watershed in terms of their influence. Expressive individualism in particular found a willing advocate in the youth counterculture, which glorified the discovery of the self through the spontaneous expression of feelings and the cultivation of inner experience. Even the more political and moral side of the 1960s did not escape the ethos of expressive individualism, especially among white middle-class youth. Protest against the war in Vietnam and support of the civil rights movement frequently were tinged with traces of rebellion against all authority and the projection of a utopian state in which the inner self would no longer be constrained by external forces.[26]

While the values and beliefs of the counterculture found their home initially among middle-class youth, they quickly spread throughout much of American culture. Once the political divisiveness of the war was ended, even those who had supported the American cause in Vietnam began to adopt expressive values first given shape in the counterculture. Sexual freedom and experimentation, for example, were no longer strictly a youth phenomenon. The quest for self-fulfillment began to flourish.

The mainline churches were particularly vulnerable to the ascendancy of modern individualism. Many of their members, especially adolescents and young adults, were caught up in the values and beliefs of the youth culture. The church was viewed with great suspicion. It was identified with the old civic faith, which seemed to lend its support to the Vietnam War and to racism; its old-fashioned morals seemed to contradict the search for inner meaning and self-expression. Worst of all, it seemed to foster conformity of thought and action that was out of touch with the individual's quest for self-fulfillment

The mainline churches lost many of their young members during this period, and it is by no means clear if those people will return to the churches of their childhood during their parenting and mid-life years. Even worse, the mainline churches lost their nerve during this period. It is not as if many of the criticisms raised by young people during the 1960s were not accurate. Coming at the end of a decade of Eisenhower-style Christianity, the creativity and moral outrage of youthful dissenters served as a badly needed judgment on the church's complacency. In attempting to accommodate these criticisms, however, the mainline churches internalized much of the modern individualism that undergirded the counterculture and social protest movements.

In particular, three influences on the mainline churches began to be felt during the 1960s.[27] First was a renewed emphasis on personal experience. While an important role for individual religious experience was nothing new to American religion, it was now given greater impetus, especially in light of the emphasis on belonging during the 1950s. Many Americans now became deeply involved in spiritual disciplines and growth groups that were designed to help deepen their awareness of God's presence in their own lives. This is indicative of a much broader concern with the self's own experience and fulfillment. At the level of popular culture, a kind of theological apologetic was made that argued for the crucial role of religion in the cultivation of the self's spiritual fulfillment or faith development. The role of religion in enhancing personal experience was now celebrated.

A second influence on the church, closely related, was the identification of the emancipation of the self with salvation. In intellectual circles, the influence of Latin American liberationist and North American feminist theologies was now being felt for the first time in this country. Both rightfully called attention to social-ethical imperatives on behalf of the poor and oppressed that are central to Christianity.

However, their calls for liberation were frequently taken by many in the mainline churches to mean little more than an affirmation of psychic liberation from social roles and mores. A legitimate call for the oppressed to become subjects of their own history was transposed into an emancipatory quest for self-fulfillment. Salvation came to be closely identified with the individual's growth toward wholeness, a trend reinforced in unfortunate ways in certain streams of the pastoral care and counseling movement.[28]

A third influence was the widespread fear of institutional authority, which portrays individuals as standing over against large-scale bureaucratic institutions.[29] After the Second World War, many intellectuals portrayed individuals as thwarted by monolithic, impersonal institutions that do not allow them to express their "real selves." People are seen as forced to play a role at work, for example, that may or may not have anything to do with their own inner sense of meaning and fulfillment. Social convention becomes a burden to be escaped.[30] During the 1960s, this fear of authority and distrust of social convention led to a desire to overturn tradition at every level. From worship to pastoral conversation to the marriage ceremony, religious ritual and practice were to become vehicles of individual expression; otherwise, they were seen as thwarting the self.

The mainline churches' internalization of these themes represents a high degree of accommodation to modern individualism. The overall effect has been to weaken further the already limited authority of the church and its representatives. Modern individualism makes the self the arbiter of life's meaning and purpose. Any sense of an authoritative tradition that stands over against and redefines personal needs and values is regarded with deep suspicion.

All too frequently, mainline churches have come to view their ministries primarily in terms of meeting needs as they are defined by individuals who are members or potential members. In formulating their programs in such a manner, these churches are in great danger of losing their teaching authority and overadapting to the surrounding culture by locating authority in the individual believer, not in the church or the Bible.

Similarly, this internalization of modern individualism poses severe problems for the church's ability to foster a genuine sense of community among its members. As Roof and McKinney point out:

> Privatized faith in the extreme knows little of communal support and fellowship; it is not a shared faith and thus is unlikely to inspire strong group loyalties and commitments. To the contrary, such individualism thrives on freedom from group constraint.[31]

In the face of weakened communal bonds, the church finds it virtually impossible to exert any real identity-shaping influence on its members. It confirms or blesses an identity that is formed elsewhere or shores up that identity in the face of life crises.

A staggering 76 percent of all church members now agree that an individual should arrive at his or her own religious beliefs independent of a church or synagogue.[32] Similarly, 70 percent of all church members believe that an individual can be a good Christian or Jew without attending a church or synagogue. Such statistics reveal the extent to which modern individualism has made its way into the mainline churches. The threat this poses to a vital teaching office is real.

Increasingly, there is a recognition from many different quarters that modern individualism is an inadequate way of understanding the problems and possibilities of modernity. As Bellah and his colleagues saw time and again in their research, the language of individualism simply cannot bring into focus certain moral dimensions of human experience, dimensions many persons intuitively recognize as important but are unable to describe adequately when using individualistic categories. Two fundamental problems with this cultural tradition can be identified.

First, modern individualism artificially abstracts the individual from the social context that provides the conditions for the formation and sustenance of the self. Preferential understandings of social life and morality make the individual primary and society secondary and derivative, which simply does not reflect the ways that social conditions undergird individual freedom.

This severely diminishes the role of the teaching office in the church's life. The social sources and supports of individual belief are removed from view. The individual is left to sort out those ideas he or she holds to be true, nervously starting from scratch in deciding what to believe. There is no sense of participation in a living tradition and wider community that can engage the problems of the present on the basis of a reinterpretation of its inherited beliefs.

A second criticism points to the fact that modern individualism has not proven adequate to the task of confronting the persistent reality of individual and communal evil so evident in the modern world. Devoid of substantive definitions of the good that give direction to what persons ought to prefer, it abandons individuals to their own resources in determining their moral values and principles. Typically, in recent American life, this leaves the individual appealing either to some form of self-interest (that which benefits me or those whom I care about) or to "feelings" and "needs" that are determined intuitively.

There is little recognition of the ways persons persistently curve in upon themselves and stand in need of forms of moral guidance that refer them to the needs of others, especially those beyond their immediate purview. It is no accident that American political life has been unable to form effective responses to the growing reality of domestic and international impoverishment. When modern individualism constitutes the "first language" of public moral discourse, there is an absence of substantive moral criteria by which good and evil are discerned and moral sacrifice fostered.

Unfortunately, the church's teaching office, under the influence of modern individualism, is vulnerable to this criticism. In spite of overwhelming evidence that the solitary person is not capable of resisting the seductive beckoning of evil, the church is frequently unwilling to teach with declarative force the kinds of beliefs and values that are consistent with the gospel. Where it should guide its members and participate in the moral discourse of the broader culture, it remains silent or equivocates. Sermons offer broad theological generalizations and leave it up to the individual to relate them to his or her life in the world.

At least in part, the current crisis of the teaching office in mainline Protestantism stems from its inability to respond to these two fundamental weaknesses of modern individualism. Too frequently, the church has capitulated to modern individualism in American life, presenting its message and its programs as one more avenue by which individuals can meet their needs. When it does so, the church abdicates the fundamental authority of its teaching office, derived from God's authoritative address to humanity in Jesus Christ.

The Lure of Counter-modern Authoritarianism

Modern individualism represents only one threat to a vital teaching office in Protestantism. Equally dangerous is the lure of counter-modern authoritarianism. If the internalization of modern individualism represents one of the ways that the mainline churches have responded to modern culture, the attempt to define the church over against modernity and reassert traditional forms of authority represents another.

Cultural accommodation is only one strategy religion can choose in the face of the pressures of modernization. To a great extent, this has been the strategy of the mainline Protestant churches in this century. Modern individualism has been internalized to the point of corroding any sense of a vital, authoritative teaching office in the church. When communal attachments are weak and the individual is the arbiter of life's meaning and purpose, what is the point of structures that can teach authoritatively?

In the face of declining membership, a loss of power and influence in the broader culture, and a problematic relation to the old civic faith, many in the mainline churches are beginning to criticize the direction these churches have taken. In many instances, these criticisms are grounded in the ideas of conservative Protestantism. To what extent do they point the mainline churches in helpful directions?

On the surface, contemporary conservative Protestantism seems to be calling for a reassertion of authority that would fit quite nicely with the rehabilitation of the teaching office of the mainline churches. A deeper look at the cultural and religious traditions lying behind its recent criticism of the mainline churches, however, raises real questions about how helpful it would be for the mainline churches to carry out the conservative program.

The current revival of "born again" Christianity is living proof that modernization does not necessarily lead to a diminished role for religion in contemporary life. Modernity breeds its own discontents: weak communal bonds, individual loneliness, a migratory existence, and the threat of planetary annihilation, to name but a few. As James Davison Hunter, Peter Berger, and others have pointed out, conservative Protestantism represents an increasingly prominent type of response to these discontents: counter-modernization.[33]

One need not look far for examples of this worldwide phenomenon. The Shiite revolution in Iran represents an explicit rejection of the modernizing tendencies of the Shah. The astounding resurgence of indigenous religion in Africa and the parallel growth of the "spiritual" Christian churches are also examples of this phenomenon. Similarly, the fundamentalist and Pentecostal churches have constantly grown over the past decade throughout Latin America.

All of these exhibit strong counter-modernizing tendencies. They explicitly formulate their identity and program in opposition to certain features of modern life. In the face of cultural pluralism and its relativizing of all religious traditions, counter-modernizers affirm the authority of the one true faith. In the face of structural pluralism, with its tendency to confine religion to the private sphere, they frequently attempt to reassert the authority of a particular religion for society as a whole. If modernization means the rationalization of more and more spheres of life, counter-modernizers resist this by positing a religious authority that is not subject to modern inquiry in any form.

Counter-modernizing groups, thus, explicitly define themselves over against modernity. Of particular concern for our purposes is the constant tendency toward authoritarianism in such groups. As Weber clearly saw, in traditional societies the authority of social roles and moral norms is taken for granted. Life can be this way and no other, for other possibilities are not clearly perceived. It is precisely the taken-for-granted authority of social and moral norms that modernity calls into question. Items as fundamental as sex role behavior of men and women no longer follow prescribed lines.

In the face of the potential relativization of traditional authority, counter-modernizing groups attempt to reassert the objective authority of the religious tradition. Almost inevitably, this reassertion takes on reactive overtones. It is the reassertion of something that has been doubted or called into question. Like a believer who temporarily wavers in the faith but comes back to the fold filled with absolute certainty, counter-modernizers reassert traditional forms of authority with a force and rigidity they did not possess in traditional society. Faith is identified with conformity to social norms and theological beliefs. Submission to group norms is demanded. The role of struggle, doubt, and questioning as important dimensions of faith is eliminated. Lost is the capacity for self-criticism and for openness to the expansive insights of other perspectives.

Not all counter-modernizing groups are authoritarian. But there is a consistent tendency in this direction, largely because of the reactive nature of these groups' responses to modernization. As used here, counter-modern authoritarianism refers to those religious groups in the modern world that define themselves over against various trends of modernization and reassert religious authority in an authoritarian fashion. In general such groups have attempted to do one of two things: (1) restore the moral and religious tradition in society as a whole (as in Iran) or (2) construct subcultures within the broader society that shelter their members from the influences of modernity. Both forms of counter-modernization can be found in America today.

In contemporary American life, conservative Protestantism represents a cultural tradition that comes closest to embodying counter-modernizing authoritarianism.[34] This is a broad generalization, to be sure. Conservative Protestantism represents a large and variegated cultural tradition, including at least four different religious and theological streams: the Baptist tradition, the Holiness-Pentecostal tradition, the Anabaptist tradition, and the wing of the Reformation-Confessional tradition that has internalized American revivalism.[35]

While there is great diversity in this tradition, it can be identified by a distinctive doctrinal and behavioral set of beliefs and practices.[36] Doctrinally, it places great emphasis on: (1) belief that the Bible is the inerrant Word of God, (2) belief in the divinity of Christ, and (3) belief in the importance and power of Christ's life, death, and physical resurrection for the salvation of the human soul. In addition, conservative Protestantism is far more likely than other branches of Christianity to view the devil as a personal agent actively involved in the world, to interpret the Adam and Eve story literally as an accurate account of the creation of the world, and to emphasize life after death.[37]

In terms of social norms and practices, this tradition places great emphasis on an experiential, personal relationship with Jesus Christ as the sole means of salvation and on the proselytizing of those who are not converted to the basic beliefs of evangelical faith. Its adherents are more committed to traditional norms of work and family than other branches of Christianity.[38] By and large, they are more conservative than their counterparts on issues of sexual morality, the role of women, abortion, divorce, and homosexuality.[39]

While diversity exists within this cultural tradition on these issues, James Hunter argues that conservative Protestantism "represents a relatively cohesive moral order."[40] There is coherence between its basic theological beliefs and its social and moral norms. This should not be surprising, for it has self-consciously viewed itself as the guardian of Protestant orthodoxy in this century, giving much attention to the maintenance of the purity of its beliefs and practices. Sociologically, orthodoxies are unique because of the special significance they give to the symbolic boundaries constituting the tradition they guard and hand on.[41]

American conservative Protestantism as an orthodoxy in this sense is the result of a particular history. Its preoccupation with symbolic boundaries is mostly a defensive response to the loss of cultural power and prestige that took place during the latter part of the nineteenth century. Marsden and Hunter make convincing cases that, contrary to many interpretations, the evangelical form of conservative Protestantism did not represent a sectarian form of Christianity during the nineteenth century but constituted the mainstream of American life.[42] It was only with the rise of liberal theology, the social gospel movement, and modern biblical criticism that it was displaced as the driving intellectual force of the mainline churches. Even on the level of popular culture, its conservative morality and supernaturalism began to lose ground.

Conservative Protestantism's response to its loss of social status was to intensify its lines of cognitive and cultural defense. The fundamentalist-modernist controversies of the 1920s are an example of the aggressive counterattacks certain streams of conservative Protestantism chose to undertake. Fundamentalism began to make its presence felt. The symbolic boundaries were tightened in an effort to identify the "pure and true fundamentals" of the faith, which were not subject to modern critical reason.

At this point conservative Protestantism began to take on many of the features of other counter-modernizing movements, especially in its fundamentalist forms. It began to form a subculture in our society that attempted to insulate its members from the perils of modern life. "Christian" radio stations, colleges, bookstores, and schools began to appear in which "Christian" orthodoxy and its accompanying morality could be maintained. Research indicates that conservative Protestantism was most successful at maintaining its worldview during this century among those portions of the population exposed *least* to modernizing trends through higher education, occupation, and so forth.[43]

New research indicates a shift in this trend. In the face of the widespread changes in traditional morality throughout American culture during the 1960s and 1970s, the conservative alternative has gained increased plausibility for many members of society whose social location in the past would not have made them susceptible to the counter-modernizing arguments of this cultural tradition. Changes in attitudes toward the role of women, divorce, premarital sex, homosexuality, and work were threatening to large segments of the American population. Much of contemporary conservative Protestantism's program is directed against precisely these issues in the attempt to buttress traditional norms. Its appeal has broadened considerably among those who are resistant to the changes these cultural trends represent. In other words, it no longer seems to be the case that this cultural tradition appeals primarily to those who are farthest removed from modernization. In a time of rapid cultural change and experimentation, its counter-modernizing approach has become increasingly plausible to many who have come to view the moral ethos of contemporary America as collapsing.

It is legitimate to ask whether this cultural tradition can harness the potentially devastating forces that modernity has unleashed or can incorporate the positive dimensions of modern life. The problem with "counter" positions of all sorts is their inability to recognize and account for the many ways they are dependent on that which they are opposing. Two major problems with this cultural tradition can be noted, problems that limit its usefulness in the rehabilitation of a vital teaching office in the contemporary mainline Protestant churches.

First, conservative Protestantism's counter-modernizing effort to represent orthodoxy consistently denies the many ways that it is historically conditioned and mediated. Timeless truths from an inerrant Bible are offered as the hallmark of orthodoxy. What must be bracketed out in order to maintain this position are the ways that beliefs, in every age, are limited by the particularities of historically conditioned language and worldviews. Conservative Protestantism is no different in this respect. It only pretends to be different.

In point of fact, it is deeply influenced by the modern world it is attempting to "counter." Of great importance in this regard is the extreme emphasis on enhanced subjectivity characterizing contemporary conservative Protestantism. Being "born again" is frequently presented as guaranteeing one personal happiness, inner peace, and, in its more perverse forms, worldly success. A rehearsal of how one's faith has enhanced one's emotional life is almost a mandatory feature of contemporary conservative witness.

Even when the more vulgar forms of this emphasis are not

present, the centrality of the individual's personal relationship with Jesus Christ remains an identifying feature of contemporary conservative Protestantism. Indeed, it has come to occupy such a position of importance in this cultural tradition that it represents an exaggeration of the rightful place of personal piety in the Christian life. It is not difficult to discern in this preoccupation with subjective experience the legacy of revivalism given new shape in response to the pervasive loneliness and anomie that accompany the institutionally fragmented world in which we live. It is an unacknowledged response to modern life and not the hallmark of Protestant orthodoxy, as it is so frequently portrayed.

Similar accommodations to modern forms of thought are present in the highly simplified codification of conversion and spirituality characteristic of contemporary conservative Protestantism.[44] The core beliefs of Christianity are reduced to a set of steps or laws that the believer must move through or accept in order to be saved. In the face of cultural pluralism, Christianity is distilled to its essence in what Anton Zijderveld calls the "primitivization of reality": the reduction of perceptions of reality to highly simplified forms as a way of coping with the complexities and abstractness of modern life.[45] This simplification of Christianity affords increased efficacy in marketing the gospel in a pluralistic cultural setting.

These acquiescences of conservative Protestantism to modern culture at the level of popular belief and practice are repeated at the level of its intellectual history. The doctrine of inerrancy, for example, gained prominence at about the same time the doctrine of papal infallibility was given official definition by the Roman Catholic hierarchy. Both can be viewed as rearguard actions in response to modern inquiry into traditional sources of religious authority. The Reformers' affirmation of the primacy of scripture is now transposed into a defense of the inner consistency of every biblical statement and the scientific authenticity of its accounts, items that were not at the heart of the Reformers' original intention.

Counter-modernizing forces inevitably presuppose certain dimensions of that which they oppose. They are forced to deny this dependency, however, in an affirmation of pure faith. The pretense of an unmediated orthodoxy severely limits conservative Protestantism's capacity to be self-critical and to take seriously the insights of other perspectives. The rehabilitation of the teaching office in mainline Protestant churches would do well to incorporate more directly an awareness of the fact that this office inevitably is conditioned by culture and history. The teachings it offers are not timeless. Nor are they derived directly from scripture. They are always the product of a finite interpretive process. The teaching office must begin its interpretation on the basis of a received tradition, but at no point must it ignore the fact that this tradition is the product of particular historical conditions which have limited its capacity to define and articulate the truth of the gospel. This is an insight that conservative Protestantism has difficulty acknowledging.

A second major weakness of contemporary conservative Protestantism is its tendency toward authoritarianism. While this characteristic is not universally present, a defensive, reactive relationship to the surrounding world and an attempt to serve as the guardian of "true" Christianity have consistently led this cultural tradition toward theological and social authoritarianism. When the "what" of Christianity is thought of as timeless and unchanging, the "who" determining this "what" almost invariably is granted more power and authority than any individual or institutional office warrants.

Perhaps the most alarming manifestation of this tendency has been documented by a body of research that indicates a strong correlation between membership in conservative Christianity and a willingness to suspend the civil liberties of minorities.[46] The willingness of persons to identify their own position unequivocably with the will of God results in a readiness to see others as deviant or even evil when they do not think or act in accord with supposedly biblical norms. This sort of attitude is repeated in many Christian schools and congregations, which place a high premium on behavioral conformity and the acceptance of a clearly defined set of theological beliefs.

In contrast to this approach, the teaching office of mainline Protestantism faces the task of formulating an authoritative teaching office that does not lapse into authoritarianism. Historically, classical Protestantism has placed emphasis on the authority of representative bodies with the ability to define beliefs and set moral guidelines. The community's right and obligation to formulate normative beliefs and practices have been balanced by a recognition that these are fallible and may be in error. A role for individual dissent and diversity is given credence, not as an absolute seat of authority over the community but as a legitimate expression of the role of individual conscience in the personal appropriation of the faith and as a potential source of prophetic criticism. The mainline churches would do well to attempt to maintain this delicate balance between individual conscience and communal authority in their efforts to rehabilitate a stronger teaching office.

In summary, two criticisms can be raised of conservative Protestantism as a cultural tradition: (1) its preoccupation with the maintenance of orthodoxy has rendered it unable to acknowledge and account for the ways that it is historically mediated and (2) it has a consistent tendency to move in the direction of theological and social authoritarianism. While the mainline churches have much to learn from conservative Protestantism's critique of modern culture, it is unlikely that they will find in this cultural tradition the resources necessary for a revitalization of their own life.

At an earlier point in this century, Protestant theology briefly began to rediscover its roots in the great Reformers, Martin Luther and John Calvin. This theological impulse barely moved beyond the intellectual centers of Protestantism to influence the life and practice of actual congregations. In part, this was because of its inability to converse meaningfully with the practical theological disciplines that are largely responsible for mediating the insights of scholarly theology to the church. Commonly known as neo-Reformation theology or neo-orthodoxy, this theological movement found expression in the thought of theologians like Karl Barth, Emile Brunner, H. Richard Niebuhr, Dietrich Bonhoffer, and Reinhold Niebuhr. While very real differences separate the thought of these theologians, each called for modern Protestantism to recover a profounder sense of the biblical faith as it was mediated through the theological traditions of the Reformation.

This task still awaits the mainline churches. Perhaps their shifting role in contemporary American life will serve as the occasion for the recovery by these churches of a deeper grounding in their Reformation roots and a lessening of dependence on the surrounding culture. If this were to take place, it might well be that these churches would come out of the transitions they currently are experiencing with a more authentic Christian witness in American life. An important part of the mainline churches' recovery of their Reformation heritage is the uncovering of a dynamic understanding of the teaching office in the church. The traditions of the Reformation offer them an understanding of teaching authority that represents an alternative to modern individualism and counter-modern authoritarianism. We now must begin to bring more clearly into focus the possibilities of a revitalized teaching office.

3

A Teachable Spirit

The task before the mainline Protestant churches is to seek a third way beyond the cultural traditions of modern individualism and conservative Protestantism. They would do well to explore anew their Reformation heritage and the forms of thought and life the Reformers envisioned. While it is neither possible nor desirable to leap back across the centuries to the Reformation period and bring forward in an unreconstructed manner its forms of church life, mainline churches will find the great thinkers of this period to be rich dialogue partners in their attempt to respond to the peculiarly "modern" questions they face today.

Seeking a Third Way

Of special importance is the mainline churches' need to carry out more adequately the three tasks that lie at the heart of the teaching office: (1) the determination of the normative beliefs and practices of the church, (2) the reinterpretation of these beliefs and practices in shifting cultural and historical contexts, and (3) the determination of educational institutions, processes, and curricula by which these beliefs and practices are handed down from generation to generation and appropriated in ever deeper ways across the lives of individual Christians.

Until the mainline churches face up to their need for normative beliefs and practices that bind together congregations and denominations through a common story and vision, a *consensus fidelium*, they will be subject to the relativism inherent in radical individualism and the authoritarian reactions to this relativism. As sensitive ministers and educators know all too well, many in their congregations today prefer simplistic answers to no answers at all. Until these churches begin to reinterpret the central teachings of the church in ways that address not only the everyday problems facing their members but also the broader global issues that often do not lie within their immediate purview, Christianity will continue to be confined to the private sphere. The Reformers' understanding of vocation will be lost: the belief that all of life is under the dominion of God, and Christian calling is to be worked out in every sphere of life.

Until these churches recover a broader sense of the ecology of educational institutions and agencies by which their identity-shaping beliefs and practices are taught, they will continue to rely in an unrealistic way on the congregational setting and its Sunday school program as the primary means of teaching in the church. The potentially expansive dialogues between individual and congregation, congregation and denomination, denomination and ecumenical Christianity, church and seminary, and seminary and university will not be realized. Conditions rife with individualism and ripe for authoritarianism will continue to be prevalent.

Only as the mainline churches adequately address the three tasks of the teaching office will they begin to find a way beyond individualism and counter-modern authoritarianism. This is by no means an easy task. It will take all the creativity that theologians, ministers, Christian educators, and lay leaders can muster. It will take the recovery of classical religious traditions that have long gone unnoticed but that stand solidly in the heritage of the Reformation.

At the heart of the establishment of a vital teaching office in the mainline churches is the need to recover a nonauthoritarian understanding of teaching authority. This need can be put in the form of a question: How can mainline denominations and congregations determine the normative beliefs and practices that lie at the heart of their teaching ministry while maintaining a noncoercive stance in their teaching? These churches must learn to speak and teach with authority. True authority, however, elicits respect and attentiveness on the basis of superior wisdom and truth. It is essentially persuasive, not coercive.

There are two important dimensions to the successful emergence of this sort of teaching authority in the mainline churches: (1) the nurture of a piety that is characterized by a teachable spirit and (2) the formation of institutional structures and relationships that allow different authorities located at various levels of church life to engage in a mutually expansive and corrective dialogue through which the church is taught what it is and what it is to do. The first of these dimensions is the focus of the present chapter, while the latter is dealt with in chapter nine.

A few words about the structural dimensions of a renewed teaching office will indicate the general contours of what we have in mind. Piety and communal structures go hand in hand. The piety of a teachable spirit cannot be evoked and sustained without an institutional matrix that embodies a nonauthoritarian teaching authority. It is important to recognize the role of authoritative offices and agencies beyond the congregation. There clearly is a role for such structures in the thought of Luther and Calvin.

The voluntary principle of denominationalism in American religion has focused the educational ministry of the church almost exclusively on the congregation. This unconsciously has been internalized by Protestant Christian education in this century. Much of its attention has been focused on the local church, with little sense of the broader ecology of institutions and offices by which the church carries out its teaching ministry.

In the field of education, it is Lawrence Cremin who has advocated most vigorously an understanding of education that does not focus exclusively on the school but on "a broad range of educational associations and institutions and the diverse interrelationship between each of these associations and institutions."[1] It is somewhat ironic that persons like John Westerhoff, who drew on Cremin's insights in looking at the breakdown of the educational ecology in contemporary America, deemphasized schooling but did not move beyond the congregation as the central unit of the church's teaching ministry.[2] The need to rehabilitate meaningful exchange between a wide variety of institutions in the church's teaching ministry simply did not come into focus.

In ways that are consistent with the heritage of the Reformation churches, mainline Protestantism can formulate a nonauthoritarian teaching office only if it recognizes the ecology of institutions by which its teaching ministry is carried out. This educational ecology includes a role for, among others, seminaries, denominational agencies and offices, and ecumenical councils, as well as congregations. Only when healthy communication is established between a variety of different teaching authorities in the church, each having a distinctive contribution to make, will a vital teaching office begin to emerge. At least some of the problems inherent in American denominationalism can be overcome through institutional structures and relationships that modify the overly strong emphasis on the individual and the congregation that is a part of this religious pattern. The recognition of a healthy ecology of institutions in the teaching office is especially important in the face of the "new voluntarism" that has emerged in the last two decades.[3]

One of the tasks before the mainline churches, then, is primarily structural: the establishment of attitudes and relationships between a variety of ecclesiastical institutions that compose the broader ecology. A second, correlative task is the nurture of a renewed sense of piety in the mainline churches, a piety that is characterized by a teachable spirit. The term "piety" is one of long-standing importance in Protestantism, being used by the early Reformers in place of the Roman Catholic concept of "spirituality" because of the latter's association with a doctrine of sanctification that seemed to imply the earning of God's favor. Piety focuses on the individual's deepest response to the divine. It deals with matters of the heart, the seat of human emotion and action. It has been described as being composed of two dimensions: attitudes and dispositions.[4]

"Attitudes" are an individual's basic posture toward the world or some part of it, including a constellation of beliefs and emotions that have relative persistence through time. A woman's attitude toward her father points toward the consistent pattern of emotions and beliefs that characterize her relationship to him. She may believe that he is a selfish, vindictive man who has never concerned himself with anything but his career, leading her to relate to him with anger and fear on a regular basis.

"Dispositions" refer to an individual's readiness to act in certain ways. While particular actions are not determined by dispositions, dispositions lead an individual to act along certain lines with some consistency. A man may have the disposition to act on behalf of persons in need, for example, something that is seen in his frequent participation in church soup kitchens and night shelters. This disposition, however, does not predetermine how he will respond to a particular set of circumstances that may arise on a given evening in one of these settings.

While human beings have attitudes and dispositions in relation to many matters, these things become piety when they are directed toward God. An individual's piety is composed of those attitudes and dispositions that constitute and flow from his or her relationship to the divine. It points to the consistent posture an individual holds toward God and the attitudes toward God's world that flow from it. It points to the patterns of action that characterize this relationship, including involvement in such things as worship, the religious community, moral endeavor, and civic commitment.

Protestant theologians have described Christian piety in somewhat different ways. John Calvin, for example, defines it as "that reverence joined with love of God which the knowledge of his benefits induces."[5] A contemporary Protestant theologian, James Gustafson, defines piety as the attitude of reverence, awe, and respect toward God requiring that human activity be ordered properly in relation to what can be discerned about the purposes of God.[6]

Mainline Protestantism desperately needs an awakening of the piety of its members. At least in part, the recent interest in spirituality is a recognition of this fact. It is essential, however, for mainline Protestant churches to do more than borrow techniques and methods of spirituality from other religious traditions. It is far more important that they recover an authentic sense of the piety of their own heritage. Reformation piety is characterized by a *teachable spirit*, a phrase coined by John Calvin. This spirit is grounded in a profound awareness of human sin and finitude and the need for individual Christians to depend on the objective means of grace found in the church. It represents a real alternative to much of the piety that is operative in American Christianity today.

Augustinian Piety

Calvin's understanding of the piety of a teachable spirit is part of a broader tradition first given shape in the thought of Augustine of Hippo in the third century. This Augustinian strain of piety, as historian Perry Miller calls it, has appeared in a variety of times and places throughout the history of the church.[7] It consistently has been characterized by three particular emphases: (1) a sense of the transcendence and majesty of God, (2) a belief in the radical sinfulness of humanity, and (3) an understanding of regeneration as the fragmentary restoration of humanity's original nature. These serve as the "deep structure" of Augustinian piety that lies beneath the differences in language and practice that have characterized it across the centuries. Each contributes in an important way to

the characterization of Christian existence, in terms of a
teachable spirit.

At the heart of Augustinian piety is a profound awareness of
the qualitative distinction between the Creator and the created. God as the maker and sustainer of all being utterly transcends the finite world. The transcendent God remains
incomprehensible to humanity; God's being and ways are finally a mystery that must be accepted and not probed with
undue curiosity. This strain of piety thus combines a sharp
awareness of God's transcendent majesty with a reticence
about human speculation concerning things divine. Piety must
confine itself to the knowledge God has provided.

This awareness of the qualitative distinction between the
Creator and the created is the most important grounding
point of a teachable spirit in this strain of piety. Humanity,
as a part of the finite created order, stands in relation to God
as student to teacher. The student comes with certain innate
gifts and capacities, but these are useless unless they are
shaped and developed under the instruction and guidance of
one who is more knowledgeable. God is sovereign, majestic,
transcendent. Humanity can only understand God and itself
if it is open to the teaching of the One who brought it into
being.

This understanding of the need to be teachable in relation
to the Author of all being is intensified by a second element of
Augustinian piety: a profound awareness of human sin. The
self-consciousness and inward probing of the heart that make
Augustine peculiarly "modern" are part of a piety that is
shaped by a profound awareness of the radicality of human
sin.[8] Calvin and the Puritans are well known for this emphasis.

Though created good, humanity is seen as falling of its own
choice into corruption and as deserving of the worst of punishments. The doctrines of original sin and total depravity give
intellectual expression to this sensitivity. So complete is human sinfulness that every vestige of human cooperation in an
escape from this predicament is eliminated. God alone in the
atoning work of Christ and the continued operation of the
Holy Spirit is the author of reconciliation. Indeed, this strain
of piety has been so concerned about protecting the absolute-
ness of God's work in saving sinful humanity that it has been
willing to project election and damnation back into God's
eternal decrees.

In its awareness of the radicality of human sin, the piety of a
teachable spirit finds a second grounding point. Not only must
finite human beings be taught who they are and who God is by

their Creator, they also stand in desperate need of such help. The teaching they need is that upon which their eternal destiny depends. In and of themselves, however, human beings do not possess the desire to be taught. This must be created by God through the work of the Holy Spirit. A teachable spirit is a gift. Though humanity's need for teaching is absolute, its recognition of this need and the desire to be taught ultimately must be created by the Spirit of God because of the depths of sin.

The third element of Augustinian piety—its understanding of regeneration—likewise serves as a grounding point for a teachable spirit. Out of compassion, God bestows grace and enables persons to respond with belief. This involves a two-fold process, the offer of forgiveness that God alone extends through Jesus Christ and the simultaneous empowerment of the believer to a new life of obedience. Though the original nature of humanity cannot be completely restored in this lifetime, owing to the continuing power of sin, it can be restored in part. In Calvin and his followers, this possibility gave rise to a strong affirmation of the third use of the law and a recognition of the importance of ecclesiastical structures of authority and accountability in the Christian life. Christians need to be taught by such external helps. If they approach the law and the teachings of the church with a teachable spirit, they will receive the help necessary to enable them to restore in part the original nature of humanity that has been distorted in sin.

Calvin and Teachability

Of all the persons and movements embodying the Augustinian strain of piety, John Calvin has probably done more than any other single person to describe its fundamental tenets in terms of teachability. At the very heart of Christian piety, he believed, stands a teachable spirit. In its relation to the transcendent, sovereign God, sinful humanity must be teachable, especially those whom God has called to a new life.

In one of the few instances where Calvin describes his own Christian experience, he portrays his conversion as a *conversion to teachableness (conversion ad dociliatem)*. As he puts it in the introduction to his commentary on Psalms:

> And first, since I was too obstinately devoted to the superstitions of Popery to be easily extricated from so profound an abyss of mire, *God by a sudden conversion subdued and brought my mind to a teachable frame* which was more hardened in such

matters than might have been expected from one at my early period of life. Having thus received some taste and knowledge of true godliness, I was immediately inflamed with so intense a desire to make progress therein, that although I did not altogether leave off other studies, I yet pursued them with less ardour.[9]

Calvin is describing here his movement from Roman Catholicism to Protestantism, something that took place during his young adult years. He was studying law at the time of his conversion, in accordance with his father's wishes. While he continued these studies, his conversion immediately gave him the motivation to study scripture and theology. Calvin's use of the phrase "a teachable frame" points to his willingness to suspend old beliefs and open himself to the forgiving and transforming grace of God. The reception of a teachable spirit gave him the zeal to pursue the "knowledge of true godliness" that he might make some "progress therein."

In a closely related fashion, Calvin frequently uses the image of teachability in his commentaries to describe accounts of conversion found in scripture.[10] In describing the call of James and John, for example, he writes that they receive commendation for their teachability *(docilis)* and ready obedience, because they are willing to leave all worldly affairs at the command of Christ.[11] Similarly, the Ethiopian eunuch in Acts is said to show a teachable spirit when he asks Philip to explain the meaning of the scriptures to him, an attitude Calvin recommends to the Christians of his own day.[12]

The idea of conversion as conversion to teachableness is an important one for us to reclaim. Too often in American Protestantism, conversion has been seen as a kind of end point, the decisive moment when salvation is procured. In Calvin's thought, however, it is portrayed as a kind of starting point. The converted are compared to students who are driven by a zealous spirit to learn more. They recognize their need for instruction and are granted the motivation and capacity to pursue it.

A teachable spirit is not to be confined to the first stages of the Christian life, however. It is not merely a part of the excitement and zeal that many newly converted Christians feel.[13] Rather, it is an attitude that characterizes piety throughout the Christian life. As Christians develop in faith, they become *more* teachable, not less.

What the Holy Spirit brings in conversion is a fundamental reorientation of the mind and heart away from a preoccupation with the self to a desire to live to God. Persons must now learn to find security not in themselves but in God's providential care, to find the justification of their existence not in their own projects and causes but in God's free gift of acceptance in Jesus Christ, to find the pattern of a new life not in their own insights but in the moral law as found in Jesus Christ and the Decalogue. This is a fundamental, lifelong task, focusing on the renewal of the mind and heart. To have reverence and love toward God is to recognize God as the ultimate teacher, creating an attitude of openness and dependency on God as the One who instructs those whom he has called throughout their lives.

What is jarring to modern sensitivities about all this, however, is the way that Calvin links teachability so closely to attitudes of docility, modesty, and tameness. This linkage is seen in the various adjectives he connects to a teachable spirit: modest, gentle, open, tame, and ready. For example, church members are described as needing a "gentle and teachable spirit" in relation to ministers.[14] Similarly, scripture is said to call for a "modest and teachable reader."[15] The very word *docilis*, which is translated "teachableness," points toward this connection. Etymologically, it uses the same Latin stem as our English word "docile" and originally described the attitude of persons who are apt to learn and especially attentive to instruction.

In an era that places such emphasis on human freedom and liberation, it seems hard to imagine that docility, modesty, and tameness are characteristics central to the Christian life. Yet this is precisely what Calvin seems to imply in his use of teachability. Ultimately, this grows out of his recognition of the qualitative distinction between Creator and created, Reconciler and reconciled. The modesty, tameness, and docility of a teachable spirit are based on a recognition of the finitude of all human knowing and the ways that it is distorted by the reality of human sin. It rests on a recognition of self-limitation and self-deception and the need for modesty with regard to what one can claim are God's intentions.

Clearly, there is a wrong sort of docility and submissiveness. Modesty or docility that simply reinforces the social oppression of certain groups is a capitulation to sin, not genuine piety. Such modesty or tameness would represent little more than the internalization of oppressive images that distort the true humanity of individuals or groups whose worth is grounded in their creation by God, not their social definition. Submissiveness to racism, sexism, or social class is not what is

meant by docility and tameness. Nor can it be identified with
the piety of a warm heart found in much popular religion.
Such warm-hearted religion views docility in highly subjective terms, identifying the work of the Holy Spirit with inner
peace or an intuitive sense of what should be done in situations of choice. The piety of a teachable spirit as found in
Calvin's thought is something quite different. A teachable
spirit strives to be docile before God; but God, in Calvin's
view, has bound Christians to the ordinary means of grace
found in the church's life. These represent objective checks
on and helps in the Christian's struggle to hear God's Word
and to obey God's will. Teachability before God thus leads to
a teachable spirit in relation to the objective means of grace.

Those objective means of grace that Calvin links explicitly
to a teachable spirit are scripture and duly constituted leaders
in the church. Teachability before God leads to a proper modesty before and openness to the instruction offered by these
authorities in the Christian life. The Bible and church leaders,
of course, are never to be confused with God. Yet they do
have a proper role in the communication of God's truth.

Above all other authorities in the Christian life, scripture is
to be approached with a teachable spirit. As Calvin puts it,
"For our wisdom ought to be nothing else than to embrace
with human teachableness and at least without finding fault,
whatever is taught in Sacred Scripture."[16] In Part Two of this
book we will discuss more fully the centrality of the authority
of scripture in Calvin's theology. What is important for the
present is to grasp the way he linked a vital Christian piety to
the ongoing study of the Bible. Christians are to approach
scripture with a teachable spirit, for here the truths about
God necessary for salvation are revealed.

Incorporating this tenet would bring about a major shift in
the current practices of the mainline Protestant churches. At
present, only the members of conservative churches read scripture with any kind of regularity.[17] Of those persons who identify themselves as liberal Protestants, an astounding 59.4
percent read the Bible less than once a month; 14.5 percent
read it one to three times a month; 17.6 percent read it one to
three times a week; and only 8.5 percent read it daily.[18]
Clearly, the authority of scripture has declined seriously in the
minds of many in the mainline churches. In contrast, Calvin
viewed a laity instructed in scripture as the very foundation of
the success of the Reformation. Only a congregation whose piety is shaped by the teachings of scripture can resist the shifting
winds of social convention and doctrinal heresy. It is the lan-

guage of scripture that provides the church as a community with a common framework so it can discuss and debate issues.

Surely, a renewed piety in the mainline Protestant churches will only emerge through the restoration of a teachable spirit toward the Bible among clergy and laity. A piety that is truly reverent toward God will lead Christians to apply themselves "teachably to God's Word," as Calvin once put it, for scripture is preeminent in authority in the Christian life.[19] Without a fundamental shift in the way that most persons in the mainline churches view scripture and an accompanying refocusing of the educational ministry of the church on the mastery of its basic content, it is highly unlikely that the problems facing mainline American Protestantism can be overcome. What good is an emphasis on persuasiveness in teaching authority if those who are being persuaded are grounded solidly not in a biblical faith but rather in social convention? How can individuals and congregations contribute to the formation of a consensus on matters of faith and morality if they do not share a common language based on scripture?

While teachable toward God, thus, Christian piety is bound to objective authorities by which God's Word is revealed. Scripture is preeminent among these authorities in Calvin's view. His understanding of a teachable spirit, however, did not stop here. In ways that stand in sharp contrast to attitudes prevalent in many mainline churches, he also advocated teachability in relation to ministers and theologians. In Book IV of the *Institutes,* he repeatedly points to the benefits of a piety that is teachable in relation to the ordained leadership of the church. As he puts it at one point:

> Meanwhile, anyone who presents himself in a teachable spirit to the ministers ordained by God shall know by the result that with good reason this way of teaching was pleasing to God, and also that with good reason this yoke of moderation was imposed on believers.[20]

He even goes so far as to write:

> Again, this is the best and most useful exercise in humility, when he accustoms us to obey his Word, even though it be preached through men like us and sometimes even by those of lower worth than we. . . . But when a puny man risen from the dust speaks in God's name, at this point we best evidence our piety and obedience toward God if we show ourselves teachable toward his minister, although he excels us in nothing.[21]

The fundamental theological affirmation that lies behind Calvin's position here is his belief that God is most likely to be found in the preaching and teaching of the Word. It is the office of the ordained minister to carry out this task in public worship and his or her teaching ministry. The members of the church should approach such preaching and teaching with the expectation that they will find God there. Even a "puny man" who "excels us in nothing" should be approached with openness and a readiness to hear God's Word.

Clearly, Calvin is linking teachability to the *office* of ministry and not to the personality of any particular person. God has established offices in the church as vehicles of divine truth. The legitimate authority of the ministerial office, however, is qualified in many ways by Calvin. Ministers are bound to the teachings of scripture and its communal interpretation by representative bodies of the church.[22] Their authority does not reside in their own opinions. They can be corrected by their colleagues. Their teachings can be tested by the congregation against scripture. Nonetheless, they are normally to be approached with a teachable spirit, for God has bound Christians to the ordinary means of grace, which include the preaching and teaching of the gospel by ordained ministers.

In a closely related fashion, theologians also are to be approached with a teachable spirit. Calvin describes his own purpose in writing the *Institutes* as being "to lead by the hand those who are teachable."[23] He frequently concludes his discussions of a particular doctrine by saying that what he has written will suffice for those who are teachable.[24] Theologians, like ministers, are viewed as possessing special competence in handing on and interpreting the central tenets of the faith. They are not to be ignored or taken lightly.

Once again, the piety of a teachable spirit is firmly linked by Calvin to more objective authorities in the church's life. He is not advocating blind obedience to ministerial leadership or to the theologians of the church. He is, however, arguing that the fundamental attitudes and dispositions of Christian piety should be shaped by a dialogue with ecclesiastical authorities who possess special competence in interpreting the meaning of scripture and theology and relating them to the contemporary situation. These leaders play a special role in articulating the cumulative wisdom of church tradition and the community's interpretation of scripture through the ages. Both of these are desperately needed in mainline Protestantism today in order for it to chart a third way between individualism and authoritarianism.

The emergence of an attitude of teachability toward ministers and theologians, however, is not dependent solely on changes in church members and congregations. It also rests on the demonstration of competence by such leaders, the foundation of true authority. This involves not only scholarly competence but also competence in grasping the basic problems before the church today and addressing them in ways that are genuinely helpful. Calvin viewed his own theology as engaged in the formation of piety and the edification of the church.

There is little doubt that the voluntary pattern of American denominationalism will continue to set the terms of contemporary Protestant Christianity in America. But there also is little doubt that unless this pattern of religious life is transformed in basic ways, it will not prove adequate to the challenges before the mainline churches. Barring fundamental change, these churches are likely to continue down the private, individualistic path that many are already traveling. More than a few are likely to react to the problems created by this position by harkening to conservative Protestantism's attempt to counter the vicissitudes of modernity.

Between individualism and authoritarianism lies a third way. It is the way grounded in the Reformation traditions out of which mainline Protestant churches originally emerged. Central to these traditions is an understanding of Christian piety as possessing a teachable spirit, a spirit that is modest in its claims for itself and high in its regard for the teaching of God. It is a piety that is teachable in relation to the authorities of scripture, ministerial leadership, and theology, for each has a proper role in the communication of God's truth. Such a piety cannot be evoked and sustained without the emergence of institutional offices and agencies with the competence and right to teach with authority. A teachable spirit is deeply and inextricably dependent on structures of teaching. It is to the history of such structures in the church that we now turn.

PART TWO

Discovering
the Teaching Office

4

Structure and Spirit

In *The Vindication of Tradition,* Jaroslav Pelikan argues that a great irony characterizes the modern West.[1] Just as intellectuals are once more beginning to rediscover the importance of tradition as an intellectual category, the central traditions of our civilization are in a state of disarray. In making this point, Pelikan shares an anecdote from Richard Altman's account of the making of *Fiddler on the Roof.*[2] Altman writes, "I don't know who finally made the discovery that the show was really about the disintegration of a whole way of life, but I do remember that it was a surprise to all of us. And once we found that out—which was pretty exciting—[Jerome] Robbins said, 'Well, if it's a show about tradition and its dissolution, then the audience should be told what that tradition is.' . . . Tradition was the key to *Fiddler's* meaning."

Altman's story serves well to introduce Part Two. If we would understand the dissolution of the teaching office in contemporary American Protestantism, we must first understand the classical understandings of this ministry in Roman Catholicism and Protestantism and their background in the New Testament and early church history. Although our discussion must deal with a wide range of complex material in a relatively short space, a real effort has been made to avoid an unfair caricature of the different positions. The early phases of the struggle between the Reformation and Roman Catholicism were highly polemical and frequently led to exaggerated criticisms on both sides. While it would not be helpful to pretend that real differences between these two traditions do not exist, we must explore these differences less in a spirit of polemics than in honest searching among fellow believers. Both sides have something to learn from such a conversation.

Reopening the Question of the Teaching Office

Since its inception over two hundred years ago, the Sunday school movement has exerted an enormous influence on the teaching ministry of the Protestant churches.[3] This has especially been true in the United States, where it was a part of the evangelicals' attempt to convert the population of the American frontier. During the latter part of the nineteenth century, the mainline denominations assimilated many of the structures of this movement, which had become de facto the dominant style of education in their churches. Through denominational curricula, an attempt was make to exert greater control over the kinds of things that were taught in what came to be known as the church school.

While the theology of the Sunday school has varied over the years, the basic pattern of Christian education it engendered has not. Primary focus is placed on teaching that takes place on Sunday morning before or after congregational worship. This pattern is familiar to virtually anyone who attends a Protestant church in the United States today. Over the last two decades, there have been serious questions about using the Sunday school as the primary means of teaching in the church. To a large extent, the debate has focused on whether the Sunday school is viable when its former cultural supports are no longer in place.[4] Greater attention should be paid, in this view, to the congregation as an agent of socialization or faith enculturation in a society that projects multiple, frequently non-Christian values.

Counter arguments of two sorts have been raised. According to one line of thought, education can never be reduced to socialization. Rather, it is a distinctive function within the life of a community, pursuing an end—like intentional belief formation or a dialectical reconstruction of the tradition—that can be distinguished from the processes of socialization per se.[5] The Sunday school constitutes one important agency through which education in the church can take place.

Others have argued in favor of the Sunday school on more pragmatic grounds. Outside of worship, it remains the time when more people are gathered together with the professed purpose of learning than at any other moment in the church's life. Moreover, a clear-cut correlation has been made between the vitality of the church school and a congregation's ability to attract and keep new members.[6] To undercut support for this agency is to cut the nerve of the church's teaching ministry.

These issues are of fundamental importance, especially the

question of the nature and purpose of education within the ongoing life of a community. However, the debate has been limited in two ways.

First, it has tended to assume that the primary focus of the church's teaching ministry is the congregation. To that extent, it presupposes the decentralization inherent in the voluntary pattern of church life in this country. Historically, however, the congregation has not been the exclusive agent of the church's teaching ministry. It has been only one of multiple offices and agencies by which the church has determined its normative beliefs and practices, reinterpreted these beliefs and practices in shifting cultural and historical contexts, and formulated institutions, processes, and instructional material. By broadening the horizon of the teaching office beyond the congregation, we gain a more realistic understanding of where the source of difficulty lies in mainline Protestantism's contemporary teaching ministry. Changes on the level of the congregation are important, but they are only part of the picture.

A second problem with the recent debate is the fact that it frequently has been carried out on nontheological grounds, in terms of historical, philosophical, or social scientific analyses. All of these are important—crucially important. It is virtually impossible to carry out reflection on the church's teaching ministry without interdisciplinary dialogue at some point. But the question is, At what point?

Since the advent of the religious education movement earlier in this century, the effort has been made to establish religious education as an independent discipline, a kind of subdiscipline of education. Empirical, social scientific investigation of how people learn, philosophical and anthropological analyses of education, and psychological investigations of the self have tended to set the terms by which the church's teaching ministry is understood.

Major gains in our understanding of the church's educational ministry have resulted from this sort of sustained scientific and philosophical inquiry. Unfortunately, however, it has also resulted in a tendency to place theology in a secondary position. This presents a problem. Theology must have the first and last word in our understanding of the church's teaching ministry, although it must also carry on a sustained conversation with social scientific and philosophical resources.

Chapters 6 and 7 will discuss the theological understanding of the church's teaching ministry as it is found in the thought of Martin Luther and John Calvin. In examining the theology of the two central figures of the Protestant Reformation, we are not merely indulging in an act of historical recollection, we are attempting to discover patterns of thought and action that have something to say to mainline Protestant churches today. The Reformers' theology is not irrelevant, it is foundational to traditions that are still alive and unfolding.

An examination of the gradual emergence of the teaching office in the early church, and of the various forms that it has taken across the centuries, will place Luther's and Calvin's thought in context. We will discover that from the very beginning of the church's life a tension has existed in the teaching ministry between structure and Spirit. The former places emphasis on the need for institutional roles and agencies by which the church can teach with authority; the latter on the role of the Holy Spirit as the teacher of every individual believer. The teaching office of the church has worked best when it has been able to balance both these emphases; it has lapsed into individualism or authoritarianism when one or the other has been given too much prominence. Mainline Protestant churches would do well to harken to the history of this tension in the church's teaching ministry as it struggles to formulate a new understanding of the teaching office today.

Teaching in the Ministry of Jesus

In an age of specialization, it is tempting to read into the New Testament forms of ministry that only emerged at later points in the church's life. Such is the case with the church's teaching ministry. In recent years, a number of scholars have attempted to argue that a clear distinction between Jesus' teaching and preaching ministries can be found in the Gospels.[7] His teaching ministry is said to be directed to those who already have faith, focusing on moral exhortation and instruction in the Christian life. Preaching, in contrast, is thought to focus on the public announcement of the coming kingdom of God and is directed to those who are not yet disciples.

This kind of distinction has been widely challenged.[8] Even a cursory reading of the Gospels reveals Jesus as teaching in a variety of locations: in Temple and synagogues, on hilltops and mountains, in villages, among crowds, at the lakeside and seaside, from a boat, in houses, and as he was walking from community to community. Moreover, teaching is not always restricted to believers but is aimed at anyone who wants to listen. Furthermore, there is little evidence that

Jesus' teaching was confined to moral exhortation or cate-chetical instruction. While there can be no question that Jesus is portrayed as teaching about the moral life, as in the Sermon on the Mount, he also is portrayed as teaching about the kingdom of God, the significance of his death, how to pray, the proper interpretation of certain passages from the law and the prophets, and a wide variety of other subjects. Frequently, he enacts his teaching parabolically, as in his table fellowship with undesirables and even in his healings.

We simply cannot find the kind of sharp demarcation be-tween Jesus' teaching and preaching ministries that we might be comfortable making on the basis of current practices in the church. During Jesus' lifetime a rich mix of educational activi-ties was present in Judaism, and these diverse teaching styles and contexts are reflected in his teaching and that of the early church. Noting the wide variety of styles during this period is instructive. There was teaching during worship on the sab-bath, involving the interpretation of scripture—a pattern re-flected in Luke 4. There was more formal schooling for students who attached themselves to rabbi-scholars and learned particular ways of interpreting the law. Informal teaching was available in the synagogue courtyard or the cen-ter of the village for anyone who wanted to listen. Traveling teachers sent out from Jerusalem frequently would oversee educational programs for adults in the synagogues. Instruction for children and youth varied from place to place and fre-quently was centered in the home.

Reflecting this pluralistic mix of activities, preaching and teaching in the Gospels are not sharply separated. Teaching takes place in Jesus' ministry in a wide variety of contexts and for a variety of purposes. At times it is virtually indistinguish-able from preaching and focuses primarily on a sharing of the coming kingdom of God. We cannot find in Jesus the clear distinctions between teaching and other forms of ministry that we have come to expect.

Rather, a clearer demarcation of the various forms of ministry only took place as part of the church's gradual organization of itself as an ongoing community. Specialized roles and offices began to emerge that pursued certain tasks on behalf of the community as a whole. Teaching now was seen as a special gift of the Spirit or as related to a special office within the church. Of importance in this regard was the early church's struggle to maintain both continuity with the original message of Jesus and unity as it expanded into diverse cultural situations.

Structure and Spirit:
Models of the Teaching Office in the Early Church

The relationship between Jesus' authority as a teacher and that of his closest disciples was paradoxical. On the one hand, Jesus is portrayed as claiming for himself a kind of authority in his interpretation of the received tradition that goes far beyond that which even the most learned rabbi or apostle would have assumed. It is he who truly interprets and fulfills the law and the prophets. He is the teacher par excellence. Indeed, at one point Jesus tells his disciples, "But you are not to be called rabbi, for you have one teacher" (Matt. 23:8).

On the other hand, it is clear in Paul's letters and in Acts that great importance was attached to the teaching authority of the apostles. They had been commissioned and instructed by Christ for a special teaching ministry: They were to hand on all that Jesus had taught them. In Mark 6, for example, the disciples are sent out two by two to practice the ministry they will carry out when Jesus is gone. In verse 30, we are told, "The apostles returned to Jesus, and told him all that they had done and taught." In the so-called great commission at the end of Matthew, the eleven disciples are told, "Go therefore and make disciples of all nations, baptizing them in the name of the Father and of the Son and of the Holy Spirit, *teaching them to observe all that I have commanded you*" (Matt. 29:19–20, emphasis added).

Throughout the New Testament, the apostles are commissioned to teach. They are presented as holding a distinctive kind of teaching authority as eyewitnesses of Jesus and as persons who had been commissioned by him. Their death caused great problems for early Christianity. Now that those who could teach with the authority of eyewitnesses were gone, how would continuity with the message of Jesus be maintained?[9] Competing teachings about Jesus' life and death are already evident in Paul's epistles. How could the church decide which of these teachings were in continuity with Jesus' own teachings and those of the apostles? What was to prevent Christianity from becoming a series of isolated sects, each with its own doctrines and practices?

The problems of continuity and unity lie at the heart of emerging understandings of the teaching office in the early church. We find a wide range of answers to these problems in the New Testament, reflecting the diversity that existed in the early church. Briefly, two different understandings of the teaching office in the New Testament can be outlined, repre-

senting vastly different models of the church's teaching ministry. To a certain extent, they represent two extremes. The
Pastoral epistles—First and Second Timothy and Titus—offer
a model of the teaching office defined largely in terms of
structure. The Johannine literature—including the Gospel of
John and First, Second, and Third John—offers a model governed by a strong conception of Spirit. The tension between
structure and Spirit is something that has plagued the
church's teaching ministry throughout Christian history. We
find this struggle present already in the very different understandings of the teaching office that the Pastoral and Johannine trajectories of Christianity represent.

The Pastoral Epistles: The Dominance of Structure

The Pastoral epistles respond to the problems of continuity
and unity in the church by establishing structure. These letters portray Paul as near death and turning toward those he is
leaving behind. He charges Timothy and Titus to preserve the
apostolic heritage against false ideas and teachers by ap-
pointing designated elders or bishops who will serve in a su-
pervisory role (Titus 1:5, 7).

At the heart of these leaders' ministerial office is the task of
teaching the sound doctrine they have received from Paul
through Titus and Timothy. As Paul writes in Titus 1:9, "[The
bishop] must hold firm to the sure word as taught, so that he may
be able to give instruction in sound doctrine and also to confute
those who contradict it." Timothy and Titus are to "follow the
pattern of the sound words which you have heard from me" (2
Tim. 1:13) and to "guard the truth that has been entrusted to
you" (2 Tim. 1:14).[10] They are to hand on these "sound words"
to specially designated leaders in the church, and the teaching of
these authoritative leaders will preserve congregations against
disintegration and the threat of false doctrine.

The Pastoral epistles are written during a situation in which
teachers are introducing new ideas, involving "vain discussion" and "myths and endless genealogies" (1 Tim. 1:4–7). In
2 Timothy, those who are affected by such teachings are said
to possess "itching ears" (4:3). The letters make a connection
between bad doctrine and immoral behavior. Apparently, an
early version of Christian gnosticism has already appeared and
is beginning to win a following. Such teachers of false doctrine
are to be "silenced" by representatives of the apostolic faith
(Titus 1:11). The world-negating teaching of the Gnostics is to
be opposed by an affirmation of Jesus' full incarnation into the

created order, an affirmation based on the belief that "everything created by God is good" (1 Tim. 4:4).

In the Pastoral epistles, the answer to the crisis posed by the passing of the original apostles is given in terms of structure: Clearly designated leaders who can offer authoritative teaching that stands in continuity with the apostolic heritage are to be appointed in every congregation. The Pastorals represent one of the most important trajectories of the teaching office that emerged in the early church, informing both Roman Catholicism and Protestantism at various points in church history. In the face of the extremes of individualism and authoritarianism prevalent in America today, this model of the teaching office brings into focus the authority of the bishop, the minister, and other designated church leaders.

Those who occupy positions of leadership in the church are charged with the task of preserving and reinterpreting the "sound doctrine" that has been handed down by the apostles. This model of the teaching office invites Protestants, especially, to ask themselves whether they have not been too quick to reject the importance of ecclesiastical structures that can introduce the church in every age to the classical expressions of the faith, teaching with an eye to the "far" tradition and encouraging each generation of Christians to resist faddish and even false teaching.

Clearly, however, this model has certain weaknesses. At its worst, its centralization of teaching authority in specially designated ministerial offices designed to guard the faith can give rise to very real distortions. A necessary protection of the faith in times of crisis becomes normative for the church's ongoing life. Officially controlled teaching gives rise to censorship, excommunication, and conformity based on coercion. New teaching is too quickly identified with false teaching. A sharp demarcation is made between those designated leaders who can teach with authority and a passive church membership whose only contribution is to receive obediently what comes from "on high." These weaknesses raise the basic question of whether the model of the teaching office represented by the Pastoral epistles does not unduly tie the work of God's Spirit to institutional roles and structures This is a key issue in the struggle between structure and Spirit in the teaching office.

The Johannine Literature: The Dominance of Spirit

We find a radically different understanding of teaching in the Johannine literature. Here the role of the Spirit is crucial in defining how authoritative teaching continues after the apostles' death. Moreover, there is something of a diminution of the role of specially sanctioned offices in the church. In a sense, all are equal before God in the Christian community. The Spirit is not mediated to the community of faith through ecclesiastical structures.

It is impossible, of course, to examine this rich and complex literature in any depth. However, certain themes are relevant for our understanding of the nature of the teaching office in this trajectory. As many scholars have pointed out, the ecclesiology of the Gospel and letters of John is dominated by its unique Christology. Far more than in the synoptic Gospels, Jesus' preexistence with the Father is emphasized. The Word is portrayed as becoming flesh to reveal the Father to those who believe. Judgment is seen as taking place not just in the future but in the present, as persons respond in faith or disbelief to Jesus.

It was precisely this high Christology, placing so much emphasis on Jesus' preexistent equality with God, that got the Johannine community in trouble with the leaders of the synagogue. The synagogue leaders saw such an affirmation as idolatrous, as denying the most fundamental tenet of Israelite faith: The Lord our God is one. Strong evidence exists that the Johannine community had already been cast out of the synagogue when the Gospel of John was written because of its christological affirmations. This is why the Gospel is so polemical, with its hostile portrayal of "the Jews" and those believers who refuse to confess Jesus openly for fear of being cast out of the synagogue. Raymond Brown argues that this situation of conflict even shapes the way the Gospel portrays Jesus, underplaying his humanity and overplaying his divinity so as not to give the synagogue opponents any ammunition.[11]

Two themes that are especially important for our purposes are the great emphasis placed on the individual's personal relationship with Jesus in John's ecclesiology and the role of the Holy Spirit as a continuation of the presence of Jesus. While the Gospel of John clearly has room for the corporate life of Christians, it uniquely places emphasis on each disciple's personal and ongoing relationship to Jesus. The statement "I am the vine, you are the branches" (15:5) implies a relationship in which the disciple must continue to be attached directly to Jesus in order to stay alive. This personal relationship outweighs all distinctions flowing from special offices in the church. It is not Peter who is dominant, for example, but "the disciple who loved Jesus," representing every disciple who stands in a close relationship to the Lord.

The Holy Spirit as a continuation of Jesus' presence is a closely related theme. The Spirit in John is identified as the paraclete. The word stems from *kletos,* meaning "called," and *para,* "alongside." The image has a legal background: When people are in trouble, they call a counselor or advocate to stand beside them in court. This fits the life situation of the Johannine community, in which its members were having to defend themselves for their christological views. Their help in the face of situations of controversy was the paraclete-Spirit dwelling within each disciple.

John portrays the Spirit as playing a representative role. Just as Jesus represents on earth the Father who sent him, the paraclete represents Jesus who sent him. The Spirit continues Jesus' presence. An especially important representative role of the paraclete is that of teacher. In John 14, the paraclete is described as the Spirit of truth who will remind the disciples of the things Jesus taught them: "But the Counselor, the Holy Spirit, whom the Father will send in my name, he will teach you all things, and bring to your remembrance all that I have said to you" (14:26). In chapter 16 (vs. 12–14), the Spirit is described as contemporizing Jesus' teachings in order to enable them to face the things they will encounter:

> I have yet many things to say to you, but you cannot bear them now. When the Spirit of truth comes, he will guide you into all the truth; for he will not speak on his own authority, but whatever he hears he will speak, and he will declare to you the things that are to come. He will glorify me, for he will take what is mine and declare it to you.

If the Pastoral epistles portray the teaching office in terms of designated elders who are to teach and guard the apostolic faith, the Johannine literature thinks in terms of the divine teacher in the heart of every believer. Paradigmatic in this regard is 1 John 2:27: "The anointing which you received from him abides in you, and you have no need that any one should teach you; as his anointing teaches you about everything, and is true, and is no lie, just as it has taught you, abide in him." The reference to anointing here refers to the reception of the Holy Spirit. Those who have this Spirit are taught directly by Jesus; they have no need for a teacher. Indeed, in 3 John 9–10, Diotrephes is criticized for taking on a role that seems to resemble that of a presbyter-bishop.

Clearly, in the Johannine literature, the teaching office is thought of in terms of Spirit, not structure. All disciples who abide in Jesus have within them his Spirit, which serves as an inner witness to bring to mind the things he has taught. Teaching is tied to Spirit, not structure.

But just as there were weaknesses in the Pastoral epistles' model of the teaching office, there also are problems with this model. When the teacher is the Spirit in the heart of each believer, what happens when those who possess the paraclete disagree with one another? Both sides can make an appeal to the Spirit. How can a determination be made as to which teaching stands in continuity with Jesus? There seems to be no clear answer to this question. Indeed, precisely this problem emerged in the Johannine community, as we see in the letters of John.

In the Johannine epistles, it is no longer the Jews who are the main antagonists, as in the Gospel of John, but a group of secessionists within the community itself. This is the threat being countered by the epistles' author. As Brown points out, the secessionists reflect certain weaknesses inherent in the Christology and ecclesiology of the Gospel of John.[12] Its diminution of Jesus' human characteristics, for example, lends itself to a gnostic Christology in which Jesus as the divine revealer comes to impart knowledge but whose earthly career and death are not significant. Hence the letters charge the secessionists with not taking Jesus seriously "in the flesh" (1 John 4:2; 2 John 7).

In the face of a group within the community that can also claim the Spirit's witness, the author of the epistles begins to appeal to the "message which you have heard from the beginning" (1 John 3:11), highlighting the importance of Jesus' atoning sacrifice on the cross and his ethical teachings. Even in the midst of this schism, however, he remains bound to the Johannine tradition's emphasis on the Spirit as the internal teacher whom believers receive with their anointing (1 John 2:27). Surely the successionists can claim the same teaching authority. A Spirit-oriented model of the teaching office seems unable to resolve the difficulty of uncontrollable divisions in the church.

Structure and Spirit: Both played important roles in models of the teaching office that emerged in the early church. In the presentations of Roman Catholic and Protestant understandings of the teaching office that follow, we would do well to keep in mind the diversity represented by the Pastoral epistles and the Johannine literature. These two very different trajectories are legitimate forms of the church's teaching ministry that emerged out of the struggle to determine how continuity and unity could be maintained in the early church once the original generation of apostles had died. The diversity they represent will bring into focus different elements that must find a place in our model of the teaching office, if it is to be viable for the American Protestant church today.

5

Magisterium: The Teaching Office in the Roman Catholic Tradition

The struggle between structure and Spirit has characterized the teaching office throughout church history. It is a struggle found within the various traditions comprising Christianity and between them as well. This chapter will examine the emergence of the teaching office in the Roman Catholic tradition. From a Protestant perspective, it would be easy to call the developments that are recounted here "the triumph of structure." The argument might be made that the understanding of the teaching office that emerges in this story unduly ties the work of the Holy Spirit to institutional roles—the pope and college of bishops—while scripture tells us that the Spirit blows where it wills, as the Gospel of John points out.

It is best to resist the temptation to fall into such stereotypes. Roman Catholicism's understanding of the teaching office is far more complex than most Protestants realize. Moreover, we must not oppose structure and Spirit in a manner that unconsciously reflects Protestant presuppositions, especially if we would enter sympathetically into the Roman Catholic view of the teaching office. Roman Catholics view the emergence of clearly defined ecclesiastical structures, which can teach the universal church with authority, as the work of the Holy Spirit. They are the outgrowth of Christ's promise to the church: "Lo, I am with you always, to the close of the age" (Matt. 28:20). As such, the teaching office in this tradition rests on a belief in the church's "indefectibility," a belief that God will not only preserve the church in existence until the end of time but also maintain it in truth.[1]

Over the centuries, Roman Catholics have come to refer to the teaching office in their tradition as the *magisterium*. Both in antiquity and in the Middle Ages, the title *magister* was frequently used to refer to the leader in a wide variety of activities and areas.[2] A *magister* of the military, for example, referred to a military leader. The closely related term *magisterium* designated the dignity or office of a *magister*, referring especially to the rights and responsibilities involved. The *magisterium* of a military leader, for example, referred to those rights and responsibilities afforded him by his rank.

As this expression gained currency in the Roman Catholic Church, it gradually came to be applied almost exclusively to the teaching function of ecclesiastical leaders and eventually to the church hierarchy itself. In this chapter, *magisterium* refers to the teaching function of the Roman Catholic Church as it is carried on by specially authorized members of the church hierarchy. The contemporary form of the Roman Catholic *magisterium*, however, is not the only model of the teaching office that has existed in this tradition. Indeed, there is more than one model of the teaching office present in this tradition even today. It is important to view the emergence of the structural elements that have come to characterize the teaching ministry of Roman Catholicism in terms of developments that were already taking place during the first centuries of its existence.

The Early Church

The story of the early church is one of becoming both catholic and Roman.[3] Each development deeply influenced the understandings of the teaching office that emerged in the Roman Catholic tradition. We will focus first on the emerging catholicity of the church during the first centuries and then examine how the church became Roman, granting special importance to the leadership and teaching authority of the bishop of Rome.

Emerging Catholicity

The term "catholic" means here an affirmation of both particularity and universality.[4] Catholicity in this sense is not a quality characterizing the Roman Catholic Church alone. Identity focuses on selfsameness through time. The identity of a person, for example, refers to those features of the personality that endure. The central focus of the church's identity is its unique trust in and loyalty to Jesus Christ as the Son of God. Universality refers to "that which impels the church to embrace nothing less than all mankind in its vision and in its appeal."[5] It refers to the church's extension in time and space. A catholic church is not turned in on itself in a sectarian fashion. Catholic Christianity seeks to relate its unique faith in Jesus Christ to all persons, all cultures, all phases of life, all historical eras.

Not every form of Christianity that emerged in the early church was catholic in this sense. Christian gnosticism, in its various forms, was typically so world negating that it did not really strive to relate Christ to every dimension of life. It is not hard to see, however, that the combination of identity and universality that catholic Christianity represents was present in latent form in the ministry and message of Jesus.

Jesus' missionary activity serves as a good example. On the one hand, Jesus maintained his identity with Judaism, addressing much of his teaching and preaching to the children of Israel. On the other hand, the universality of his message is clear in his willingness to preach to the Samaritans, the tax collectors, and other supposedly unrighteous classes of people. Moreover, during the forty days of resurrection appearances, explicit reference is made to a worldwide mission.

Both identity and universality are present in Jesus' ministry. Christianity became catholic as a result of a dynamic in the life and work of Jesus himself. The various understandings of the teaching office that have emerged in the Roman Catholic tradition are an attempt to remain faithful to this catholicity. Across the centuries certain structures evolved in an attempt both to preserve identity by guarding the original message of Jesus and the apostolic church and to strive for universality by reinterpreting and developing this message in the face of new cultural and historical contexts. In Roman Catholic thought, the teaching office represents a divine gift to the church, and God has bound the Holy Spirit to it in a special way. Believers can look with confidence to those who carry out this ministry for truthful teaching.

The single most important development in the emergence of the teaching office was the centralization of the teaching authority of the office of bishop. Initially, this took the form of authority accorded bishops who supervised individual churches or metropolitan areas, a trend we saw emerging in the Pastoral epistles. As the church expanded, regional leaders emerged whose responsibilities went beyond individual congregations and municipalities. What is important here is the crucial role of the bishop in the church's teaching ministry. This office was charged with the task of conserving and handing on the apostolic faith from generation to generation.

While a full-scale theology of apostolic succession emerged only gradually over the course of several centuries, certain trajectories of Christianity at an early stage began to grant the office of bishop a special teaching authority, which was seen as standing in continuity with that of the apostles in the primitive church. The teaching authority of bishops has consistently been an important element in Roman Catholic models of the teaching office. But how episcopal teaching authority is conceived in relation to the bishop of Rome, general councils, and the universal practices and beliefs of the laity has varied greatly across history.

The Link with Rome

An account of these different models must, by necessity, begin with the story of how the catholic church became Roman. It would be misleading to think of this as a two-step process. The church did not first become catholic and then become Roman. In the process of becoming catholic the church in the west also became Roman Catholic. What does this mean? During the first five or six centuries of the church's life, the church in Rome and its bishop increasingly came to be viewed as holding a position of primacy in the church's teaching ministry. How did this happen?

Initially, Jerusalem held a position of primacy among the various apostolic congregations. The book of Acts states it was a council in Jerusalem that settled the controversy as to whether Gentiles first had to become Jews by being circumcised before they could become Christians. Primacy among the apostles was accorded to Peter. It was to Peter that Jesus addressed these words, "I tell you, you are Peter, and on this rock I will build my church, and the powers of death shall not prevail against it" (Matt. 16:18). In Acts, Peter is portrayed as the dominant figure in the Christian community. It is he who first preaches the gospel after Pentecost; he who must be convinced by the Holy Spirit that the gospel should be preached to the Gentiles as well as the Jews; he who is named first in the various lists of the apostles.

A variety of traditions both inside and outside the New Testament magnified the place of Peter as first among the apostles and as holding primacy in the early church.[6] Over a period of time, this primacy was transferred to Rome. By the fourth and fifth centuries, certain Roman bishops argued for a position of authority over all other bishops on the basis of being Peter's successors. This is referred to as the Petrine function or ministry. Just as Peter initially held a special position of importance in the early church, the bishop of Rome or pope, as the occupant of Peter's "chair," was seen as carrying out this same special ministry. Among a variety of reasons for this, three are especially important for our purposes.

First, there was a close identification of Peter with the church in Rome. Quite early in the church's life, traditions emerged that portrayed both Peter and Paul as traveling to Rome, where they were placed in prison and eventually martyred. Rome took on the prestige of these two great apostles. Irenaeus goes so far as to write that the Roman congregation was founded by Peter and Paul.[7] The emperor Constantine erected a basilica over the spot where Peter was thought to be buried, drawing attention to Peter's connection to Rome and serving as an especially important shrine for Christian pilgrims.

Second, political factors gradually enabled the bishop of Rome to seek and win primacy in the church.[8] The destruction of Jerusalem in A.D. 70 diminished the power of the Jerusalem church. As Christianity spread around the Mediterranean, it organized itself into several patriarchates. Four were in the east: Alexandria, Jerusalem, Antioch, and Constantinople. Only one was in the west: Rome.

It was to the west that much of the population would move. Islam's rise during the seventh and eighth centuries severely diminished the political power and freedom of the eastern patriachates. Even before this, with the fall of the Roman empire, the bishop of Rome had been given a great deal of political power in the west, taking over many of the empire's administrative and juridical functions.

Equally important is a third factor: the orthodoxy of the Roman church. In the first centuries of the church's life, theologians of Alexandria and Antioch engaged in one conflict after another, arguing over such crucial things as the nature of the Trinity and the person of Christ. Time and again, Rome was able to offer theological formulas accepted as orthodox by large portions of the church.

When the church met in Chalcedon in A.D. 451, for example, the theological formula that finally prevailed came from Leo, Bishop of Rome. Frequently, bishops and theologians who were declared unorthodox by eastern churches and stripped of their ecclesiastical office appealed to Rome to overturn these decisions. Indeed, Athanasius was received to communion by the Roman bishop Julius after he had been formally excommunicated by Greek synods.

All these factors—an identification of Peter's leadership

with the church in Rome, political developments that enhanced the power of the Roman church, and the consistency
with which the bishop of Rome was able to represent orthodoxy in the midst of doctrinal controversies—conspired to
make the bishop of Rome the most important leader in the
Western church. At the very heart of the special prerogatives
granted to this bishop was teaching authority in matters of
doctrine and morality.

In the eyes of Roman Catholics, these developments are not
accidental, as we have noted. They are the work of the Holy
Spirit. Human factors can be pointed to, to be sure. But there
is confidence that God's Spirit has worked through these human factors to bring about certain structures in the church
that allow it to be maintained in truth and thereby to survive
as the church. As Pelikan has pointed out, an "organic" view
of the church's history is operative here: Christianity is not
identified simply and completely with primitive Christianity
or even the gospel, in the same way that a great oak cannot be
identified with a tiny acorn.[9] Those of us who are Protestant
cannot scoff at such faith, especially if we are honest about the
all-too-human factors that went into the process of determining the canon, the central authority of teaching and preaching
in the Protestant tradition.

Models of the Teaching Office

While there was a steady trend toward acknowledging the
primacy of the bishop of Rome in the teaching of faith and
morals, this did not (and does not) immediately and necessarily result in a monarchical understanding of the papacy and its
teaching prerogatives. A monarchical model of the teaching
office, described in greater detail below, views the pope as
teaching with supreme authority, at times even infallibly, by
divine right. A monarchical, infallibilist understanding of the
teaching office in the Roman Catholic Church is a relatively
recent phenomenon, only strictly defined as such at Vatican I
during the late nineteenth century. While certain elements of
this model were in existence quite early in the Roman Catholic tradition, it was not dominant; indeed, even when it became so in recent centuries, it was not the only model present.

The Conciliar Model

Several other models of the teaching office in the Roman
Catholic tradition can be sketched briefly. At several points in

the history of the Roman Catholic Church, ecumenical councils have been viewed as possessing supreme teaching authority. While the bishop of Rome may have authority to call and preside over such councils, he functions as "first among equals." By himself, he cannot teach definitively; this is a privilege reserved for councils. Hence, in this model, supreme teaching authority is located in the College of Bishops when they are gathered together in official session representing the universal church. Frequently, such councils consult or include leading theologians in the church.

Often referred to as conciliarism, this understanding of the teaching office has struggled with the monarchical model throughout church history. At times, this struggle has been undertaken in the name of a representational understanding of teaching in the church.[10] The bishops gathered in council are seen as representing the beliefs and practices of the churches over which they preside. The activity of the Spirit in the church as a whole is acknowledged, including the beliefs and practices of the laity and the more systematic reflections of theologians. In the latter Middle Ages, this representational emphasis drew on certain principles of constitutionalism that were present in the secular sphere, calling for a more limited, delegated view of authority in the church.[11] The bishops were to consult the *sensus fidelium*—the sense of the faithful—on matters of belief and practice.

At other times, the College of Bishops has itself been viewed as invested with the authority to teach the truth infallibly under certain conditions. Here, councils teach by divine right through the power of the Holy Spirit in a manner comparable to the pope in a monarchical model.

The Twofold Model

During the Middle Ages, what is sometimes called a twofold model of the teaching office emerged, representing an alternative to both monarchical and conciliarist models. The relative independence of the monasteries and medieval universities allowed theology to develop some autonomy in relation to the church hierarchy. At various points, the theology faculties of the universities were viewed as possessing a teaching authority that functioned alongside of and, at times, even in opposition to that of the pope and the College of Bishops.

This twofold model is reflected in the theology of Thomas Aquinas, who distinguished between the *magisterium cathe-*

drae pastoralis, the teaching ministry of the bishops, and the *magisterium cathedrae magistralis,* the teaching ministry of the theologians.[12] At its best, this model viewed the theologians and the church hierarchy as playing distinguishable but interrelated roles. Theologians were charged with the task of asking questions of faith in terms of the canons of rationality then operative in the university, frequently leading them to pursue lines of thought that both challenged and extended the received tradition. The pastoral leadership was charged with teaching in ways that maintained continuity with the past and nurtured the present life of the church.

During the late Middle Ages, the universities played an increasingly important role in defining orthodoxy, with several general councils submitting their teachings to universities for approval before officially publishing them.[13] It is frequently forgotten that Luther's theses were first condemned by several theological faculties before he was officially excommunicated. During the fifteenth century, reform councils were viewed along the lines of a parliament or estates-general, with theological faculties receiving corporate invitations to attend. A model of the teaching office in which theologians play an important role is not foreign to the Roman Catholic tradition, even if this might seem to be the case at times in the contemporary church.

The Monarchical Model

The model of the teaching office that is frequently seen by Protestants as *the* exclusive model of the teaching office in the Roman Catholic Church is that of a monarchical papacy. While certain elements of this model were in existence quite early in the Roman Catholic tradition, it did not fully come into its own until after the Reformation. As Dulles points out, it can be seen as moving through two distinct phases, the Counter-Reformation and Neo-Scholasticism.[14]

In both phases, increasing emphasis is placed on the church hierarchy as the exclusive agent of teaching authority in the church. Teaching is viewed juridically, along the lines of legal decisions that are handed down and must be obeyed as law. A lack of assent to duly constituted teaching authority implies a lack of reverence and is punishable according to prescribed procedures. Howland Sanks has provided a helpful description of the basic features of this model, describing it in terms of its sociopolitical structure, its understanding of authority, and its view of truth.[15]

The sociopolitical structure operative in this model is that of monarchy, as we might expect. The pope rules by divine right. He does not receive his authority from the body of Christ but directly from God. Councils and theologians possess no comparable teaching authority. Indeed, it is the pope and the pope alone who can teach the church with supreme authority. Authority in this model is structured hierarchically. It is best conceptualized as a pyramid whose peak pierces heaven itself.[16] Subordination of the lower to the higher in a clearly defined chain of command holds the universal church together. Moral force and intellectual persuasion are less important than juridical authority. The understanding of truth that characterizes this model, especially in its Neo-Scholastic form, is static. A correspondence theory of truth is operative with propositional teachings offered by the *magisterium* viewed as corresponding to the divine order of things. All notions of historical and cultural relativism are eliminated, as well as the possibility that such teachings might be in error.

The Fallibilist Model

This monarchical model of the teaching office has been challenged from a number of different directions in recent Roman Catholic theology, recalling emphases that were important in earlier models. Hans Kung and others have argued for a "fallibilist" model of the teaching office.[17] Rather than continuing to justify previous errors made by popes and councils, Kung argues, the church should drop notions of infallibility altogether.[18] The church is maintained in truth in spite of its errors. In Kung's view, the indefectibility of the church does not depend on persons who can teach without error. The church's teaching ministry should be viewed in more dialogical and participatory terms, with the laity, priesthood, and members of the hierarchy, including the pope, each playing important roles.

The Liberationist Model

While operating out of a very different theological and philosophical perspective, the proponents of liberation theology can be seen as offering a challenge to the monarchical papacy that is similar to Kung's.[19] In ways that are reminiscent of the importance of the *sensus fidelium*, this approach places emphasis on the ability of members of the church to interpret scripture directly. Priority, however, is given to the capacity of the "struggling poor" to hear and respond to the message of Jesus, which is seen as addressed, first and foremost, to the poor and as biased on their behalf.[20]

It is no accident that this model and Kung's have met such resistance from the church hierarchy. They both represent a direct challenge to the teaching authority of the monarchical papacy. Both undercut the notion that the papacy is the key office by which the church is maintained in truth. In the case of liberation theology, the poor, not the pope, hold a position of "epistemological privilege." In Kung's case, the pope functions only as one of many sources of authoritative teaching in the church, and a fallible one at that.

The "Moderate Infallibilist" Model

A second line of thought, also in tune with long-standing elements of the teaching office in the Roman Catholic tradition, is increasingly coming to serve as a genuine alternative to the monarchical model. It is what George Lindbeck has labeled the model of "moderate infallibilism."[21] Like Kung and the liberation theologians, this model wants the teaching office to become less absolutist and authoritarian. In contrast, however, it believes the infallibility of the teaching office points to something that is basic to Roman Catholic identity: the belief that certain designated church leaders, with the help of the Holy Spirit, have the ability to teach without error under certain conditions, that the church might be maintained in truth.

Unlike strict monarchicalists, however, this model affords importance to the whole people of God, placing emphasis on both the *sensus fidelium* and collegiality among the church hierarchy. The former harks back to more representational models of the teaching office, positing a crucial role for the "sense of the faithful," aroused by the Spirit, in the "reception" of official teachings. Teachings by the hierarchy that are not accepted by the people of God over a period of time are not seen as true to the deposit of faith.

An emphasis on collegiality shifts the focus of the teaching office away from a preoccupation with the pope and onto the importance of the bishops as a whole in defining truth and handing it on to the faithful. Moreover, the need for collegiality between bishops and theologians is also emphasized, recalling certain elements of the medieval twofold *magisterium*.

Representatives of moderate infallibilism, like Avery Dulles and Karl Rahner, are cognizant of the dynamic, historical nature of truth and reject the static understandings frequently characterizing the monarchical model.[22] In contrast, the teaching office is viewed as crucial precisely because of the historical nature of truth. Doctrine develops; it must be reinterpreted anew in every age. The teaching office is charged with carrying out this task. At its best, this office does not impose beliefs and moral directives in an authoritarian fashion but, through persuasion, represents a unifying center in the church, providing a common authoritative body of teaching that sustains the church as a community of moral and theological discourse.

In the view of moderate infallibilists, church teaching is infallible only when solemn definitions are rendered. Such definitions of the faith are offered solely in instances of extreme duress, when the church's identity is at stake. More frequently, the teaching office offers noninfallible teaching, providing guidance to the faithful that is not binding in the same way. According to this line of thought, even when the *magisterium* does teach infallibly, this does not mean that its teachings cannot be reinterpreted. Indeed, they must be, as they are brought into new cultural and linguistic frameworks. It is the *meaning* of infallible teaching that is without error, not the particular linguistic expressions used to state this meaning. Such statements are by definition historical and limited and may even have been poorly formulated in their original form.[23]

Frequently, Protestants view the teaching office of the Roman Catholic tradition only through the eyes of the media or the highly charged polemics of the Reformers. True to its inner genius, Roman Catholicism has developed in response both to Protestantism and to modernity. Indeed, it is developing still. In light of the extremes of individualism and authoritarianism in American Protestantism today, there is much to be learned from a tradition that acknowledges the importance of certain structures in the church in maintaining both a sense of tradition and the ongoing reinterpretation of that tradition. While Protestantism must take issue with Roman Catholicism's understanding of the teaching office at crucial points, it should not do so without first acknowledging this tradition as a legitimate expression of the Christian faith.

6

Martin Luther's Break
with the Roman Catholic *Magisterium*

For many Protestants it is surprising to learn of the diverse
forms of the teaching office in the Roman Catholic tradition. It
may be even more surprising to learn that the teaching office
is a topic of import and debate in Protestantism as well. However, the nature and authority of the church's teaching office
lay at the heart of the Reformers' disagreements with Rome. It
was a central part of their broader attempt to develop a new
theology and new structures for the church's life.

Debate Over Teaching Authority

At stake in the Reformers' effort to redefine the teaching
office was the doctrine of justification by faith. In the face of a
monarchical papacy that claimed for itself the power to define
articles of faith infallibly and to demand obedience to the
church's teachings as a condition of salvation, the Reformers
rejected the authority of the *magisterium*, arguing that it
usurped prerogatives that belong to Christ and Christ alone.
The structures of the teaching authority that confronted them
were viewed as oppressive not merely in a political sense.
They were seen as theologically oppressive, setting themselves up as the mediator of salvation when Christ alone is the
true mediator, burdening the consciences of the faithful with
onerous beliefs and practices when the hallmark of true faith
is Christian liberty, and making human traditions and teachings the norm of faith when scripture alone is the final rule of
faith and life.

It was inevitable that the Reformers would confront the
question of the church's teaching office in their conflict with

Rome. The Roman *magisterium* was quite clear about the grounds of its teaching authority. By what authority did the Reformers dare to offer their teachings? Repeatedly, Luther faced arguments like the following: "The church, the church: Do you suppose that God is so merciless that he would reject his whole church for the sake of a few Lutheran heretics? Do you suppose that he would leave his church in error for so many centuries?"[1] Inevitably, such taunts were part of a defense of the teaching authority and juridical power of the pope. Is it any wonder that on three different occasions Luther summed up his life's work as a struggle against the papacy, a struggle he bequeathed to his successors?[2] We would do well to extricate ourselves from present understandings of the teaching office in the Protestant church in order to recapture something of what was at stake in the Reformer's efforts in this area.

One piece of Reformation history typifies a widespread understanding of teaching authority in the Protestant church today. It centers on Luther's closing remarks at the Diet of Worms in 1521. Having been excommunicated by the pope and seen his teachings condemned by the University of Paris, Luther was called before the Diet by Emperor Charles to account for his position. He was only allowed to answer two questions put to him: Did he acknowledge the books that were published under his name as his own? Did he stand by their content or wish to recant?

In the forceful conclusion of his response, Luther replied, "Unless I am overcome by the testimony of Scripture or by clear reason (for I believe neither the pope nor councils by themselves), I remain conquered by the Scriptures which I have adduced. As long as my conscience is captive to the words of God, I neither can nor will recant, since it is neither safe nor right to act against conscience. God help me. Amen."[3]

Luther's appeal to conscience here seems almost paradigmatic of teaching authority in the American Protestant church. Is he not arguing that individual conscience is to reign supreme, that it is more authoritative than any ecclesiastical structure, including specially designated leaders, councils, and denominational confessions? Do not persons stand in an unmediated relationship to God, with salvation essentially a transaction between the individual and God? Is not the private interpretation of scripture the right of every individual believer?

This kind of interpretation of Luther makes Spirit absolutely dominant over structure, as these themes were developed in chapter 4. God's Spirit is located primarily in individual consciences, giving persons the right to resist any attempt by church structures to limit or shape their beliefs and behavior. The Spirit's empowerment of individual freedom is made the hallmark of Protestantism.

And yet this portrayal has more to do with the contemporary church than with Luther. It is to view Luther through the eyes of modern individualism. While the Spirit's empowerment of individual conscience does have a role in Luther's thought, it is only one of a cluster of relative authorities in the church's life, all of which are subordinate to and derivative from the authority of the gospel. In the passage just quoted, Luther's appeal to conscience is subordinated to scripture. Moreover, his appeal to conscience is not primarily to the authority of the Spirit-filled individual over against the religious establishment. It rests on his responsibility as a doctor of the church commissioned to nourish the faith and life of the people.[4] His appeal to conscience only makes sense when it is placed in a larger field of authorities found in his thought as a whole.

In a very real sense, we must "widen the gap between the centuries," to borrow a phrase from New Testament scholar Krister Stendahl.[5] We must step outside of what we think we know of the Reformers and encounter their thought afresh. In so doing, we will discover a complex understanding of the relationship between structure and Spirit in the proper exercise of teaching authority in the church.

For what Luther and Calvin took away with one hand, they were forced to give back with the other, albeit in a distinctly new form. It was one thing for Luther to challenge the structures of the Roman Catholic Church in the name of the freedom of God's Spirit, as he did in *The Babylonian Captivity*, and quite another to face the task of building structures that could sustain the doctrine and life of the Reformation in the newly emerging churches.[6] No sooner had Luther and Calvin begun to extricate themselves from Roman authority than they were faced with the Anabaptists and their emphasis on the unmediated role of the Holy Spirit in the Christian life. In the Reformers' rejection of this form of Christianity, they were forced to reaffirm the relative importance of councils, church tradition, the ordained ministry, and theological doctrines and confessions. How they reaffirmed these structures of the church while attempting to maintain the freedom of God's Spirit can teach Protestant mainline churches much today.

Luther's Struggle with the Papacy

It was no accident that Luther's theological and ecclesiastical reform brought him into conflict repeatedly with the papacy, for the papacy was the seat of symbolic and political authority in the church of his day. In large part, Luther constructed his own understanding of the teaching office in opposition to the papacy. It is illuminating to follow the stages through which he moved.

The overall pattern of Luther's relationship to the papacy has been aptly characterized as a movement from internal ambivalence to unrelenting, highly polemical rejection.[7] What is especially important for our purposes is the shift in the configuration of authorities, which Luther deemed important in the church's definition of articles of faith and its guidance of the moral life of its members. From beginning to end, Luther viewed multiple authorities as having roles to play in the teaching office: scripture, tradition, ministerial offices, individual conscience, and church councils. The relative weight assigned to each of these authorities, however, shifted markedly over the course of his reform. Largely, this shift was prompted by his struggle with the model of authority represented by the papacy.

Indications are that Luther harbored an ambivalence toward the papacy long before his disaffection became public. His early struggles over the possibility and efficacy of confession became related, in his mind, to papal authority through the writings of Jean Gerson.[8] An influential proponent of conciliar authority, Gerson argued that unless disobedience to the church's laws was deliberate, it was not a sin and hence need not be confessed.

In Luther's view, this freed him and other church members from the need to confess every sin and relaxed the influence of church authorities over the most intimate details of a person's life. In general, Luther's difficulties with the penitential practices of the church seemed to raise questions in his mind about the church hierarchy that sponsored such practices.

These reservations remained private during the first part of Luther's career. Upon the completion of his doctorate and the acquisition of the titles "teacher" and "preacher" in 1512, Luther began to sound a theme that was to characterize his entire work as a Reformer. In his lectures and sermons, he criticized the laxity of the clergy. By their office, he said, they are charged with the task of nourishing the members of the church with the word of God. If they, in their conduct and public ministry, are deficient in this task, who will feed God's people?

Is was precisely this sense of responsibility for the nourishment of the faithful that led Luther, as a doctor of the church, to criticize the widespread practice of selling indulgences. The purchase of an indulgence was thought to release the buyer from the need to do penance for a predetermined number of sins. In his earliest public criticisms of the clergy, Luther also criticized this practice as promoting laxity among the laity, creating the false impression that persons could buy their way into heaven, as expressed by the common rhyme; "As soon as the coin in the coffer rings, the soul from purgatory springs."

What particularly rankled Luther was the practice of plenary indulgences, a special category that was supposed to cancel the guilt and mandatory punishment of *all* sins. On March 31, 1515, Pope Leo X authorized the sale of plenary indulgences in the German provinces to raise money for a new basilica of St. Peter. John Tetzel was sent as the official indulgence preacher. In his 95 theses and letter to Albert, the archbishop of the area, Luther politely but pointedly protested this practice. The whole idea of indulgence-selling represented an abdication of the central responsibility of the clergy: the preaching of the gospel that could assure the faithful of the love of God. He called on the archbishop to remove this threat to the faith of the people.

Almost immediately, Luther's protest was construed as an attack upon the prerogatives of the pope. This was the case not only with Tetzel, who rightly pointed out that he was not acting on his own authority, but also with Prierias and Cajetan, members of the church hierarchy, who were subsequently sent by Rome to examine Luther on this matter.

Two things are important to note about Luther's understanding of papal authority at this stage. First, he publicly maintained an affirmative stance regarding the papal office. He did not reject the papacy as such at this point. Second, he placed the authority of the papacy in a broader constellation of authorities. He recognized the authority of scripture, past and present councils, the church fathers, and the pope.[9]

Luther felt that the truth about matters like indulgence-selling should emerge from a *consensus* of all of these authorities. In his view, the pope, both as a person and as an office, does not possess absolute teaching authority. He can teach and demand obedience to beliefs and practices only if they are articulated by a variety of authorities in the tradition. In arguing in this fashion, Luther is not far from those medieval conciliarists who advocated a representative understanding of teaching authority in the church.[10]

As the controversy over indulgences unfolded, Luther became increasingly aware that the truth of scripture, the church fathers, and church councils might have to be defended against the present pope. He was particularly appalled by the fact that the representatives of the pope who examined him and the official pronouncements that refuted his position made virtually no references to scripture and did not develop a rational justification for their position. It was as if appeal to the authority of the pope alone were enough to settle the matter.

A decisive step was taken by Luther in his debate with John Eck at Leipzig in 1519. Eck had written a series of pamphlets critical of Luther's position that defended the authority of the pope. Eck was officially commissioned to defend the church against Luther, and the two met for debate. During the course of their exchange, Eck attempted to link Luther with John Hus, who had been condemned as a heretic by the Council of Constance. Luther was faced with a choice: either disavow any relationship to Hus or admit that a council could err.

He chose the latter. Indeed, in the following months, he openly identified himself with Hus's views of the church. Eck also forced Luther to affirm that the simple meaning of scripture could stand over against the views of the church fathers. Clearly, the weight within Luther's consensus of authorities had now shifted toward scripture.[11] It was the norm against which all other norms were to be measured. Neither pope nor council could define articles of faith that stood in opposition to the teachings of scripture.

Coupled with this emphasis on the priority of scripture among the various authorities in the life of the church was a positive criterion for the proper conduct of the ministerial offices in the church. Their sole reason for being was to nourish and sustain the church through the proclamation of the word as it is witnessed to by scripture. The pope, church councils, and priests all have their authority *within* the word. Only to the extent that they exercise this function do they possess the rightful, derivative authority that is their due in the ongoing life of the church.

On the basis of this new consensus of authorities in which scripture is dominant, and an accompanying understanding of the ministerial office as a servant of the word, Luther was now ready to sharpen his attack on the ecclesiastical structures of authority that confronted him. In three works written in

1520, *The Papacy at Rome, Address to the Christian Nobility*, and *The Babylonian Captivity*, he began to take aim at the papacy itself.

No longer was it a matter of the improper exercise of the office that was at fault; it was the very office itself. The papacy leads Christians to give respect to human authorities that should be reserved for Christ and Christ alone, he said. By making obedience to questionable doctrines and practices of the church a condition of salvation, the church hierarchy tyrannizes the consciences of the faithful. Most importantly, Luther took exception to the substance of the church leadership's teaching and preaching. The papacy's claim to be the living voice of Christ had led it to define beliefs that were contrary to the gospel as contained in scripture. It had set itself above scripture, resulting in perversion of the gospel itself

In short, not only did the papacy exercise its office badly but the office itself had a demonic effect on the people of God. As early as 1515, Luther had stated the belief that the antichrist might be at work in the church hierarchy. He now had no reservations about identifying the papacy and the work of the antichrist. The pope was portrayed as seducing souls away from the gospel and into allegiance with the devil. This was a theme Luther sounded repeatedly in the latter part of his career. To the end of his life, he remained resolute and at times virulent in his rejection of the papacy. Even the extremes of the Anabaptists did not lead him to retreat to a softer position.

Obviously, Luther's conflict with the authority of the papacy goes far beyond his concern with the teaching office as it was exercised by the Roman hierarchy. But it is clear that at the heart of his conflict with Rome was a rejection of its understanding of teaching authority. This conflict played an important role in forcing Luther to form a positive conception of the teaching office. By turning to an examination of his position in a more systematic fashion, we will gain insight into how he saw the complexity of the teaching office. We will also gain insight into the great distance between the tenets of his thought and the actual conduct of the mainline Protestant churches today.

Luther's Theology of the Cross
and the Priority of the Gospel

Georg Hofmann rightly points out that it is a mistake to view Luther's highly polemical rejection of the papacy as a battle against every form of teaching office and teaching authority:

> The subjectivistic interpretation of the Reformation which sets the individuality of conscience absolutely against that which is objectively binding . . . is and remains a misunderstanding resting on profound misinterpretation. . . . Luther did not fight against every form of teaching authority and binding doctrine in general, but only against the kind of and manner in which teaching authority in his time confronted him.[12]

If this is the case, on what basis does Luther establish the objective authority of the church's teaching office? The answer can be found in his understanding of the gospel and the importance of scripture as its witness. In this section, we will examine the gospel in relation to the broader theme of Luther's theology of the cross. In the next section, we will turn to his understanding of the relationship between the gospel and scripture.

The central question facing the teaching office is, How are the normative beliefs and practices of the church determined and reinterpreted through the ages? In Luther's view, the key to answering this question lies in the absolute priority of the gospel in the Christian life. The gospel provides the church with the only knowledge necessary for salvation. It may not answer all questions about all matters, but it does offer the crucial knowledge necessary to salvation. Moreover, the gospel is self-authenticating. It does not need an interpreter, such as the *magisterium*, which stands above or outside of it; its truth grasps those whom it addresses and renders understandable all that is necessary for eternal life. It needs faithful witnesses, not interpreters. As one contemporary Lutheran scholar put it; "In short, the teaching office is essentially an instrument to guard the preaching office, which was instituted by God to evoke faith in the promise that human beings are saved without human merit."[13]

Luther's understanding of the teaching office is based on his affirmation of the absolute priority of the gospel in the Christian life and the distinctive kind of authority it has in human experience. To grasp how he develops this affirmation, we need to understand something of his theology of the cross. First, however, we must make a few comments on Luther's understanding of the gospel.

The gospel, of course, refers to the good news of the forgiveness of sins that God offers to an undeserving, sinful humanity through his Son, Jesus Christ. Luther typically develops the meaning of the gospel in contradistinction to the law. While the ceremonial and moral law of Israel sets forth the will of God, it does so primarily in a negative fashion, depicting standards that humanity, in its sinfulness, cannot possibly fulfill.

Thus the essential function of the law in Luther's view is to convict humanity of its sinfulness and create an opening in which the gospel may address those who recognize their need. On this basis Luther develops the contrast between the righteousness of works and of faith. Obeying the moral precepts of the law is impossible. Righteousness simply cannot be earned in this fashion; it can only be *imputed* to those who believe—that is, God applies the righteousness won by the obedience of Christ to those who cling to him in faith.

Luther's Theology of the Cross

An essential part of Luther's presentation of the distinction between the law and the gospel is his theology of the cross. To a certain extent, Luther develops this theme in relation to his rejection of natural theology. While natural reason can know *that* God is, it can not know *who* God is. Indeed, natural reason under the conditions of sin ends up playing a kind of religious blindman's buff, grasping after God but inevitably grabbing hold of something else. God can only be known in the divine self-disclosure of Jesus Christ.

What we find in Jesus Christ, however, is not what we would expect of God. Natural reason portrays God in terms of glory and majesty. Jesus Christ reveals God in terms of weakness and suffering. This is especially the case when we focus on the cross of Christ. Here, in unsurpassable fashion, God is manifesting love for humanity. But it is precisely here that God appears most helpless, suffering an ignoble death at the hands of evil human forces.

Hence the cross of Christ, Luther believes, contradicts the world's standards. The gospel is foolishness in the world's eyes. It puts an end to self-confident human reason. It forces believers to adopt a paradoxical view of ultimate reality. Truth about God is hidden under its opposite. Where the world sees suffering and humiliation in the cross, the eyes of faith see the power of God. Where the world sees defeat, faith sees victory over the power of sin and death. There is no way for natural reason to move directly from the logic and reality of the world to this sort of understanding of God. God's wisdom is foolishness in the world's eyes, revealing and concealing itself in its opposite.

The Priority of the Gospel

Luther's theology of the cross has great implications for his understanding of the teaching office. Most importantly, it places all human wisdom and authority, including that of the church, in a subordinate position to the gospel. When any authority attempts to set itself up outside of the gospel, it falls prey to the wisdom of the world. This is especially the case for the church's teaching authority. Its power and authority must reflect the *theologia cruxis*. Its greatness lies in its weakness: When it does no more than follow after and witness to the gospel, it is truly authoritative; when it humbly serves the word, it grasps a wisdom that surpasses all human knowledge.

Any notion of a teaching office that stands above and authorizes the gospel is rejected by Luther. No office or council or theology can define, on its own, articles of faith. Rather, the gospel itself teaches us of God, providing all we need to know for salvation. Hence, Luther could write the following:

> Therefore if we teach anything contrary to the Word of God, neither I nor the church nor the fathers nor the apostles nor even an angel from heaven should be believed. . . . No one likes to say that the church is in error; and yet, if the church teaches anything in addition or contrary to the Word of God, one must say that it is in error.[14]

The primary function of the teaching office is simply to communicate the gospel it has received. Very early in the Lutheran tradition, this insight led to an important distinction between those things that are necessary to salvation and those that are *adiaphora*—"things which make no difference."[15] Luther's basic quarrel with the Roman Catholic *magisterium* was that it constantly confused these two realities. By placing its teaching authority above the gospel, it said that belief in articles of faith and obedience to church practices not an original part of the gospel were essential to salvation. God's saving truth was confused with human traditions.

Human traditions are necessary to the well-being (*bene esse*) of the church but are not a part of its essential being (*esse*). For the church to exist, it must teach. It must test its present proclamation against the gospel again and again. It must hand on to the next generation a tradition of interpretation by which scripture is grasped. It must engage issues that are not directly addressed by the Bible. The church must teach or it will die.

But at no point, Luther argued, should the church claim for

itself the kind of infallibility found in the Roman *magisterium.*
Its doctrinal formulations, moral teachings, and ecclesiastical
structures are all to be clearly distinguished from the gospel
itself. The gospel and the gospel alone is infallible.[16] As
Gritsch points out, "While Lutherans have always affirmed
the *function* of teaching authority in the Church, the specific
form of this function is an *adiaphoron*."[17] The teaching office
or function is a part of the church's essential being, but the
particular structures developed to carry out this ministry and
the teachings the church offers at any given time are not. No
single office or agency is invested with the same kind of teaching authority that is present in the Roman papacy. Rather, the
teaching office may be carried out through a variety of structural arrangements

In comparison to the *magisterium* of the Roman Catholic
tradition, the teaching office in the Lutheran church seems
"fluid, variable, and well-dispersed."[18] This is no accident, for
Luther affirms a variety of ecclesiastical authorities that may
play an important, if penultimate, role in the exercise of the
church's teaching ministry. In part, this is a function of his
qualified acceptance of certain principles of conciliarism
found in the late Middle Ages

The Authority of Scripture

The authority of scripture is an important part of Luther's
understanding of the teaching office. Indeed, *sola scriptura*
was one of the great rallying cries of Luther's reform. Scripture alone is the decisive norm in determining the normative
beliefs and practices of the church. Althaus states this quite
nicely in terms of our argument:

> The Scripture is the record of the apostolic witness to Christ
> and is as such the decisive authority in the church. Since the
> apostles are the foundation of the church, their authority is ba-
> sic. No other authority can be equal to theirs. Every other au-
> thority in the church is derived from following the teaching of
> the apostles and is validated by its conformity to their teaching.
> This means that only the Scripture can establish and validate
> articles of faith. The Scripture offers all that is necessary to
> salvation.[19]

Scripture stands in a special relationship to the gospel, and
the church in its attempt to teach the gospel faithfully is bound
to the unique authority of scripture. And yet we must be care-
ful here, for Luther was not a biblicist in the modern sense. He

made distinctions between and within books of the Bible on the basis of a "christological canon."[20] The authority of scripture is based on its gospel content. Its various writings are to be evaluated entirely in terms of "what conveys Christ."[21] As Luther writes, "All the sacred books agree in this, that all of them preach and inculcate Christ. And that is the true test by which we judge all books, when we see whether or not they inculcate Christ. For all the Scriptures show us Christ."[22]

While scripture is uniquely authoritative in Luther's thought, he does not identify the gospel with the words of the Bible in any straightforward manner. The gospel is the heart of scripture, the center from which all its contents are to be interpreted. Moreover, in Luther's view, the gospel is found primarily in the living proclamation of the church. As Braaten puts it, "The living Word of preaching is the basic form of the gospel; the Scriptures are the written form which has become a necessary aid in the ongoing oral proclamation of the church."[23]

Two things are thus apparent about Luther's understanding of the authority of scripture. First, what is truly authoritative about scripture is its material content, its witness to the gospel. Second, by basing the authority of scripture on its gospel content and arguing that the gospel was and is primarily a living word of proclamation, Luther emphasized what we might call today the *existentiality* of scripture. Only when scripture enables the living word of God to become a transforming event in the existence of actual human beings does it exercise its proper authority. Its authority exists *in actu,* in the act of enabling the ongoing proclamation of the gospel to take place.

We can now see how Luther's belief that the teaching authority of the church is based solely on scripture rules out certain models of the teaching office. Any model must be rejected that sets up an office in the church above or outside scripture, claiming the authority to define as necessary to salvation additional articles of faith that go beyond its gospel content. This was Luther's basic argument against the Roman Catholic *magisterium* of his day. His scripture principle also rules out models that set the Holy Spirit as a special religious experience over against scripture. The essential teachings of the church are contained in scripture, and it is the primary work of the Spirit to bring these to life in the minds and hearts of believers. Hence neither isolated individuals nor single congregations can base their teachings primarily on new revelations that come directly to them.

In contrast, the teaching office is based on the authority of

scripture as it witnesses to the gospel and allows living proclamation to take place from age to age. Its authority resides not
merely in repeating the words of the past, however true to
scripture they may be, but in teaching and preaching on the
basis of the words of scripture in ways that allow the gospel to
come to expression today.

In short, the most important task of the church's teaching
office is to ensure that the church has a living witness to the
gospel in its preaching and teaching. This is no simple task. As
Luther recognized, it necessitates a role for penultimate authorities in the church's life who assist the church in carrying
out its teaching ministry.

Penultimate Authorities in the Teaching Office

It is clear that Luther ascribes a unique kind of authority to
scripture in the determination of beliefs and practices that are
necessary to salvation. He goes so far as to argue that scripture
interprets itself from its own center, the gospel of forgiveness
definitively given expression in Jesus Christ. All other authorities in the church's teaching ministry are penultimate in comparison. They can carry out their task as a living witness to the
gospel only in that they are based on scripture.

This led Luther to reject all traditions and authorities that
claim a salvific function belonging solely to the preaching and
teaching of the gospel. But what if there are disagreements in
the church as to the meaning of the gospel? In any given congregation, who is to decide what theological position should
prevail? Questions such as these arise again and again in the
actual life of the church. Luther himself faced such questions
as he confronted the task of giving structure to the newly
emerging Reformation churches. It is one thing to argue that
the church's teaching ministry is primarily charged with the
task of ensuring the preaching and teaching of the gospel. It is
quite another to sort out how this is best done in the actual
structures of the church's life.

While Luther was not systematic at this point, his thought
as a whole indicates a place for a number of penultimate authorities. The most important of these are church councils,
the consensus of tradition, office-bearers, the congregation,
theological doctrines, and individual conscience. The fact that
Luther was not specific as to the role each of these should play
in the teaching office's protection of the gospel has led to
innumerable conflicts in the Lutheran church. Do church
councils have teaching authority over that of congregations,

allowing binding beliefs to be formulated not only by ancient ecumenical councils but also by contemporary synodical bodies? What measure of freedom does individual conscience retain? What role does the congregation have in such matters?[24]

It is not my intention to provide definitive answers to these questions. Indeed, it is my belief that Luther himself does not provide definitive answers. In a sense, the actual form of the church is *adiaphora,* as we have pointed out. Luther did not believe that there is a divine blueprint for the church, even in scripture. It is fair to ask, however, whether there are not basic principles which inform Luther's affirmation of multiple penultimate authorities in the church. This is especially important in attempting to grasp what kind of teaching authority these subordinate offices and structures possess.

Jaroslav Pelikan once wrote, "We Protestants must discover what made the Reformation possible, while Roman Catholics must discover what made the Reformation necessary."[25] He was pointing to the fact that Protestants frequently act as if the Reformation emerged out of nothing, having no real continuity with previous generations or the ancient church. It is particularly important to overcome this tendency in attempting to make sense of Luther's affirmation of various structures and offices in the church that possess teaching authority. While he advocated no single plan for the church, he did draw on certain traditions already present in medieval Christianity to determine the principles by which these authorities function.

John McNeill makes a convincing case that both Luther and Calvin were informed by certain principles of conciliarism in their depiction of church order, and his basic argument will be followed here.[26] As we saw in chapter 5, conciliarism arose in opposition to the monarchical understanding of the papacy that began to emerge during the Middle Ages. These two forms of teaching authority rested on opposing principles of government, monarchical absolutism and conciliar constitutionalism. The former grants authority and power to a ruler who is not responsible to the ruled, governing by divine right; the latter views power as resting in the people and sees them as governing through delegated and responsible bodies.

During the latter part of the Middle Ages, conciliarism existed in a wide variety of forms. In one form, the argument was made that only councils possess infallible power to define articles of faith and morality. In another, a conciliar form of secular government was advocated, while a monarchical form of the papacy was upheld. In still another form of conciliarism, church councils were viewed as representative bodies and were granted real but fallible authority in defining the church's teachings.

This third position, McNeill argues, was most influential on Luther's thought. In the early phase of his conflict with Rome, Luther repeatedly called for a free general council to settle the dispute. Although he did not press this appeal in the latter part of his career, it was because he felt that a truly free council could not be convened. He remained a conciliarist, though a disillusioned one.

Luther's conciliarism was appropriated in terms of the theological themes we have already examined. Fallible representative forms of authority are desirable because scripture alone is finally authoritative as it witnesses to the gospel and makes living proclamation possible. In a sense, we might say that Luther's is a qualified conciliarism. It functions less as a simple affirmation of the role of councils per se than as a principle that undergirds his view of every authority in the church. It is especially important in his view of the teaching office. All teaching authority is *representative* and *fallible.* Moreover, there is a need for multiple authorities in the church, for no single office or agency should be identified too closely with the lordship of Christ.

These multiple teaching authorities are best pictured as functioning within a dialogical model of the teaching office. No single authority can lay exclusive claim to the definitive conservation and interpretation of scripture. As each attempts to teach, it must confront other authorities in the church which can correct, expand, and confirm its understanding of Christian teaching. All must base their authority on the conformity of their teachings to scripture. In matters that are *adiaphora,* these authorities play an important role in guiding the church but must always make it clear to themselves and to others that their teaching is not to be confused with matters necessary to salvation.

Several of the more important teaching authorities in Luther's thought can be described. A qualified conciliarism can be seen in each of these areas.

Councils

We have noted how this understanding of teaching authority is present in Luther's views of councils. He criticized the Council of Constance as fallible in its condemnation of Hus. Yet he called for a general council to settle the indulgence-selling controversy. He accepted the authority of the three ecumenical councils of the ancient church and the doctrines of the Trinity and the twofold nature of Christ they articulated. Yet he recognized that the conceptual framework of these councils went beyond what was directly present in scripture, and he was willing to quibble with their language at points. Their authority lay in the fact that what they taught was in conformity to the basic substance of scripture.

We see more than a mere affirmation of the penultimate authority of councils here; we see a conciliar principle at work: Ecclesiastical authorities are representative of the church as a whole and have a real but fallible right to teach the church. We see a similar principle at work in Luther's affirmation of the authority of consensus in the church.

The Consensus of Church Tradition

In a manner that is somewhat different from Calvin's, Luther did not profess to ground all church structures in biblical precedent. He called for a reform of church tradition only at those points where it conflicted with the gospel.[27] Especially in his fight with the Anabaptists, he argued for practices in the church on the basis of their "catholicity." Infant baptism is a particularly important case in point. Since scripture gives no definitive guidance on this matter in Luther's view, the church must rely on the fact that it has been "practiced since the beginning of the church" and has been "accepted among all Christians in the whole world."[28] The Anabaptists were the innovators in this regard, and the burden of proof rested on them.

This affirmation of church tradition might seem strange if we view Luther only through a relatively narrow understanding of *sola scriptura*. What is at work here, however, is an application of the conciliar principle identified above: Truth is to be found in the consensus of the universal church. While scripture should have the final say on matters in which it teaches clearly, in those places where it does not, the church's "catholic sense" should be consulted in the determination of beliefs and practices.

Theology and Doctrine

Theology and church doctrine are similarly granted a real but penultimate authority in the church's ongoing life. Theology, Luther believed, is necessary for the clarification and interpretation of the teachings of scripture. Its authority resides not in its originality but in its ability to render meaningful the original message of the gospel. As Althaus puts it, "The authority of the theologians of the church is relative and conditional. Without the authority of words of scripture, no one can establish hard and fast statements of dogma in the church."[29] As contemporary Lutherans are quick to point out, in this perspective doctrinal formulations are confessions and doxologies, rather than promulgations of infallible dogma: "They function as guides for the proper proclamation of the gospel, the administration of the sacraments, and the right praise of God rather than as statements which are themselves objects of faith."[30]

Inherited confessions and creeds are frequently the work of representative church bodies and serve as guides to the interpretation of scripture. Their value lies in their ability to summarize and bring into focus the teachings of scripture, serving as a tradition of interpretation. They teach the members of the church what doctrines are central to scripture and how they are interrelated, but they are not a substitute for an original reading of scripture.

Similarly, the work of individual theologians plays an important teaching function. Luther viewed his theology primarily as an attempt to set forth the various teachings of scripture. Moreover, he often distinguished his own opinions from what he could say on the basis of the bible. The theologian is to measure the church's beliefs and practices again and again against the biblical witness, engaging in both a critical and a constructive task. While unwilling to claim infallibility for theology and doctrine any more than for any other ecclesiastical authority, Luther was quite clear that the question of truth is at stake in the theological enterprise. At times, the theologians of the church must engage in controversies that are crucial to the preservation of the church's life.

The Congregation

We see an affirmation of the authority of the congregation and its office-bearers that is similar to what was described earlier. They too occupy an important, if penultimate, position in Luther's thought. Luther placed great emphasis on the church as a congregation, not as an institution or church hierarchy. He focused his interpretation of the church on the Apostles' Creed and its affirmation of the "communion of saints." The visible church is a concrete fellowship or priesthood of believers in which goods and burdens are shared.[31]

It is on the basis of the conception of the congregation and its ministry that Luther based his understanding of its teaching authority. Although he is not always completely consistent about the teaching authority of the congregation,[32] he was insistent throughout his career on the important place that the congregation plays in both teaching the basic beliefs of the church and evaluating the teachings offered by other ecclesiastical offices and agencies, including its own minister.

Especially during the early phases of the Reformation when the newly emerging Reformation churches were faced with a transitional period in which Roman Catholic priests continued to hold jurisdiction in certain areas, Luther strongly affirmed the ability of the congregation to judge church teaching for itself. In one such situation in Leisnig, Luther wrote a pamphlet for the Christian population with the long title, "That a Christian Assembly or Congregation Has the Right and Power to Judge All Teaching and To Call, Appoint, and Dismiss Teachers, Established and Proven by Scripture."

In this pamphlet, he argues that the true church only exists where the pure gospel is preached. Priests who preach another gospel have no real authority. Moreover, the members of the church will recognize true teaching when they hear it. Drawing on John 10, he writes:

> Bishops, pope, scholars, and everyone have power to teach, but the sheep should judge whether they are teaching Christ's voice or the voice of strangers. . . . That is why we let bishops and councils conclude and establish whatever they want; but if we have God's Word on our side it should be up to us, and not them, to decide whether it is right or wrong, and they should yield to us and obey our word.[33]

To the extent that a congregation is grounded in the gospel, it has not only the right but the obligation to judge the teachings of other authorities in the church. Drawing on 1 Thessalonians 5:21 ("but test everything; hold fast what is good"), Luther goes on to write:

> See, he does not desire any tenet or teaching to be obeyed unless it is heard, tested, and recognized as good by the congregation that hears it. For this testing is not the concern of the teachers; rather, the teachers must announce beforehand that one should test. So here too judgment is withdrawn from the teachers and given to the students among the Christians.[34]

Similar passages can be found throughout Luther's writings. A clear affirmation of the congregation's right to judge and test the teachings offered by other authorities in the church is seen here. Luther did not absolutize the congregation's right in this regard, however, especially if the body of his thought is taken into account. His conflict with Karlstadt and the Peasants' War made him more cautious in affirming the ability of a single congregation to interpret scripture for itself and judge definitively the offerings of other authorities.[35]

In the end, the conciliar principle seems closer to his final thought. Bodies and offices beyond the congregation, which are representative of the church as a whole, are viewed as having an important role to play in the teaching office. Church councils and the consensus of church tradition through the ages can potentially save a congregation from a provincial understanding of Christianity, bringing to mind certain aspects of the gospel it has neglected or lost. The congregation, however, is to judge all such teaching. After all, they too have the ability to interpret scripture and may very well have to stand up against a church council or an inherited tradition on behalf of the gospel.

The Ministry

This tension between the ability and right of the congregation to determine its normative beliefs and practices and the role of ecclesiastical structures that are representative of larger dimensions of church life is brought into focus in Luther's understanding of the authority of the ordained minister. Over the years, scholars have identified two positions in his thought on the nature and authority of office-bearers in the church, positions not easily reconciled.

In one line of thought, Luther views the office of ministry in basically a representative fashion. The priestly ministry is given to the congregation as a whole, and the minister is called to a special public ministry within the church by the congregation. All functions of ministry remain invested in the congregation, and the ordained ministry is established solely because of the need for order in the congregation. Office-bearers represent the community and do everything in its name. The only distinction between clergy and laity is the public character of the ordained ministry.

This line of thought is quite consistent with the conciliar principle that we have found elsewhere in Luther's thought. The minister's authority is delegated by the congregation, whose own ministry is represented in this special function. The congregation retains the right to call, dismiss, and judge the teachings of such persons on the basis of its more fundamental priestly ministry.

In the second line of thought, however, the ordained ministry is viewed as directly instituted by the express command of Christ and not mediated through the congregation. It serves a special role in the preaching of the gospel, which is the sole means by which the church is established.[36] A congregation's need for the gospel is so fundamental that God has mandated the setting aside of persons who are specially qualified for this task. Indeed, the ordained ministry constitutes the fifth mark of the church and is distinguishable from the priesthood of all believers.[37] God did not merely give the word and sacraments to the church but also instituted the public proclamation of the word and the proper administration of the sacraments. Luther writes, "As he has bound the Holy Spirit to the Word, so he has bound the proclamation of the Word to the institution of the ministry."[38] Without the exercise of the public office of ministry, a congregation will not be able to carry out its own priestly ministry properly, for it is dependent on the continual nourishment of the preached word.

There is thus a tension in Luther's depiction of the authority of office-bearers in relation to the authority of the congregation.[39] Seemingly, strict conciliarism is qualified by emphasis on the direct institution of the office of ministry. Delegation of authority gives way to a succession of apostolic witnesses who are bound to the gospel of Christ. This is a healthy tension, however, protecting against the tendency of strict congregationalism to make the minister a mere functionary of the people and the proclivity of a hierarchical ministry to destroy the authority of the congregation.[40]

It is precisely this sort of tensive quality in Luther's thought that makes his understanding of the teaching office so dynamic. Authority to define the normative beliefs and practices of the church and to provide guidance on matters in which salvation is not at stake is located in multiple structures and offices, none of which can be reduced to another. Such authorities are representative, to be sure. But they owe their ultimate loyalty to the gospel as witnessed to by scripture. They play their proper role, not by a slavish dependency on those whom they represent but by trying to conserve and interpret the gospel faithfully.

The Individual Christian

A final brief word must be said about the liberty of the individual Christian and the role of conscience in all this. By now it should be apparent that Luther's understanding of

Christian liberty should not be identified with modern individualism. The priesthood of all believers, for example, does not mean that individuals are their own priests, directly related to God. Rather, all are given the task of ministry for others. At no point are individuals abandoned to their own resources, including their consciences, to determine Christian truth. They are situated in a concrete fellowship of believers that is itself open to an ongoing interchange with past and present church councils, the inherited catholic tradition of the church, and office-bearers who are bound to the gospel.

Luther developed his understanding of Christian liberty not to set believers free to determine their own beliefs but to free them from the oppressive domination of a teaching authority that substituted its own decrees and laws for the gospel. Every form of teaching authority that sets up human tradition in Christ's place must be rejected outright. There is a certain sphere of life inside and outside of the church that is set free from a direct correlation to matters of salvation. In this sphere, matters are *adiaphora.* They may be extremely important, but no single avenue of thought or action can be identified as necessary for salvation. The individual must struggle to discern what is the most faithful response as a member of the church and as a forgiven sinner. As a forgiven sinner, he or she is freed to take the risks inherent in all human choice. As a member of the church, he or she is part of a tangible fellowship that will provide authoritative, if fallible, guidance in the exercise of such liberty.

While a single individual may have to resist all authorities in the church on behalf of the gospel, as Luther himself did, this is not the ordinary situation of the believer. Moreover, such dissent is not grounded in the right of every individual to determine his or her own beliefs and actions but in the individual's conscience as it is bound to the word of God. On behalf of God and, ultimately, on behalf of the church, the individual may dissent. But this is an emergency situation, not the norm.

After Luther

We have examined Luther's understanding of teaching authority in terms of his theology as a whole. Luther did not write a single work, like Calvin's *Institutes,* that can be consulted for a systematic discussion on his position on any given topic. What we find is a persistent, unfolding series of reflections on the church's teaching authority. Luther could not escape this issue, for his reform was constantly confronted with the institutional and theological reality of the papacy. If he would challenge the church of Rome, then he must challenge the ways it justified its authority and formulate an alternate understanding.

It would be misleading for us to leave the impression that Luther's reflections fit neatly together in a clear-cut model of the teaching office. What we have seen are a set of emphases that appear repeatedly in Luther's thought over the course of time: The gospel alone is infallible, scripture must be interpreted christocentrically, various penultimate authorities are ordered under scripture as it witnesses to the gospel. There are real tensions in Luther's thought, and the history of the Lutheran church reflects these tensions. At various points, teaching authority has resided in the episcopacy, the Biennial Convention, confessional statements, the congregation, ordained ministers, and leaders of synods. Each of these can claim legitimacy on the basis of some part of Luther's thought.

No single form of teaching authority, however, can legitimately claim to represent Luther's model of the teaching office definitively. While the function of teaching is a part of the *esse* of the church, the specific form it takes is a part of its *bene esse*. This may be the most important by-product of the lack of systemization and the internal tensions that characterize Luther's thought. It forces those who would take him seriously to engage the form of the teaching office as an open question.

A number of contemporary Lutheran scholars have begun to pursue this open question. Carl Braaten has asked whether the occupants of positions in the church bureaucracy have not begun to take on a kind of teaching authority that excludes the theologians of the church.[41] George Lindbeck has questioned whether every community ultimately affirms certain propositions as infallible and necessarily needs some form of authority to guarantee its identity, continuity, and unity.[42] Eric Gritsch has argued that Lutherans must ask whether the gospel needs a *magisterium* in order to be authentic.[43]

For our purposes, what is important is to grasp how Luther's understanding of the church's teaching office raises questions about contemporary American Protestantism. Obviously, Luther was writing in a different context, one in which territorial churches were dominant. Nevertheless he points toward a style of teaching authority that stands between the extremes of individualism and authoritarianisim.

We have seen repeatedly that Luther's affirmation of the

unique authority of the gospel as witnessed to by scripture does not rule out penultimate authorities in the church's life. The church's teaching authority is dispersed and relativized, but it is not thereby negated. The individual Christian is situated among a concrete fellowship of believers who are in dialogue with a tradition of biblical interpretation and agencies that represent the catholic sense of the church. Confessional statements and theology are viewed as important but relative guides to the interpretation of scripture. Neither the individual nor orthodox belief is given exclusive teaching authority.

In Part Three a model of the teaching office will be projected that harks back to certain themes found in Luther's thought. It is precisely the tensive, multifaceted nature of his writing on the teaching office that makes his work such fertile ground for rethinking the nature of the teaching ministry in the church today.

7

The Teaching Office in the Thought and Practice of John Calvin

It is no simple matter to move from the thought of Martin Luther to that of John Calvin. Robert Johnson once characterized the shift from Luther to Calvin as a movement "from the complicated to the complex."[1] What he had in mind was the more systematic quality of Calvin's thought, the simple fact that Calvin began a process of intellectual ordering of the Protestant faith that went beyond the more occasional quality of Luther's work. While Luther and Calvin share much in common, issues of genuine substance separate the two men. In assessing Calvin's understanding of the teaching office, it will be helpful to keep in mind some of these basic differences.

Between Luther and Calvin

While something of an oversimplification, it is possible to characterize the differences between Luther and Calvin in terms of a common question: How does each conceptualize sin and what sort of soteriology does each frame in response? Throughout Luther's thought, it is the theme of works righteousness that repeatedly appears in his characterization of sin. This leads him to place absolute priority on God's justification of the ungodly in every aspect of his theology. In contrast, Calvin characterizes sin more in terms of idolatry, the placement of some finite object or concern in God's place.[2] This leads him to conceptualize the benefits of salvation in terms of the restoration of God to a proper position of sovereignty in a person's life.

Luther's emphasis on justification leads him to view both the law and sanctification somewhat differently from Calvin.[3] The law and the gospel serve as contrast terms in his thought, with the first or pedagogical function of the law playing the primary role.[4] It is to serve as a mirror of our sins, teaching us of our fallen nature and driving us to the gospel. There is no way to move from the good works of the law to the forgiveness of sins offered freely in Jesus Christ. The Christian always lives in the tension between the kingdom of God, which comes into this world as the alien righteousness of Jesus Christ, and the kingdom of the world, which remains under the curse of the law.

Calvin's understanding of sin as idolatry and his emphasis on the restoration of God to a proper position of sovereignty lead him in a somewhat different direction. A far more positive role for the ordering of ecclesiastical and secular life under God is advocated. In the final analysis, the law and the gospel are not in opposition. The law is a sign of God's gracious care for the elect, providing guidance for the proper ordering of human life. Its pedagogical purpose is "accidental," emerging only after the Fall. For the elect, the law regains its original function, guiding and spurring them on to obedience. It is this third use that is primary in Calvin's theology.[5]

This affirmation of the positive, ordering functions of the law leads to a stronger, more active understanding of the church's teaching ministry than is found in Luther. It has a role to play in assisting the elect in appropriating their salvation and ordering their lives according to the pattern of the law. Calvin went so far as to portray the church as having a teaching role in society, something that undoubtedly is based on his understanding of the continuity between the law implanted originally in all persons in conscience and its clarification in the moral precepts of Israel and Jesus.[6]

Calvin's attempt to formulate educational institutions and practices for both the church and the general population of Geneva is an expression of his commitment to structures that give expression to the church's teaching ministry. He too was forced to struggle with the question of the relationship between structure and spirit in the teaching office. His response to the set of issues this involves is highly suggestive, not only for churches grounded in the Reformed tradition but for all of mainline Protestantism as it struggles to find a way between the subjectivity of individualism and the authoritarianism of counter-modernism.

Calvin's Doctrine of Word and Spirit

As we saw in chapter 6, Luther focused on the unique authority of scripture in his response to the dilemmas posed by the tensions between structure and Spirit in the teaching office. A role for ecclesiastical structures by which the church teaches authoritatively was affirmed but placed in a subordinate position to the authority of scripture as it "conveys Christ." Likewise, the Spirit was seen as bound to the gospel content of scripture and its proclamation. The church cannot claim the authority of the Spirit to authorize teachings that are contrary to scripture. Both the Roman Catholics and the Anabaptists, Luther believed, bind structure and Spirit to scripture insufficiently.

Calvin's understanding of the authority of scripture in the life of the church is virtually identical with Luther's on a general level. In a fashion that is perhaps more systematic than Luther's, he develops a comprehensive doctrine of word and Spirit that serves as the basis of his understanding of the church's teaching office. From beginning to end, he believes, the teachings of the church are bound to the authority of scripture. As he writes:

> Let this be a firm principle: No other word is to be held as the Word of God, and given place as such in the church, than what is contained first in the Law and the Prophets, then in the writings of the apostles; and the only authorized way of teaching in the church is by the prescription and standard of his Word.[7]

Calvin believed that he was simply following the pattern Jesus had set up in his own ministry, expressed in the dictum, "My teaching is not mine but his who sent me."[8] The power of the church, as such, is "enclosed" within God's word. As Calvin puts it at one point: "God deprives men of the capacity to put forth new doctrine in order that he alone may be our schoolmaster."[9]

Calvin binds the work of the Holy Spirit to scripture and not to particular church structures and offices. It is precisely this point that led him to reject so vociferously the Roman Catholic *magisterium* of his day. As he writes:

> If we grant the first point, that the church cannot err in matters necessary to salvation, here is what we mean by it: The statement is true in so far as the church, having forsaken all its own wisdom, allows itself to be taught by the Holy Spirit through God's Word. This, then, is the difference. *Our opponents locate the authority of the church outside God's Word; but we insist that it be attached to the Word, and do not allow it to be separated from it.*[10]

Word and Spirit are bound inextricably together. The proper teaching authority of the church is located *within* the more fundamental teaching authority of the word and Spirit. If the Holy Spirit is the primary teacher of the church, the written word is its basic subject matter. It is no accident that Calvin repeatedly employs phrases and metaphors that focus on teaching to describe the activity of both the Spirit and the word in relation to the church. He is establishing the unique teaching authority that these two possess in contrast to that of the *magisterium.* The Spirit is bound to the word and not to a particular office or agency in the church.

How does Calvin describe the relationship between the word and Spirit? The Spirit *attests* to the authority of scripture; and scripture *tests* the Spirit.[11] It is the internal witness of the Spirit alone that establishes the word as authoritative. The authority of the church does not establish its teachings as true. Only the Spirit of God working in the minds and hearts of those whom God has called can *attest* to the authority of scripture as containing the knowledge necessary for salvation. The authority of the church's teaching office is placed beneath or within scripture.

But the converse is also true. The written word *tests* the Spirit. One of Calvin's favorite descriptive words for the Spirit is "Teacher." But the teaching of the Holy Spirit does not take place apart from the written word.[12] The Spirit does no more than bring to life the already given teachings laid down in scripture. It does not add something new in the work of councils or other agencies of teaching. Hence, scripture must be used to *test* when and where the church's teachings are actually formulated under the power of the Spirit.

In his doctrine of word and Spirit, Calvin binds both the authority of the Holy Spirit and all ecclesiastical structures that claim to speak on the Spirit's behalf to the written word. But how does this binding take place? Does Calvin subscribe to an understanding of verbal inerrancy that allows the church, under the power of the Spirit, to determine clear, propositional teachings about God that must be accepted as orthodox in every age? Two issues are important in giving answer to these questions: (1) Calvin's understanding of the relationship between the gospel content of scripture and scripture as a whole, and (2) the relative importance of Calvin's discussion of the inspiration of scripture within his broader understanding of its salvific function.

The first of these issues points to a contrast between Luther and Calvin. Calvin was more reticent than Luther to posit so absolutely a canon within the canon.[13] In Calvin's theology, scripture's gospel content does not overshadow the importance of the rest of its teachings. The gospel is seen as found at every point in God's dealings with the covenant people, from God's gracious promise to Abraham down through the entire history of Israel. Christ allows us to see more clearly the gratuitous mercy of God that has been operative at every point. Scripture in its entirety witnesses to Christ. Christ, as the focal point of God's unmerited love and forgiveness, has priority in Calvin's thought, but not in a way that leads to denigration of any of its parts.

This does not mean, however, that Calvin advocates an understanding of scripture based on a theory of verbal inerrancy in which every part of scripture is seen as miraculously testifying to Christ. Rather, Calvin's affirmation of scripture as a whole is a function of a broader theological conviction: that God accommodates to a sinful, finite humanity in different ways during different ages but remains the self-same triune God. This leads us to the second issue: his understanding of scripture as inspired and its salvific function.

At various points in his thought, Calvin describes the role of the Spirit as the author of scripture, using language implying that the words of scripture are the very words of God. There is no consensus among scholars as to whether Calvin is advocating biblical inerrancy at these points. Dowey and Polman, among others, argue that, in fact, he is.[14] The view accepted here is that of Wendel and McKim.[15] They argue that such a doctrine would be incompatible with the critical methods of biblical interpretation that Calvin took over from humanism and constantly employs throughout his commentaries.[16] Calvin, they argue, views scripture along the lines of the rhetorical principle of accommodation, a theme that will be discussed more extensively later. God has accommodated himself to the needs of humanity by employing human authors to express the divine message under the Spirit's guidance in human forms of thought. As such, the Bible is like a mirror; it reflects something but does not impart the thing itself and is not to be confused with the God whose image is found within its words.

Whether one accepts this interpretation of Calvin or not, it is important to see that Calvin's understanding of scripture focuses primarily on its *salvific function*, not its formal authority as an inspired document. Even those like Dowey and Polman who claim that Calvin adopts a theory of verbal inspiration are clear about this.[17] Its teachings are given with the purpose of transforming the sinful orientation of the human heart and assisting the elect in recognizing that God holds a rightful position of sovereignty over every aspect of their lives. A doctrine of biblical inerrancy is not necessary for scripture to fulfill this task. Indeed it can be positively harmful, to the extent that it leads to an authoritarian understanding of the teaching office that results in a narrow, overly cognitive understanding of faith.

While the cognitive dimensions of faith are important to Calvin, they are not exclusively so. Knowledge of God is always presented as part of a transformation of the basic trusts and loyalties governing a person's pattern of life. While Calvin is willing to go further than Luther in giving form to a teaching office that plays an active role in the ordering of the individual's and the church's life, he does so in a way that humanizes both those doing the teaching and that which is taught. This becomes clear in his understanding of the church's teaching authority.

The Authority of the Church

Calvin identifies three forms of authority in the church: the power to teach doctrine, to legislate laws regulating the church's life, and to carry out church discipline.[18] The teaching office of the church falls under the first of these and consists of two basic tasks: the authority to lay down articles of faith and the authority to explain them.[19] Before examining more directly what Calvin means by these two tasks it is important to gain an understanding of his view of church power and authority in general.

Calvin begins his discussion of the church and its powers in Book IV of the *Institutes* by distinguishing between the visible and invisible church. This is essentially an eschatological distinction. The latter alone is the true church, composed entirely of God's elect and enjoying the complete benefits of grace in the fullness of God's kingdom. Only the invisible church can be affirmed as one, holy, apostolic, and universal.

This distinction, however, does not lead Calvin to denigrate the role of the empirical or visible church. On the contrary, it is described as the very "mother" of believers. R. N. Hunt once wrote of Calvin, "For all his abhorrence of Rome, he was after his manner as good a Churchman as any Pope."[20] Hunt is pointing to the fact that Calvin placed a great deal of emphasis on the real, though limited, authority of the visible church.

One of the keys to interpreting Calvin's understanding of the authority of the visible church is to see the way it is based on his belief in God's accommodation to finite, sinful humanity, a theme we noted in conjunction with his doctrine of scripture.[21] Accommodation was a principle of rhetoric Calvin learned from his humanistic education in France. It referred to the speaker's need to bridge the gap between the subject matter being presented and the audience being addressed. An adept speaker should be able to present a complex, learned subject to an audience that is relatively uneducated and with little prior knowledge of the topic being addressed. The speaker must take into account the capacities and the limitations of the hearers.

Calvin uses the theme of accommodation throughout his writings to describe the way the gap between God and humanity is overcome. This gap is of a twofold nature, composed of the distinction between Creator and created and the separation between a sinful humanity and a holy, righteous God. Calvin argues that God takes the finite, sinful nature of the human condition into account, adjusting to human capacity when communication with humanity takes place.

Precisely for this reason, God has chosen "to teach us through human means" rather than "to thunder at us and drive us away."[22] The knowledge given in revelation is governed by the moral and noetic limitations of the human condition. God does not communicate all things about the divine being but accommodates to human need and communicates only what is necessary for the salvation of sinful, finite human beings. The divine rhetoric is "scaled down" to human capacity and need. Scripture is one form of accommodation. The church is another. The church's authority, as such, resides in its use by God as a means of accommodation. God has chosen the church to be a means of grace, communicating the promise of forgiveness and assisting in the process of sanctification in ways that are appropriate to human need and ability.

As a means of divine accommodation, the church's authority can be said to possess four characteristics.

First, the church's authority is *derivative*. The church is an instrument God uses to call and transform the elect. Its authority is that of a means of divine accommodation, not an end in itself. As we have seen, Calvin binds the authority of the church to the teachings of scripture. Its structures can claim the power of the Spirit only in that the laws they legislate, the doctrines they teach, and the discipline they enact are consistent with scripture. The church's authority is derivative.

Second, the church's authority is *fallible*. Though God uses human words and agencies to come near to humanity, these means of grace remain finite and sinful. God accommodates to human capacity; God does not eradicate it. The treasure of the gospel is preserved in an earthen vessel. A distinction is maintained between the church and God. No claim to infallibility can be made on behalf of any office or person in the church's life.

Third, the authority of the church is *dispersed.* Since Christ alone is the sole head of the church, Calvin is reticent to place exclusive authority in any single agency or office. He rejects the Roman Catholic argument that the papacy serves as a unifying center of church life, locating authority in a single head of the church universal. Calvin counters on the basis of Ephesians 4, in which church unity is portrayed as residing in Christ alone. As he puts it, "Do you see how he assigns to each member a certain measure, and a definite and limited function, in order that perfection of grace as well as the supreme power of governing may remain with Christ alone?"[23] As the editors of the *Institutes* point out, there is a consistent tendency toward "plural authorities" in Calvin's discussions of ecclesiastical and political forms of government.[24] Authority and power are best dispersed throughout the church in order to protect the prerogatives that belong to God alone.

Fourth, the authority of the church is *real.* In spite of the fact that church authority is derivative, fallible, and dispersed, it is to be acknowledged by the members of the church as a genuine expression of God's love and care for the church. In order to accommodate to human need and capacity, God has ordained certain offices and agencies as the normal means of grace. These are to be taken very, very seriously. Their authority is real, for "although God's power is not bound to outward means, he has nonetheless bound us to this ordinary manner of teaching."[25]

Each of these four characteristics is present in Calvin's description of the visible church's teaching, legislative, and juridical authority. They reflect the church's status as a means of grace by which God accommodates to a sinful, finite humanity. The church's authority is based solely on its ability to function in this role. It should not claim prerogatives properly reserved for God, but it should not refuse to play the important role that it is assigned.

The Church's Teaching Ministry

By this point, it should be clear that for Calvin the teaching office of the church is only one facet of the church's general power and authority and is determined by the fundamental theological themes that he uses to describe the church in general. Calvin describes the specific tasks of the church's teaching ministry as twofold: the authority to lay down articles of faith and the authority to interpret these articles.[26] These tasks are reminiscent of the historic functions of the teaching office as they have been defined in this book: (1) the determination of the normative beliefs and practices of the church; (2) the reinterpretation of these beliefs and practices in shifting cultural and historical contexts; and (3) the formation of appropriate educational institutions, processes, and material that can teach each new generation and help it deepen its faith as it matures and ages.

Calvin addressed each of these tasks in his thought and practice. There can be little question that he thought of the church's teaching ministry as a crucial part of its life. A strong case can be made that Calvin thinks of the church *primarily* as a teacher. At many points in his writing, the most important images of the church he offers focus on the nourishment and education it provides. This seems to spill over from his use of teaching-learning as a central metaphor by which to describe key facets of God's accommodation to humanity, especially to the elect. Words and phrases that have to do with teaching and learning appear again and again in the *Institutes* as describing the divine-human relationship: "pupil," "instruction," "schoolmaster," "educate," and "tutor," to name only a few.[27]

God is presented as being like a teacher, using the ordinary means of creation to communicate knowledge appropriate to the capacities and needs of the pupils. The proper human attitude toward this knowledge is one of "teachableness." Both in heart and in mind, human beings are to acknowledge their dependency on the teaching of God, limiting their understanding of God's nature and will to the positive guidance that is provided and refraining from unnecessary speculation beyond what is offered.

In an analogous fashion, Calvin frequently uses teaching-learning imagery to describe the nature of the church. In a remarkable passage in the *Institutes,* he unfolds his understanding of the church by comparing it to a mother.[28] The visible church is to be the mother of believers, because "there is no other way to enter into life unless this mother conceive us in her womb, give us birth, nourish us at her breast, and lastly, unless she keep us under her care and guidance until, putting off mortal flesh, we become like the angels."[29]

As he continues to unpack what is meant by this metaphor,

Calvin weaves in language that describes the teaching function of the church: "Our weakness does not allow us to be dismissed from her school until we have been pupils all our lives."[30] He goes on to write, "We see how God, who could in a moment perfect his own, nevertheless desires them to grow up into manhood solely under the education of the church."[31]

This interweaving of maternal and educational imagery is not uncommon.[32] The church is the appointed means of grace to which the elect are bound in order to receive the "spiritual food" of the gospel and the edification necessary for their growth in Christ. The church is their teacher because God himself has chosen to instruct them through this agency in ways that are appropriate to their need and capacity. In describing both God and the church in terms of teaching-learning imagery, Calvin goes far beyond a depiction of the teaching ministry of the church per se. His use of this sort of imagery so frequently in his writings, however, underscores the importance he attaches to this particular ministry.

At various points, Calvin discusses the structures by which the church can exercise the teaching office, describing the role of ministers, doctors, councils, tradition, and conscience in terms of their teaching function. Each has an important role to play in defining the normative beliefs and practices of the church and interpreting them in the face of shifting contexts. Their authority, however, always retains the characteristics of the church's authority in general: It is derivative, fallible, dispersed, and real. These characteristics are evident in two of the most important agencies of the teaching office discussed in depth in the *Institutes*—ordained ministers and church councils.

Ordained Ministers in the Teaching Office

Calvin explicitly links the depiction of the proper teaching authority of the ordained ministry with the theme of divine accommodation. In his initial discussion of the church in Book IV of the *Institutes*, he writes:

> Since, however, in our ignorance and sloth (to which I add fickleness of disposition) we need outward helps to beget and increase faith within us, and advance it to its goal, God has also added these aids that he may provide for our weakness. . . . He instituted "pastors and teachers" [Eph. 4:11] through whose lips he might teach his own; he furnished them with authority. . . . God, therefore, in his wonderful providence accommodat-

ing himself to our capacity, has prescribed a way for us, though still far off, to draw near to him.[33]

The authority of ministers is *real;* the members of the church are to have a "gentle and teachable spirit" that "they may allow themselves to be governed by teachers appointed to this function."[34] It is by God's design that ministers are given to the church. Just as God raised up prophets and priests in Israel in order to interpret the law, "so today he not only desires us to be attentive to its reading, but also appoints instructors to help us by their effort."[35] He decries the fact that in every age there are schismatics who resist the authority of duly appointed ministers, preferring "private reading and meditation" to public worship and preaching.[36] He warns his readers that this is "like blotting out the face of God which shines upon us in teaching."[37]

While Calvin is affirming here the genuine authority of ministers, he places this authority within clear limits. It is a *derivative* authority. This goes to the very heart of Calvin's understanding of the ordained minister's role in the teaching office. At no point is the teaching authority of ministers their own. It does not reside in their personal opinions or the latest theological fad, it derives from their faithfulness to the teachings of scripture as handed down by the church, and

> we shall not find that they have been endowed with any authority to teach or to answer, except in the name and Word of the Lord. For where they are called to an office, it is at the same time enjoined upon them not to bring anything of themselves, but to speak from the Lord's mouth.[38]

Clearly, the accent here is not on individual originality but on faithfulness to teachings that are received. Calvin explicitly links the teaching authority of the minister to scripture when he writes:

> But where it pleased God to raise up a more visible form of the church, he willed to have his Word set down and sealed in writing, that his priests might seek from it what to teach the people, and that every doctrine to be taught should conform to that rule.[39]

Not only does the authority of ministers reside in their faithfulness to received teaching, it also remains *fallible.* Subject to finitude and sinfulness, the teachings of all ministers are open to tests by other ministers and by members of the church. As Calvin writes, "But if we must accept the teaching of all pastors whatever without any doubting, what was the point of the Lord's frequent admonitions to us not to heed the talk of false prophets?"[40] Hence the church is "to test all spirits of all men by the standard of God's Word in order to determine whether or not they are from God."[41]

The authority of ministers is *dispersed*. The minister of a congregation functions within a broader configuration of authorities. The teacher must remain teachable. The teachings of church councils, theologians, and other ministers and church members all prevent any single minister from determining in isolation what the teachings of the church are to be.[42] The minister functions as part of a living tradition in which multiple authorities play a part in the interpretation of scripture.

Church Councils in the Teaching Office

We see these same four features in Calvin's discussion of the church councils. His whole discussion of councils in the *Institutes* emphasizes their fallibility, and there is little reason to tarry on this point.[43] He repeatedly points out the errors made by church councils with regard to scripture and the incompatibility of the teachings of various councils with one another.[44] What is not always taken into account, however, is the proper authority that Calvin does assign to them. As he writes, "The fact that I shall here be rather severe does not mean that I esteem the ancient councils less than I ought. For I venerate them from my heart, and desire that they be honored by all."[45] In his view, their authority is *real*; it resides in the ability to interpret scripture definitively in the face of controversy. Calvin writes:

> We indeed willingly concede, if any discussion arises over doctrine, that the best and surest remedy is for a synod of true bishops to be convened, where the doctrine at issue may be examined. Such a definition, upon which the pastors of the church in common, invoking Christ's Spirit, agree, will have much more weight than if each one, having conceived it separately at home, should teach it to the people, or if a few private individuals should compose it.[46]

Councils, which are representative of the church, have priority over individuals in such situations. It was this emphasis on the authority of gathered bodies that led to the importance of confessions in the Reformed tradition. These statements of faith serve as hermeneutical keys in the interpretation of scripture and have priority over the private interpretation of scripture by the individual.

Calvin is equally clear, however, that the authority of councils and the confessions of faith they compose are both *finite* and *fallible*. They are subject to the limitations of time and place, as well as to the vagaries of human sin that can lead to distortions of faith. He constantly stresses the *derivative* character of conciliar authority. Councils per se are no guarantee that the true faith will be articulated. Their authority is bound to the teachings of scripture. As he puts it, "Thus councils would come to have the majesty that is their due; yet in the meantime Scripture would stand out in the higher place, with everything subject to its standard."[47]

This leads Calvin to emphasize the *dispersed* nature of authority in the church. The councils have a real and proper authority over the individual and the congregation. But the individual and the congregation have a right and an obligation to test the teachings of councils because of their potential fallibility. Since their authority is derivative, they should be tested according to the teachings of scripture. Calvin writes:

> But whenever a decree of any council is brought forward, I should like men first of all diligently to ponder at what time it was held, on what issue, and with what intention, what sort of men were present; then to examine by the standard of Scripture what it dealt with—and to do this in such a way that the definition of the council may have its weight and be like a provisional judgment, yet not hinder the examination which I have mentioned.[48]

A Constellation of Authorities in the Teaching Office

Our examination of the teaching authority of ministers and church councils provides us with a broader picture of the teaching office as it is found in Calvin's thought. A variety of authorities have important roles to play in the church's determination of its normative beliefs and practices and its reinterpretation of these beliefs and practices through the ages. Ministers and church councils are only two of these authorities. Congregations, theologians, individual conscience, and church tradition also have important roles to play in the church's teaching office. Their teaching authority is real, but it is dependent on their faithfulness to scripture. Moreover, no single church authority can be raised to a position that rivals that of the Bible, for all church teaching and every church teacher are subject to human fallibility.

For this reason, the teaching office must include a constellation of authorities functioning at various levels of the church's life. Ideally, these offices and agencies will work together to articulate the central teachings by which the church is maintained as a community. But frequently it is out of the tension between the various partners in the church's teaching office that the truth emerges. Calvin was aware of the problems of the dispersement of teaching authority. But he was equally aware of what could happen when it is overly centralized, as in the Roman Catholic *magisterium* of his day. The teacher must remain teachable, for fallibility and sin are inherent dimensions of the human condition, even in the church. Even if Calvin's own practices and those of the church of Geneva did not always live up to the ideals he professed, they do not negate the fundamental insights of his theology. To this day, he remains *the* Protestant theologian of the church's teaching ministry.

Calvin's Encounter with Humanism

Calvin did not stop with a merely theoretical exposition of the church's teaching office. He worked tirelessly to develop church structures that carried out the teaching ministry of the church in a manner appropriate to their real but fallible authority. Of particular importance are two educational projects in which he invested a great deal of his energy: the founding of the Academy of Geneva and catechetical instruction among the children of the church. We gain significant insight into Calvin's understanding of the teaching ministry by examining the concrete practices he formulated in these two areas. Here we see Calvin focusing n the third function of the teaching office: The formation of institutions, processes, and material by which the church can hand on its faith from generation to generation and deepen the understanding of its members across the course of their lives.

By way of introduction, it is instructive to note Calvin's educational background. Calvin experienced firsthand the tensions between the style of education inherited from the Middle Ages and that which was emerging in France under the influence of Renaissance humanism.[49] During the latter part of the Middle Ages, a scholastic style of theology and education emerged, in large part because of the rediscovery of the writings of Aristotle during the end of the twelfth century. This style of education placed great emphasis on the study of logic and de-emphasized grammar and rhetoric, two of the major divisions of the classical *trivium*.[50]

In contrast, Renaissance humanists saw themselves as reaching behind the traditions of the Middle Ages to antiquity, especially to ancient Greece and Rome.[51] In the face of a newly emerging city culture with expanded governmental and commercial interests, they self-consciously attempted to devise a style of education that would form leaders who could combine learning and active civic participation in ways appropriate to an urban setting.[52] At the heart of their educational reform was the classical ideal of the orator-statesman. Grammar, composition, the study of foreign languages (especially Latin and Greek), the study of history (especially classical history)—all were seen as enabling eloquent, persuasive, and morally enriching rhetoric. Rhetoric was viewed as an inherently moral discipline, focusing on the art of persuading one's contemporaries to moral truths with a view to the harmonious conduct of civic life.[53]

In writing and in speaking, the principle of "authoritative usage" held sway in humanistic education.[54] Education was to expose persons to the best models available, with emphasis placed not on individual creativity but on the imitation of higher standards, which were viewed as authoritative. Classical culture in particular was looked to as providing these models in writing and in speaking. Hence, the outstanding authors of Greece and Rome were read, not merely to "broaden" the perspective of the student as in a contemporary liberal arts education but to learn proper grammar, rhetoric, and composition.

Calvin experienced both the worst of scholastic education and the best of humanistic education. It is little wonder that humanism made such a lasting impression on him. He received his first education in an endowed school in his hometown, popularly known as the School of the Capettes.[55] At the age of fourteen, he was sent by his father to the University of Paris to prepare for the priesthood. There he studied briefly under the brilliant humanistic educator Mathurin Cordier in the College de la Marche.[56] Though Calvin studied under Cordier for only a few months, it was the beginning of a long-lasting friendship. Many years later, Calvin was to entrust Cordier with the initial organization of education in Geneva, and he dedicated his commentary on the First Epistle to the Thessalonians to him.[57]

For unknown reasons, Calvin transferred to the College de Montaigu, also a part of the University of Paris. One of the strongholds of orthodoxy, this college represented many of the worst features of scholastic education.[58] Calvin stayed here for five years. At that point, his father decided that a career in the priesthood was no longer promising for his son and had him take up residence at the University of Orleans to study law.[59] This represented a shift of great importance for Calvin, freeing him from the oppressive atmosphere of the University of Paris and allowing him to encounter more directly the ideals of humanism. Of special importance was his exposure to a historical analysis of the law, something the humanists were only beginning to introduce.[60]

Calvin was forced to leave the University of Orleans rather suddenly upon learning of his father's illness and subsequent death in 1531. This left him free to pursue his own course of study. He chose to return to Paris and enter the newly established Royal College (Lecteurs Royaux) founded by one of the most influential humanists in France, Guillaume Bude.[61] This institution represented the best humanistic education available in France at that time. Here, Calvin pursued Hellenistic studies under Pierre Danes, as well as learning Hebrew.

During his sojourn at the Royal College, Calvin completed work on his first book, *Commentary on the De Clementia.* The book clearly reveals the extent to which his education had left him a thoroughgoing humanist.[62] Calvin's conversion several years later transformed his humanism dramatically. In contrast to humanism's optimistic assessment of nature and culture, he offered an Augustinian doctrine of sin. In place of its emphasis on life in this world, he put an understanding of the purpose of life as the glorification of God. Wendel surely is correct when he writes, "Before his conversion he took humanism to be the end in itself; after that event it was no more than a means; and as it has been said of him . . . 'He employs humanism to combat humanism.'"

In spite of this marked shift in Calvin's thought, humanism's influence continues to be evident in his work for the remainder of his life, especially in the educational institutions and practices he puts in place in Geneva.[63] While scripture and theology now have a position of greater importance than the insights of philosophy, Calvin is willing to use the reforms of humanistic education as a "means" of creating an educated laity and persons competent to lead the church and the community.

The Academy of Geneva

It might seem odd to focus on the Academy of Geneva before examining Calvin's proposals about catechetical instruction, for the Academy was the final major project Calvin undertook before his death. His interest in establishing a first-rate institution of education, however, was present from the very beginning of his work in Geneva. Moreover, the continuing influence of humanism on Calvin's thought is more apparent in his work on the Academy. In our examination of Calvin's educational proposals in both the Academy and catechetical instruction, we will present his thought as it unfolded. Each area provides us with great insight into the relationship between Calvin's theology of the teaching office, as described in this chapter, and the educational practices he designed to carry out this ministry of the church.

Not long after his conversion, Calvin left France for Basel, where he devoted himself totally to theology. While living in Basel, he made several trips to France. On one of these he met Guillaume Farel, who was the spiritual leader of the Protestant community in Geneva. Farel implored Calvin to return with him to Geneva and assist him in the reform of the church and city life. Calvin did so, somewhat reluctantly, beginning a relationship with this community that was to last virtually the rest of his life.

During the early stages of the reform in Geneva, Calvin wrote several documents that reveal the special importance he attached to general education and the church's stake in supporting the creation of educational institutions that were open to all. Of special importance in this regard are the *Articles Concerning the Organization of the Church and of Worship at Geneva* (1537) and *The Ecclesiastical Ordinances* (1541), both of which outline Calvin's proposed reforms for the city. When Calvin began his work in Geneva, he was faced with a paucity of educated ministers and a general population that had received little opportunity for education. Until 1502, the city had not offered systematic instruction, and, for the most part, youths were forced to go elsewhere if they desired anything beyond an introduction to Latin.[64] Believing that sound instruction of the laity in Christian doctrine was a key to the success of the Reformation, Calvin emphasized the advancement of education in both the *Articles of Organization* and *Ecclesiastical Ordinances*.

In the former, he included plans for a school that was open to all children, with the poor attending free of charge.[65] As

Calvin moved to put his proposals into practice, he enlisted the help of his old teacher and longtime friend, Mathurin Cordier.[66] In 1538, the two worked together on final plans for the school, which eventually was known as the College de la Rive. The proposed curriculum clearly indicates the conjoining of humanistic education and theological goals.[67] It included three general areas: religion, language, and human sciences, placing great emphasis on classical culture as providing the authoritative models for composition and rhetoric.[68]

At this point Calvin's work was interrupted as he and Farel were asked to leave the city because of the unpopularity of their reforms. Calvin spent the next three years in Strasbourg, where he worked closely with Martin Bucer, the leading Reformation pastor of the city. These years were crucial to Calvin's formation as a minister and exerted great influence on his understanding of the church's teaching ministry. He became pastor of a church for Protestant refugees from France.

During this period, Calvin also became involved in a college founded by Johannes Sturm, an acquaintance from his days in Paris. Sturm had established a college in Strasbourg that was based on both Reformed and humanist principles. He placed great emphasis on the study of classical culture for the acquisition of proper grammatical and rhetorical skills, arguing that Christians should be able to present their "sanctified wisdom eloquently and effectively."[69] Calvin was given a chair in exegesis in the school and began the practice of developing commentaries in conjunction with his teaching of the Bible.

Sturm's school was based on a division of pupils and subject matter according to the students' abilities. While we take this for granted today, it was something of a major reform at that time. This allowed Sturm to set up a course of study with systematic goals, testing, and promotion. These are ideas Calvin used later in the Academy of Geneva. In the Strasbourg school, kindergarten was for children under six. Gymnasium was open to students between six and fifteen and focused on linguistic studies, particularly the mastery of Latin. The upper school, or *Hochschule,* was for persons sixteen and over. It concentrated on Greek, Hebrew, philosophy, mathematics, physics, history, law, and theology.[70]

While Calvin and Farel were exiled from Geneva, the city was in a constant state of turmoil. In 1540, an official embassy traveled to Strasbourg and implored Calvin to return. Reluctantly, he did so in order to complete the reforms he had begun there. On the very day of his return, he appeared before the Magistracy and demanded that a commission of ministers and advisers be established to draft an ecclesiastical constitution. The resulting document, the *Ecclesiastical Ordinances* of 1541, was something that Calvin, in fact, wrote himself.

In this document he continued to press for the establishment of a school that was open to the population of the city. The church, he believed, has a stake in the creation of strong educational institutions, for only a literate population will be able to read scripture and theology. As Calvin points out, it is only possible to profit from the study of theology "if first one is instructed in the languages and humanities."[71] In the *Ordinances*, he even goes so far as to locate the teachers of the proposed school—the doctors—within the ordained officers of the church. Their primary task is "the instruction of the faithful in true doctrine, in order that the purity of the Gospel be not corrupted either by ignorance or by evil opinions."[72] The doctors were to be under the discipline of the church and nominated by the ministers. They also were to be subject to the approval of the city government.

It was not until eighteen years had passed, only five years before his death, that Calvin realized his dream of a fully supported academy in Geneva. The immediate impetus for his renewed work in this area was a return visit to Sturm's academy in Strasbourg in 1557.[73] Having witnessed the expansion and curricular development of that institution, Calvin was determined to press for a school of high quality in Geneva. He began by securing a piece of property and raising enough money to allow building to begin. The more difficult problem initially seemed to be procuring an outstanding faculty. A conflict between the city authorities in Berne and the faculty of the academy in their vassal city, Lausanne, led to the resignation of the Lausanne faculty, providing Calvin with a ready-made group of doctors who could teach in his school. The Academy of Geneva opened on March 16, 1559, with Theodore Beza as rector.

During the opening of the Academy, Calvin read *The Order of the College of Geneva*, which he is thought to have written.[74] It describes the administrative organization and curriculum of the school and shows the unique way the Academy attempted to bring together a Reformed emphasis on knowledge of God as the true source of all wisdom and an appreciation of the insights of humanistic educational reform.

The doctors of the school continue to be seen as representatives of the church, as Calvin had originally envisioned in the *Ordinances* of 1541. They are to subscribe to a set confession of faith and are subject to church discipline. This is consistent with the basic assumption upon which the school was founded: The teachers are, above all else, "to teach them [their students] to love God and to hate sin."[75] This did not mean, however, that the Academy was to do the work of the church. Their relationship was complementary. Religion, for example, was not even taught in the lower school. Students were involved in the singing of psalms and were examined on their understanding of the Sunday and Wednesday sermons, but this instruction was seen as complementing what they were receiving in catechism classes.

The curriculum of the Academy, moreover, was thoroughly humanistic. The lower school, the *scholar privata*, included students up to about the age of sixteen. It was divided into seven divisions, with a systematic form of examination and promotion from one division to another. The lowest three grades focused on the mastery of Latin and French grammar through the study of the Latin-French catechism. The study of French on a par with Latin was something of an innovation. During the next two years, the students were gradually introduced to Greek and encouraged to learn how to express themselves in written composition and rhetoric through an imitation of Latin and Greek authors. In the final two divisions, history and dialectics were studied.

A sample of the authors used in the curriculum gives a clear indication of the humanistic regard for antiquity that permeated the school: Virgil's *Bucolics* and *Aeneid*, the *Epistles* of Cicero, and the *Commentaries* of Caesar. These alone were studied during the first three years. When the student had mastered Greek sufficiently, he was to read Seneca, Xenophon, Polybius, Herodian, Demosthenes, and Homer, as well as the Gospel of Luke.

The upper school, the *scholar publica*, was designed to prepare persons for the ordained ministry or leadership in civic government. It was organized in a very different fashion. No divisions were established. The student registered with the rector, signed a confession of faith, and attended lectures. Public lectures were offered in the arts and theology, with the hope that law and medicine would soon be added. Overall, there were twenty-seven hours of lectures a week: three in theology; three in Old Testament; five in Hebrew grammar; three in moral philosophy (using Aristotle, Plato or Plutarch, or a Christian ethicist); five in Greek poetry, history, or orations; three in physics or mathematics; and five in dialectics and rhetoric.

The principles of humanistic education are clearly evident in the Academy of Geneva. Classical culture was held in great esteem, providing the authoritative models for grammar, composition, and verbal expression. Rhetoric, likewise, occupied a position of importance. How should we evaluate the role of humanism in Calvin's academy? In his commentary on 1 Corinthians 1:17, Calvin provides us with his own assessment of this matter. In commenting on Paul's evaluation of oratory, he points out that "it were quite unreasonable to suppose that Paul would utterly condemn these arts which, it is manifest, are excellent gifts of God, and which serve as instruments, as it were, to assist men in the accomplishment of important purposes."[76] He goes on to write:

> As for these arts, then, that have nothing of superstition, but contain solid learning, and are founded on just principles, as they are useful and suited to the common transactions of human life, so there can be no doubt that they have come forth from the Holy Spirit; and the advantage which is derived and experienced from them, ought to be ascribed exclusively to God.[77]

Clearly, Calvin is affirming the insights of the arts and sciences here. They are "excellent gifts of God." Accordingly, he is willing to draw on the insights of humanistic education in formulating the Academy's curriculum. He even goes so far as to borrow certain themes that are prominent in humanism's understanding of rhetoric to describe God's relationship to humanity, as in the theme of divine accommodation.[78] His view toward tradition is also deeply influenced by humanistic thought.

At no point, however, does Calvin ascribe the same kind of authority to the insights of the arts and sciences as he grants to scripture and Christian doctrine. Indeed, he can be quite critical of the human and natural sciences when they move beyond their proper sphere and attempt to explain life's meaning and purpose solely on the basis of natural reason.[79] It is scripture and scripture alone that can provide true knowledge of God and the world in relation to God. Calvin believed that this is true whether the focus is on the church's teaching of its own members or on the general education of the city's population. He does not live in a world in which the public domain is given over to secularized meanings. The Academy, thus, is seen as assisting persons in pursuing vocations discernible only in conjunction with the knowledge given in faith. Learning to speak well and to write clearly can assist persons in the exercise of their vocations, but this cannot tell them what their vocation is. Only Christine doctrine on the basis of scripture can do that.

Calvin's critical appropriation of humanism in his educational proposals and his long-term insistence on the church's support of and involvement in the general education of the Genevan population force us to ask some of the most difficult questions facing the contemporary teaching office. From beginning to end, Calvin viewed the foundation of the Academy as the knowledge given in Jesus Christ. While he was quite willing to draw on humanistic education to inform the school's curriculum, at no point was he willing to allow it to determine its basic purpose. This seems an impossible educational ideal in a pluralistic society in which the public schools must honor the official disestablishment of religion. Moreover, the emergence of the natural and human sciences as autonomous disciplines have increasingly made their relationship to theology unclear.

Nonetheless, Calvin's vision of a school of general education in which the knowledge given in Christ holds a preeminent position challenges the contemporary teaching office to broaden its horizons beyond an exclusive concern for the education that takes place in the church. In Calvin's view the church's teaching ministry is involved in the task of ordering the patterns of life in society beyond the church. Accordingly, it has a stake in the educational institutions of the public domain.

There is little question that the cultural context of the contemporary teaching office is quite different from the one in which Calvin worked. Yet the church's care for both the education of its members and the educational institutions of society as a whole continues to be an issue of great importance to the teaching office. With some notable exceptions, there can be little question that the contemporary teaching office has unwittingly accepted the role assigned it by a society in which religion is privatized.[80] One of the most difficult issues before mainline Protestantism today is how to move beyond this position with regard to the education of the public.

Catechetical Instruction in the Church

Almost from the beginning of his conversion to Protestantism, Calvin was involved in the teaching ministry. As he writes in the introduction to his commentary on the Psalms, "I was quite surprised to find that before a year had elapsed, all who had any desire after purer doctrine were continually coming to me to learn, although I myself was as yet but a mere novice and tyro."[81] Nor did his departure from France to Basel not long after his conversion in order to write theology diminish his involvement. Indeed, Calvin's initial work in the *Institutes* was originally viewed as an exercise in teaching. The first edition was not intended for theologians or those training for the ministry but was written

> especially for our French countrymen, very many of whom I knew to be hungering and thirsting for Christ; but I saw very few who had been duly imbued with even a slight knowledge of him. The book itself witnesses that this was my intention, adapted as it is to a simple and, you may say, elementary form of teaching.[82]

In the editions that followed, Calvin expanded the *Institutes* and adopted as his purpose the writing of a clear and comprehensive exposition of the basic doctrines of the Christian faith. He did not abandon his belief that an "elementary form of teaching" for the church as a whole was necessary. This was precisely how he viewed the role of catechetical instruction.

Calvin was himself the author of two catechisms and wrote throughout his career about the practice of catechetical instruction. Several prominent themes emerge when the body of his thought is examined. First, catechetical instruction plays a significant role in the teaching office's attempt to maintain unity both in the congregation and among the churches, providing all members with a common set of beliefs. It should not be viewed strictly in terms of its role in the individual's faith. It has a unifying function in the church's life. Second, catechetical instruction is necessary for the preservation of sound, evangelical doctrine in the church. It allows individuals and congregations to discern and resist heretical thinking. Third, the teaching of the catechism serves as a means of grace, enabling baptized children to appropriate personally the promises made on their behalf at baptism and initiating them into the ongoing process of sanctification that is nurtured through their participation in the word and sacraments of the church during their lives. We can trace these themes as they emerge in Calvin's thought.

In the *Articles* of 1537, written shortly after coming to Geneva, Calvin describes four matters that he believes are necessary to the reform of the Genevan church: the discipline of excommunication, the singing of psalms in congregational worship, the catechetical instruction of children, and the improvement of regulations governing marriage. Calvin argues that the children "ought to make a confession of their faith to the Church [for] if we truly believe with the heart, it is right that we ought also confess to with the mouth to that salvation which we believe."[83] It was precisely for this reason that "a definite catechism was used for initiating each one in the fundamentals of the Christian religion" in the ancient church and an opportunity provided for each child to "testify their faith to the Church, to which they were unable at their Baptism to render witness."[84]

Calvin's initial appeal here is not to scripture but to the fact that catechetical instruction was an important practice in the early church.[85] He goes on to link the importance of catechetical instruction to the authority of scripture. It was precisely because the word of God had been neglected in the teaching of the church and families that a need for catechetical instruction was so desperate in Geneva. He calls for

> a brief and simple summary of the Christian faith to be taught to all children, and that at certain seasons of the year they come before the ministers to be interrogated and examined, and to receive more ample explanation, according as there is need to the capacity of each one of them, until they have been proved sufficiently instructed.

All parents are expected to see to it that their children learn the catechism and are presented to the minister at appropriate times for instruction and examination.

The primary emphasis in this document is on the need for all baptized members of the church to accept for themselves at an appropriate age the promises made on their behalf at baptism. Baptized children are considered members of the covenant community and have the right and obligation of instruction in the faith. Their baptism does not preclude their need to make a personal confession of faith to the church. Calvin frequently links catechetical instruction to the baptism of infants, and it is indicative of the developmental themes he often uses to describe the Christian life. In a number of places, for example, he describes the Holy Spirit's operation in individuals' lives in terms of the slow and steady growth of a seed that is planted in them during infancy.[86] As he puts it, the "ordinary method in which God accomplishes our salvation is by beginning it in baptism and carrying it gradually forward during the course of life."[87] Elsewhere, he writes, "Infants are renewed by the Spirit of God according to the capacity of their age, till the power which was concealed within them grows by degrees and becomes fully manifest at the proper time."[88]

In the *Articles*, he also focuses on the important role catechetical instruction plays in the life of the church. Catechetical instruction is important not only for the individual member but for congregations and the church as a whole. He alludes to this in the introduction to the *Articles* when he points out that instruction of children at a "tender age" is necessary to "maintain the people in purity of doctrine."[89] Catechetical instruction that teaches the basic beliefs of the Christian community is essential "so that evangelical doctrine is not left to decay, and also that its substance be diligently maintained and transmitted from hand to hand and from father to son."[90]

Here, Calvin clearly is acknowledging a role for normative beliefs and practices in the church that attempt to maintain continuity with the original apostolic witness and affords unity in congregations and the church as a whole. Every member is to be taught "a brief and simple summary of the Christian faith" that sets forth the church's basic beliefs. In so doing, the church binds its members to the faith of the church universal, providing them with knowledge of God and an introduction to the teachings of scripture.

Having called for a "brief and simple summary of the Christian faith," Calvin set about writing a catechism, which was published in French during this same year (1537).[91] The following year he translated it into Latin "for the other churches," indicative of his hope that a common catechism might promote unity throughout the Reformation churches.[92] Titled *Instruction in Faith*, this first catechism presented the teachings of the *Institutes* of 1536 in a simplified manner.

Calvin prefaces this catechism with three brief passages of scripture from 1 Peter, each underscoring the importance of Christians' possessing a sure and certain knowledge of the basic doctrines of the Reformation.[93] Likewise, he appends two verses to the conclusion: "My people go into exile for want of knowledge" (Isa. 5:13) and "How can a young man keep his way pure? By guarding it according to thy word" (Ps. 119:9). Both are indicative of the important role Calvin accorded catechetical instruction in the long-term success of the Reformation. Shortly after Calvin wrote *Instruction in Faith*, he and Farel were exiled from Geneva. This afforded Calvin the opportunity to try out his ideas about catechetical instruction as a pastor in Strasbourg. There he made mastery of the catechism mandatory for all children, not allowing them to partake of the Lord's supper until they gave evidence of a satisfactory knowledge of its contents.[94]

In the *Ecclesiastical Ordinances* of 1541, which Calvin wrote upon his return to Geneva, he again turned his attention to catechetical instruction, writing a section in which he outlined the rationale and organization of this practice. Once more, he relates catechetical instruction to baptism, writing that only persons of faith and of the Reformed communion can serve as godparents during the baptismal ceremony "since others are not capable of making the promise to the Church of instructing the children as is proper."[95]

Calvin goes on to prescribe a series of concrete steps for the catechesis of children. All persons are to bring their children every Sunday at midday for catechism class conducted by the minister. When its contents have been mastered, the children are to recite them in their entirety and make a profession of their faith in the presence of the church. A "definite formulary" is to be composed by which all will be instructed. No children are to receive communion before they have had catechetical instruction, for "it is a very perilous thing . . . to introduce them without good and adequate instruction; for which purpose this order is to be used."[96] The discussion concludes with several organizational recommendations as to how children are to be divided up by parishes and parents held accountable for their children's participation.

Of even greater importance is the second catechism Calvin wrote around this time, *The Catechism of the Church of Geneva* (1541). Calvin had already revised the *Institutes* significantly in 1539, and the theological changes he made at that time are reflected.[97] The overall pattern of this catechism is significantly different. It follows the question-answer format Luther used in his catechisms. All in all, there are over 373 questions and answers. In the instructions he gives in the introduction, it is clear that Calvin views the mastery of the catechism as far more than an exercise in rote memorization. It is to be a living dialogue between minister and student in which the structured questions and answers serve as an occasion to examine together the basic beliefs of the church. Calvin himself divides the material into four sections to help ministers organize their teaching: faith (focusing on the creed), the law (dealing with the Ten Commandments), the Lord's Prayer (focusing on the relationship between prayer and providence), and the proper worship of God (dealing with the relationship of word and sacrament).

Of great significance is what Calvin has to say about the

importance of catechetical instruction at the beginning of this work in his letters to the reader and the ministers of East Friesland. Here he places great emphasis on the unity of belief among the faithful that instruction in a common catechism affords. Calvin says this is his chief reason for writing the Genevan catechism. In it and others like it, the church is given "the rudiments with which both the learned and the unlearned among us were from youth constantly instructed, all the faithful holding them as the solemn symbol of Christian communion."[98] Similarly, he writes in these letters that instruction in the catechism allows children to be examined "concerning the specific points which should be common and familiar to all Christians."[99]

Throughout these letters Calvin relates the unity of doctrine and belief afforded by instruction in the catechism to the common baptism, which all Christians have received. He writes:

> Since it is proper for us by every means to endeavour to make that unity of faith shine forth among us which is so highly commended by Paul, the solemn profession of faith which is joined to our common Baptism ought to be directed chiefly to this end. It might therefore be wished, not only that there exist a perpetual consent by all in pious doctrine, but that there be also a single form of Catechism for all Churches.[100]

He goes on to argue that anyone who teaches doctrine in a manner that destroys the unity of the church is engaging in an "impious profanation of Baptism" and continues, "For what further use is Baptism, unless this remain its foundation, that we all agree in one faith?"[101]

With even greater force than in his earlier writings, Calvin is emphasizing here the importance of catechetical instruction for congregations and the church as a whole. It affords a common language and set of theological convictions by which the church can order its life together. Indeed, the common mind it produces is a witness to the unity that should exist in the church on the basis of the one baptism of which all Christians partake. It is important for us to grasp the role Calvin believes catechetical instruction plays in creating church unity. Too frequently in the contemporary church, what is presently called confirmation is viewed exclusively in terms of its role in enhancing an individual's growth in faith. Arguments about when it should be offered are governed by an evaluation of when persons are psychologically ready for a more individuated faith response. Calvin's understanding of catechetical instruction does not overlook the importance of the personal appropriation of faith, as we have already seen, but it also points to the role of catechetical instruction in laying a firm theological foundation throughout the church as a whole. This theme is especially important in light of contemporary Protestantism's need to come to grips with the influence of modern individualism in its own midst.

In the final edition of the *Institutes*, Calvin writes of the importance of catechetical instruction in ways that reiterate themes we have already examined. One passage in particular is worth quoting in full:

> But the best method of catechizing would be to have a manual drafted for this exercise, containing and summarizing in simple manner most of the articles of our religion, on which the whole believers' church ought to agree without controversy. A child of ten would present himself to the church to declare his confession of faith, would be examined in each article, and answer to each; if he were ignorant of anything or insufficiently understood it, he would be taught. Thus, while the church looks on as a witness, he would profess the one true and sincere faith, in which the believing folk with one mind worship the one God. . . . There would be greater agreement in faith among Christian people, and not so many would go untaught and ignorant; some would not be so rashly carried away with new and strange doctrines; in short, all would have some methodical instruction, so to speak, in Christian doctrine.[102]

As in the introductory letters to the Genevan Catechism, Calvin places great emphasis here on the unity of faith that catechizing produces. It initiates every member of the church into the articles of Christianity on which the "whole believers' church ought to agree without controversy." Moreover, it protects Christians from being rashly carried away by the latest religious fad or teaching.[103]

Far from advocating individualism in Christianity, it is clear that Calvin, in his writings on the catechetical instruction of children, sees an authoritative role for the church in teaching the basic tenets of the faith. It is to serve as one of the most important educational practices by which the teaching office creates unity in the church. Calvin's willingness to write two catechisms so carefully and to translate them into Latin and French is indicative of how serious he was about this teaching activity. His attempts to draft ordinances for the organization of the Genevan church singled out the instruction of children in the catechism as a key part of his projected reform.

Theology and Practice in the Teaching Office

It should be clear by now that Calvin in his theology and practice advocated an extremely important role for the teaching office in the church's life. His work in establishing the Academy of Geneva and encouraging catechetical instruction in the congregations under his leadership reveals a wonderful symmetry of thought and action. His theology repeatedly draws on imagery of teaching and learning to describe the relationship between God and humanity and the overall ministry of the church. Likewise, the educational proposals he advocates clearly reveal their grounding in the basic tenets of his theology. Thought and action, theology and life, are not separated.

In the best sense, Calvin's theology is practical, guiding the reform of the church that he is attempting to put into effect. Conversely, it is also apparent that Calvin's practice is theological. It is out of the struggle to put new structures of church life in place that much of his theology is born. Theology informs practice; practice prompts theological reflection. In its struggle today to recover a more adequate teaching office, mainline Protestantism has much to learn, not only from the substance of Calvin's reflection on this ministry of the church but from the way he was able to hold together theology and the Christian life. While the contemporary church finds itself in a cultural situation that is significantly different from the one the great Reformers faced, it too must strive to bring theology and life together. Part Three concentrates on this task.

PART THREE

Recovering
the Teaching Office

8

Recovering the Teaching Office
in a New Theological Paradigm

As the mainline Protestant churches struggle to discern their role in the new religious America, it is important that they ground that role in firm biblical and theological foundations. Decline in membership and a general loss of cultural prestige and power have led many in these churches to advocate programs that will supposedly turn things around in short order. Neither quick-fix church growth programs nor a return to the "spiritual" religion of an earlier era represents an adequate response to the challenges before mainline Protestantism. The task before these churches is more difficult and probably more costly. It involves the willingness to let go of patterns of thought and action that seemed to work so well in the recent past and to search for new ones.

The Recovery of the Teaching Office

At the heart of this search is the discovery of attitudes and institutional forms that can bring into being a stronger teaching office in the Protestant mainstream. How can these churches find ways of articulating the normative beliefs and practices that lie at the heart of their communal identities? The threats of modern individualism are real. The need for communal authorities and educational practices that can bind communities together is more pressing than ever. How can it become possible for representative bodies and church leaders to teach congregations with any real authority? All too often, their teachings are either disparaged or ignored altogether.

Similarly the mainline churches face crucial issues with regard to the process of reinterpreting the faith. Questions of tremendous significance are before them. The challenge to exclusively masculine descriptions of God is just one case in point. What is the best way for the mainline churches to continue to struggle with this and other similar issues? Can it do so without losing touch with the historic sources of Christian identity? Equally important is the task of forming educational institutions, processes, and resources to teach the church. Once more, issues of tremendous consequence are before the church. The transformation of catechetical instruction into confirmation raises questions about the theological underpinnings of this practice. Is it designed for the individual's growth in faith or the community's education of a membership that has mastered a common set of basic beliefs? Can the latter be done without a catechism? What is the relationship of denominational publishing houses to seminaries? What role should seminaries play in developing curriculum, for example? To what extent should the publishing arm of the church be bound by marketing concerns?

Like a person whose identity has become uncertain, the mainline churches are tempted to look to others to find answers to these questions. It is tempting to look to the traditions of modern individualism and view the church's teaching ministry primarily as a means of helping each solitary individual formulate his or her beliefs and personal moral norms. There is much in modern society that makes this way of thinking about the church's teaching ministry seem quite plausible. It is equally tempting to react to the vicissitudes of modernity and look to the traditions of conservative Protestantism to determine the church's teaching ministry. An inerrant Bible, the reassertion of traditional forms of authority, and the demarcation of clear communal boundaries seem to be the very foundations that the mainline churches are seeking.

In the end, neither modern individualism nor countermodern authoritarianism will provide the foundations for the sort of teaching office that is needed in the mainline churches today. These are not the only options available, however. These churches can rediscover their own Reformation heritage and the unique theological bases and institutional forms of the teaching office. They can seek a third way in the contemporary American religious scene: a nonauthoritarian teaching office that recognizes the legitimate role of teaching authority in the church but locates it in multiple offices and agencies, none of which can claim infallibility. As the mainline churches struggle to define their new role in contemporary American life, they would do well to mine the riches of their own theological past.

The *rediscovery* of a tradition, however, and its *recovery* are by no means the same.[1] Rediscovery is the activity of discerning once again the meaning and power of a tradition that has been repressed or forgotten. Recovery goes further. It involves the positive evaluation and appropriation of that tradition, using what has been rediscovered to structure present patterns of thought and action. Our task in the remainder of this book is one of recovery. On the basis of our examination of the thought of Luther and Calvin, the possibility of a stronger teaching office in contemporary Protestantism will be projected.

This attempt to recover elements of the teaching office found in the thought of Luther and Calvin does not mean that we can take over in an unreconstructed form the understandings of the teaching office that have emerged from their thought. Our task is more difficult: It is the creative appropriation of Luther's and Calvin's thought to address a situation that is quite different from the one they faced. Between the era of the Reformation and our own day stands the whole process of modernization, with its scientific forms of rationality, rapid social change, and structural and cultural pluralism. Our task is to recover the teaching office and devise forms to make it appropriate today. Of great importance in this regard is the shift from an established pattern of church life to one of denominationalism. This raises both problems and possibilities for the teaching office in contemporary Protestantism.

Both Luther and Calvin wrote in the context of an established pattern of church life in which a particular church (e.g., Lutheran, Reformed, Roman Catholic) was dominant in a geographical area and supported by the civil authorities. At least in part, the ability of these churches to establish normative beliefs and practices in a given area depended on their privileged position and close ties to the state. This pattern has been supplanted by the voluntary form of American denominationalism, an outgrowth of the structural and cultural pluralism of modern life. It is neither possible nor desirable to retrieve those dimensions of the teaching office that were grounded in the established pattern of church life.

The church's teaching authority is now far more dependent upon persuasion than direct or indirect coercion in collaboration with the state. If the Genevan church could watch over the moral behavior of the entire city's population through the Consistory, today's congregation typically has neither the desire nor the means of monitoring the behavior of its members.[2] The authority of the church is largely dependent on congregations' and ministers' ability to persuade their members that the teachings they offer have an important bearing on their lives.

This emphasis on the persuasive character of teaching authority is not inconsistent with the basic contours of Luther's and Calvin's thought. In principle, both men were opposed to an identification of the church's teaching authority with any form of coercive power. The function of the teaching office is not to ensure obedience to the church hierarchy but to promote the contemporary proclamation of the gospel and to support the new life in Christ that a response of faith engenders. Only God, through the inner witness of the Holy Spirit, can determine whether or not persons will respond to the gospel and help them to grow in faith.

In the established pattern of the church, however, these theological convictions were not always embodied in the actual structures of the church's life. The church, in conjunction with the state, assumed the task of enforcing uniformity of belief and morality. Almost inevitably this led to a confusion of social convention and obedience to God. The church's determination of normative beliefs and practices became something other than an aid to the living proclamation of the gospel, coming to serve as a loyalty test or a tangible measure of authentic Christianity. This tendency became especially prevalent with the rise of Protestant orthodoxy and its internal and external battles. It was in this context that Protestants and Roman Catholics alike began a desperate search for sources of religious authority that could buttress their position against the charges of their opponents. Absolute claim matched absolute claim. Church membership became dependent on a willingness to subscribe to the normative beliefs and practices of a given group, which were now portrayed as timeless and infallible norms. The result was years of religious strife and a defensive response to modern forms of inquiry.

It is important to remember this history and the dangers that an authoritarian teaching office represents. The recovery of the teaching office cannot and should not strive to return to the established pattern of religious life that served as the original context in which Luther and Calvin worked. At its best, denominationalism represents a social form in which religious groups with differing perspectives can live together in peace. No group can claim the official sanction of the state. The resulting pluralism can lead to an unhealthy relativism, but it can also have the beneficial effect of moderating the tendency to absolutize the norms of any particular group by forcing them to take the perspectives of others into account. While these characteristics of denominationalism are closely related to the structural and cultural pluralism of modern life, they are also consistent with the most basic insights of Reformation theology: The teaching office at any given moment is a fallible human depository of cumulative wisdom. It exists in the service of the gospel, not for its own aggrandizement. When it loses the capacity for self-criticism and begins to make absolute claims, it usurps prerogatives belonging to Christ alone.

Given the constraints of denominationalism and the theological commitments of its Reformation heritage, the mainline churches would do well to view the teaching office as deeply involved in a process of *consensus formation.* As a community, the church must strive to design structures and processes by which genuine consensus about its normative beliefs and practices can be formulated. Consensus formation in any community takes place on two levels, what we will call *"issue consensus"* and *"paradigm consensus."* The second level is more important and far more difficult to achieve. The concept of "paradigm" was first used by Thomas Kuhn to describe the set of commitments that scientists possess when they carry out their work.[3] While Kuhn has used the concept in several different ways, in his most recent work he uses it to refer to the "disciplinary matrix" in which science takes place.[4] This matrix includes three things: (1) symbolic generalizations—linguistic formulations that allow communication to take place; (2) models—the use of metaphors in a sustained fashion to carry out research in which a less familiar item is seen as analogous to one that is better known; and (3) exemplars—examples of concrete problems and how they are properly solved. When the scientific community pursues what Kuhn calls "normal science," it assumes widespread agreement about each of these elements. Agreement about these matters represents paradigm consensus.

In contrast, issue consensus is more specific. It focuses on agreement about a particular issue or topic of research. Issue consensus assumes agreement on the paradigm level. Paradigms shift only when "anomalies" or problems that cannot be resolved by the existing set of assumptions become pressing and a new paradigm emerges that seems to present a more promising approach.[5]

In recent years, a number of scholars have pointed out how religious and theological communities function in a manner that is analogous to the scientific community, em-

ploying at different times in history different paradigms that
have structured the life of faith and theological reflection in
markedly different ways.[6] Each of the three elements that
Kuhn points to is present: symbolic generalizations providing a common language, preferred models, and exemplars of
problem solution.

Paradigm consensus thus refers to agreement about how
discussion and debate on matters of central importance to the
church's life should take place: what authorities legitimately
can be appealed to, what theological convictions serve as a
common framework for discussion, and what structures and
procedures are best suited to helping the church make up its
collective mind. It points to agreement about the basic framework establishing how the church carries out its ongoing work
on specific issues. Issue consensus, in contrast, refers to agreement about specific matters in the life of faith: work on a contemporary ethical issue, for example, or the design of a new
curriculum for the denomination.[7]

It may well be that the recent difficulties facing the mainline
Protestant churches will result in a paradigm shift in the way
they are structured. Real and pressing anomalies are before
these churches, anomalies that seem unresolvable in terms of
present structures and attitudes. At the heart of these difficulties is an issue that has increasingly come into focus at many
levels of the church's life: *The problematic nature of theological reflection in the contemporary church.* The church seems
destitute of a theological language, grounded in scripture and
church tradition, by which it can guide its collective life. The
recovery of the teaching office that is being called for here is
best understood as part of a broader paradigm shift that currently may be under way. In large measure this is a shift in
fundamental assumptions about the nature and purpose of
theology in the life of the church, the location of theological
reflection, and the manner by which theology makes its contribution to consensus formation in the church.

Consensus Formation and a New Paradigm
of Theological Reflection

Throughout this century there has been a widespread feeling that academic theology is unnecessarily distant from the
life of faith and is so fractured into diverse disciplines and
methods that it has lost all internal coherence. While this criticism of theology has been raised by congregations, ministers,
and theologians alike, it has taken on increased urgency and

strength in light of two recent discussions in the theological community: the problematic nature of theological education and the nature and purpose of practical theology.

While the former has been a perennial topic in this century, it has taken a new turn under the influence of Edward Farley's book *Theologia*.[8] The resurgence of interest in practical theology can be found in the work of a number of different persons. What these discussions challenge is the view that theology is solely the property of academic specialists and is best thought of exclusively in its highly technical, scholarly forms. Increasingly, there is a commitment to viewing theology as something inherent in Christian life and as taking distinctive forms throughout the community of faith.

While focusing on the problematic nature of theological education, Farley's work is significant precisely because it seeks the more fundamental assumptions that undergird what he calls the "clerical paradigm" that has governed theological education in modern times.[9] Rather than accepting the problems of the current paradigm, he calls for a paradigm shift toward recovering a much broader and richer understanding of theology than that currently in place.

Theology, Farley argues, has been understood in several different ways during the course of Christian history.[10] In the first centuries of the church's life, theology referred to two distinct realities. First, it referred to "an actual, individual cognition of God and things related to God, a cognition which in most treatments attends faith and has eternal happiness as its final goal."[11] Theology in this sense was thought to be a part of every Christian's life. It involves the personal and existential wisdom or understanding that occurs when faith becomes self-conscious and engages in deliberate processes of reflection. In terms of the concepts used in this book, it is the cognitive component of piety. It is the insightfulness and knowledge that grows out of and shapes the attitudes and dispositions of the self in its apprehension of God and the world in relation to God.

Theology was also used in a second way during the church's first centuries, to refer to the scholarly investigation of the mysteries of faith. Theology in this sense was viewed as the systematic investigation of the nature of faith along rational lines. During the Middle Ages, both of the original understandings of theology remained in force, although with some modifications. Theology as the reflective dimension of piety largely remained intact, although it was joined to an Aristotelian anthropology and viewed as a *habitus* or enduring orientation of the soul. Theology as scholarly inquiry found a home in the newly emerging medieval universities and cathedral schools, where it came to be viewed as a science.

It was primarily during the modern period that these two understandings of theology were radically altered. In large measure, these alterations took place with theology's location in the modern university. Theology as a dimension of piety disappeared altogether; the sense that theology is an inherent part of every Christian's vocation was lost. At the same time, theology as a form of scholarly inquiry began to pattern itself after the newly emerging modern sciences. It lost its character as a unified science and was dispersed among the various disciplines that had become a standard part of the modern theological faculty. Gradually, the fourfold pattern of the theological encyclopedia became the standard way of viewing the various studies of theology: biblical studies, church history, dogmatic or systematic theology, and practical theology. Each discipline was seen as having its own methods and areas of special inquiry.

This is largely the paradigm in place today. The problems it engendered are familiar to anyone who knows the modern seminary or university divinity school. The lack of integration of the diverse, highly specialized theological disciplines that typically constitute the curriculum leaves seminary students without an understanding of how their various courses cohere. Moreover, there is a wide disparity between the forms of inquiry appropriate to the scholar and the kind of knowledge and skills appropriate to professional church leadership. Seminary courses frequently are modeled after the former, with the latter typically left to the practical theological disciplines or to field work. Even worse, there is not a vital connection between theology as a scholarly enterprise and congregational/denominational life. It has become increasingly unclear in what ways theology is related to the life and work of the church.

Underlying Farley's argument is the contention that these problems cannot be overcome without a basic paradigm shift in the way theology is understood. Merely tacking on interdisciplinary courses or seminars that seek to integrate theory and practice through case-study methods is not enough. What is necessary is the recovery of theology as a fundamental dimension of piety, an inherent part of every Christian's vocation. The proper location of this sort of theological reflection is the congregation and its individual members as they interpret and respond to concrete situations in light of their faith. Farley recognizes the importance of other modes of theology, describing the distinctive focus of scholarly theological reflection and that of professional church leadership.[12] Both of these, however, are seen as contributing to the formation of the cognitive component of piety and to theological reflection in congregational life. All theology is practical in precisely this sense.

Two things are missing from this proposal, however. The first is greater specification of the distinctive mode or genre of theological reflection that is proper to ministerial leadership and the ordinary believer; the recent discussion of practical theology has its greatest contribution to make at this point, and Farley has made his own contributions to this discussion. The second missing element is a conceptual framework by which to understand the interrelationship of the different forms of theological reflection that are carried out in different settings in the church; this is the issue addressed by the recovery of a classical understanding of the teaching office of the church. The remainder of this chapter will be devoted to the history and recent discussion of practical theology, and chapter 9 will explore the possibility of recovering forms of the teaching office that are based on the Reformers' work, relating it to contemporary mainline Protestantism.

Practical Theology as a Distinctive Mode of Theological Reflection

Practical theology is a rubric that gained currency in the theological encyclopedia period when theology came to be located in the modern university. Its history reflects the narrowings and specialization Farley has accounted for in his work, a history we will trace briefly. "Practical theology" cannot be taken over from the past in an unreconstructed fashion, for there are very real problems with this theological category. Chief among these difficulties is the implication that practical theology alone deals with the life and reality of the church, while the other theological disciplines—biblical studies, dogmatic theology, church history, and Christian ethics—do not. This sort of understanding stands in direct opposition to a fundamental affirmation of Protestant theology: All theological reflection is inherently practical. As H. Richard Niebuhr once put it:

> How, then, does Protestantism raise the question of God and how does it seek and find its answers to its problems? How does

the problem of God present itself to us who work in this living tradition? It comes to us as an eminently practical problem, a problem of human existence and destiny, of the meaning of human life in general and of the life of self and its community in particular. . . . It has not sought to convince a speculative, detached mind of the existence of God, but has begun with actual moral and religious experience, with the practical reasoning of the existing person rather than with the speculative interests of a detached mind.[14]

In writing this, Niebuhr is echoing something that has been affirmed from the very beginning of Protestantism. As we have seen, Calvin viewed theology's task as the shaping of piety and the guiding of the church in its transformation of human life and society.[15] In the Protestant tradition, all theology is practical in this sense.

While it is important to begin with this fundamental affirmation, this does not prevent us from asking whether there is something valid in the gradual emergence of practical theology as a distinct focus of theological reflection. Just as we would affirm all theology as grounded in the Bible, we still recognize the need for the special forms of inquiry that are pursued in biblical studies. Just as we would affirm the dogmatic element of all theology, we still acknowledge the need for the kind of coherence and systemization that dogmatic theology pursues. In a comparable fashion, we must affirm the inherently practical nature of all theology in the Protestant tradition, while recognizing the importance of the distinctive focus and reflective style that lie at the heart of practical theology.

What is that distinctive focus and reflective style? The answer to this question is by no means self-apparent. In large measure, the recent discussion of practical theology is focused precisely on this question, and no general consensus as to the answer has emerged.[16] Important clues can be found in the history of the emergence of this discipline since the Reformation. If all theology is practical, why did something called practical theology emerge? What was its focus? Did it point to a distinctive type of theological reflection? We will discuss six stages in the history of the emergence of practical theology as a specialized theological discipline.

The Separation of Moral Theology from Speculative Theology

The first stage involves the separation of moral theology from speculative theology, what we could call today in the Protestant tradition the separation of Christian ethics from dogmatic theology. Initially, this separation took place in Roman Catholicism, growing out of the need to provide guidance to priests in carrying out their responsibilities as confessors who must assign penance.[17]

Protestantism also began to pay special attention to the moral life. Reformation churches that emerged in the generations following Luther and Calvin were faced with the charge by Roman Catholicism that their understanding of salvation undermined social and individual morality, endangering not only the church but society as a whole. In the face of this charge, Protestant theologians and ministers began to make ethics a special focus of reflection.

One such instance is the "cases of conscience" literature that began to emerge in English Puritanism shortly after Calvin's death. Calvin, we recall, completed the final edition of the *Institutes* and founded the Academy of Geneva in 1559. By 1596, William Perkins was writing widely influential books that attempted to assist persons in making moral decisions. Other notable contributors to this genre during the 1600s are William Ames and Richard Baxter. This literature retained an understanding of theology as a unified discipline. It is no accident, however, that it emphasized the *practical* nature of theology.[18]

As William Ames writes in *The Marrow of Theology* (1623), "Theology is the doctrine or teaching of living to God."[19] Shortly thereafter, he goes on to write, "Now since this life so willed is truly and properly our most important practice, it is self-evident that theology is not a speculative discipline but a *practical* one."[20] He goes on to describe theology as supplying rules for the art of living to God: "Every art has its rules to which the work of the person practicing it corresponds. Since living is the noblest work of all, there cannot be any more proper study than the art of living."[21] This notion of "rules of art" will reappear in Schleiermacher's thought.

Ames makes a distinction within theology between faith and practice, with the former focusing on doctrinal matters and the latter on the ordering of ecclesiastical and individual life before God. While theology remains "one," a recognition of distinctive foci within it clearly is present. The concern with practical moral guidance falls on the "observance" side of theological reflection, as we might expect, providing us with an important clue as to why something like practical theology eventually emerged. Theology must concern itself not only with what people believe but also with how they act and interact in their roles as parents, citizens, professionals, workers, and church members. Concern with the totality of life in Protestantism heightened as all persons and not just "the religious" were seen as having a calling. This sparked moral reflection on the duties and obligations inherent in every social role, for every sphere of life was viewed as an expression of Christian vocation.

This sort of concern with the theological and moral significance of everyday life comes directly into focus in the cases of conscience literature. It offers moral and theological guidance that is directly aimed at assisting individual Christians in "living to God" in their daily lives. William Perkins provides us with insight into how this sort of practical moral guidance was pursued in Protestantism. Perkins was responding to the charge of moral licentiousness that Roman Catholics were making against Protestants during his day. He attempts to answer this charge by describing the singular place of conscience in the Christian life.

Conscience is viewed as a part of "practicall understanding," by which a person "stands in the viewe and consideration of every particular action, to search whether it be good or badde."[22] Conscience is a natural power God has implanted in all persons to assist them in judging the moral propriety of their actions. It has various functions: accusing, excusing, terrifying, and comforting. It is especially important to note the way that conscience in the individual moral life is related to the ethical teachings the church and its theologians offer. Precisely at this point, Perkins differentiates his perspective from that of his Roman Catholic counterparts. It is impossible through moral casuistry to address every particular case that individual Christians face, he argues. Indeed, this is not the church's prerogative but the role of conscience. Conscience is "to take principles and conclusions of the minde and apply them, and by applying either to accuse or excuse."[23] He goes on to say, "Againe, conscience meddles not with generals, only it deales in particular actions."[24]

In other words, conscience is located between the general moral teachings of the church and the concrete situations that confront individual Christians in their everyday lives. No manual can address every situation. It can attempt to point out the relevant moral and doctrinal issues, but then it must step aside and let conscience do its work. The church's task is to form conscience through its teaching ministry in such a way that it can exercise its proper freedom. It is to this end that the "cases of conscience" literature was written, providing guidance on topics ranging from family life to how persons should be comforted during periods of mental distress.

It is not difficult to discern here an important landmark on the road to practical theology—and, indeed, as Christian ethics first was distinguished from dogmatic theology, it occasionally was referred to as practical theology.[25] The "cases of conscience" literature focuses on the practical moral reasoning of ministers and ordinary Christians as they strive to fulfill their vocations in the world. Theology remains one, but its practical nature is emphasized. It contributes to the art of living to God. Conscience is viewed in such a way as to make every Christian a casuist, charged with the responsibility of taking general theological and moral principles and using them to judge the moral propriety of particular actions. It is precisely these sorts of concerns that have reemerged in the recent discussion of practical theology.

A Broader Understanding of Practical Theology

The second major step in the development of practical theology was the widening of this rubric beyond its use as an occasional reference to moral theology. The Reformed theologian Gisbert Voet, or Voetius, developed and defended this broader understanding of practical theology in *Selectae Disputationes Theologicae*, published in five volumes between 1648 and 1669.[26] He points out that in the recent past practical theology has been associated with moral theology and conscience literature.[27] He argues in favor of a more inclusive understanding of practical theology that involves three things: moral theology, ascetic theology (the practice of devotion), and ecclesiastical polity (including reflection on the church's constitution and the affairs of the ordained ministry, especially preaching and catechesis). It is not difficult to see what unites these three: Each deals with a form of practice that is closely related to the actual life of the church and ordinary Christians. While Voetius continues to argue that all theology is practical ("all theology among pilgrims on earth is in its nature practical, and no portion of it can be correctly and completely discussed unless it is developed practically"),[28] he is deeply interested in developing the meaning of practical theology in the "more narrow sense," as he puts it.[29]

This definition of practical theology was relatively rare until the next century, when the inclusion of moral theology and church polity under this heading became widespread.[30] What was significant about the way Voetius began to use this category is his focus on the practice of ministry in its various forms. This represents the beginning of a shift away from the practical moral reasoning of every Christian to a focus on the leadership of the church. It is no accident that Voetius developed his understanding of practical theology in conjunction with his role as a teacher of persons seeking to enter the ministry. Practical theology focuses on the kind of knowledge and skill church leaders need in the practice of their ministries.

Schleiermacher and the Formation of Church Leadership

This emphasis on church leadership became dominant in the third stage of the emergence of practical theology. During the latter part of the eighteenth century, theology was located in the newly emerging modern universities in Germany and began to define itself along the lines of an academic discipline. (Edward Farley's work, already described, points out the significance of this period.) Only at this point was theology differentiated into the four specialized forms of research and teaching. These divisions became standard during the nineteenth century and have continued to set the basic terms defining practical theology until recently.

As theology was divided into discrete academic disciplines, it became more and more difficult to see how the different branches of theology were interrelated and in what ways they were related to the life of the church. A specific genre of literature arose to respond to these issues, the theological encyclopedia. In this literature, practical theology was defined as one of several academic disciplines with its own special focus and tasks. Without question, the most influential way of understanding practical theology during this period was offered by Friedrich Schleiermacher.

Schleiermacher described the nature and role of practical theology in his own attempt at a theological encyclopedia, *Brief Outline on the Study of Theology,* which first appeared in 1811, and in his lectures to university students, which were published posthumously.[31] He attempted to legitimate the role of theology in the modern university, making the argument that it is oriented to the education of a profession, the ministry, that is an important contributor to society. He defined the purpose and unity of the theological disciplines accordingly: Each has its reason for being in the formation of church leadership.

In defining the nature of theology, Schleiermacher makes a distinction between pure and positive sciences, placing theology in the latter. Pure science is concerned with the pursuit of knowledge in a particular area for the sake of that knowledge alone (pure research in biology, for example). Positive science cuts across several disciplines "to put together a number of elements, otherwise treated separately, by relating them to some particular practice."[32] In a very real sense, then, Schleiermacher continues Protestantism's emphasis on the practical nature of all of theology, even as he attempts to describe the distinctive contributions of each theological discipline.

Schleiermacher rejects the fourfold pattern of the theological encyclopedia that was dominant at that time, advocating a threefold pattern of philosophical, historical, and practical theology. Philosophical theology attempts to define the basic concepts by which theology carries out its work, setting forth the nature of religion and the distinctive "essence" of Christianity as a religious community. Historical theology, including both Bible and church history, attempts to trace the unfolding of that essence in history, correcting or deepening the work of philosophical theology. The two disciplines provide practical theology with a clear idea of *what* the church should be and its present historical situation. Practical theology itself focuses on *how* the leadership of the church should carry out ministry toward a more perfect state in two general areas: church service (focusing on the internal life of the congregation) and church government (focusing on the church's polity and its relation with other institutions).

Schleiermacher describes the "how to" focus of practical theology with the word *Technik*. *Technik* is the study of how to get something done, an inquiry that sets forth a theory and rules of action about how a particular practice should be pursued. Schleiermacher does not mean technique in the modern sense of a standardized procedure that can produce the same desired end in a repetitious fashion. Rather, as he puts it, "By *Technik* we refer to instruction about how to bring something about, especially when this something is not to be brought about in a manner that is merely mechanical or completely arbitrary."[33]

Elsewhere, Schleiermacher describes practical theology in relation to the "art" of ministry in ways reminiscent of Ames' understanding of theology as supplying guidance for the art of living toward God.[34] The focus of practical theology is a theory of practice in which certain "rules of art" (Schleiermacher's phrase) are set forth to guide church leaders as they carry out ministry in indeterminant situations.[35] These rules function as intermediate guidelines between the theological and ethical perspectives afforded by philosophical and historical theologies and concrete situations. As Schleiermacher points out, rules of art and the personal creativity of the church leader interact in the actual practice of the minister.[36] Good rules do not ensure that they will be used correctly. Their proper use requires a certain kind of disposition and "a talent for correctly identifying the relationships among the various factors in any situation and for making use of whatever is appropriate to produce a desired result from the situation."[37]

In principle, Schleiermacher did not define practical theology exclusively in terms of the ministry of ordained persons.[38] He was concerned that every leader of the church carry out a reflective ministry informed by all of the theological disciplines and the cumulative wisdom of past practice represented in rules of art. Moreover, he repeatedly emphasized the "evangelical spirit" of Protestantism, which should characterize leadership in every Protestant denomination, a spirit that attempts to enhance the freedom of every individual Christian.[39] It is for this reason that Schleiermacher views the overarching phrase that best captures the basic focus of ministry as the "cure of souls." He does not mean this in the modern sense of pastoral care as ministry to persons in need but as the guidance of every Christian toward a deeper and more personal understanding of the Christian faith.[40] Ideally, every Christian should benefit from the work of practical theology or, better yet, be a practical theologian.

Schleiermacher's understanding of practical theology was extremely influential in the period of theological encyclopedias. Even those persons who did not accept his threefold understanding of theology and reverted to a fourfold pattern accepted his understanding of practical theology as theoretical reflection that assists the "art" of ministry.[41] Philip Schaff, for example, defines it as follows: "Practical Theology is the science and art of the various functions of the Christian ministry for the preservation and propagation of the Christian religion at home and abroad."[42] While affirming that all theology is practical in its spirit and aim, "some parts of it are more directly practical than others, and constitute what is technically called Practical Theology."[43] He criticizes the work of those who confine practical theology to clerical duties and functions in light of his commitment to the Protestant doctrine of the general priesthood of believers, a doctrine that "implies the co-operation of the members of the congregation pastor in all departments of Christian activity."[44] Schaff's work was particularly important in mediating the conceptual framework of the German theological encyclopedia movement to the American theological community [45]

The Clericalization of Practical Theology

Both in this country and in Europe, there was a gradual tendency to limit the focus of practical theology to the tasks and functions of the ordained minister. This represents the fourth stage in the emergence of practical theology. Both Schleiermacher and Schaff resisted this clericalization of practical theology, although much of their actual work in this field was oriented toward the preparation of clergy for ministry. Some writers continued to define practical theology in this broader fashion, using the term "pastoral theology" to refer to theological reflection on clergy functions. Others, however, abandoned this distinction, limiting the focus of practical theology to ministerial activities or substituting pastoral theology for it altogether.[46]

Once again, we find important clues in the theological encyclopedia period as to what was at stake in the emergence of practical theology as a distinctive form of theological reflection. With the emergence of specialized forms of inquiry in theology, it has become increasingly difficult to affirm the unity of theology. Theology may be one, but it no longer is a simple unity. Practical theology as a distinct theological discipline emerged along with the other specialized forms of theology. Schleiermacher and those who built on his work attempted to identify what the special focus of practical theology was.

Of special importance in this regard is Schleiermacher's notion of "rules of art," which was taken up by others during this period. Ministry as an art is described as neither a mechanical repetition of techniques nor a happenstance response to different events. It is an intentional, informed response that draws on certain rules allowing for integrity and coherence as a disciplined form of practice. This notion of rules of art rightfully points to the dynamic quality of ministry as it is carried out in the midst of unfolding, indeterminant situations. This interpretation of practical theology was deficient in two respects, however. First, it did not give a clear understanding of the role of theory and research in practical theology, especially as these are carried out in dialogue with nontheological disciplines. Second, it did not have an adequate understanding of practical theology's constructive contribution to theology as a whole.

Even Schleiermacher diminishes the theoretical nature of practical theology, writing, "If philosophical and historical theology have been clearly appropriated and in the right proportion, nothing further remains of a theoretical nature in order to acquire a right conception of these tasks."[47] The role of theory in practical theology is not sufficiently acknowledged. With the rise of the social sciences, however, it became increasingly clear that the rules of art guiding practical theology must be more than the accrued wisdom of the practitioner. They also had to be grounded in the research and theoretical frameworks of psychology, sociology, and the other newly emerging human sciences. Practical theology now had to become self-conscious about how it would incorporate the insights of these disciplines into its teaching, preaching, and pastoral care. In other words, it was faced with the task of constructing an interdisciplinary theoretical basis for its ministerial practice.

Ironically, the second deficiency in practical theology's definition during this period has to do with its inadequate understanding of the contribution of practice to theory. It does not give a sense of the way knowledge, generated and tested in the midst of some ongoing form of practice, can contribute to the constructive work of theology in all its forms. It is viewed along the lines of the "theory-applied-in-practice" model. As Schleiermacher puts it at one point, philosophical and historical theology formulate knowledge and practical theology "applies this knowledge."[48] At the root of this weakness is an inadequate understanding of the theory-practice relationship.

Dialogue with the Social Sciences

These two weaknesses of the theological encyclopedia period were addressed in the fifth stage of the emergence of practical theology, which we will call practical theology in dialogue with the social sciences. Two movements in particular are representative: the religious education movement and the pastoral care and counseling movement that emerged in conjunction with the spread of clinical pastoral education. Both movements developed during the first part of this century and focused their attention on incorporating the findings of the social sciences into the practice of religious education and pastoral care, respectively. In light of our interest in the church's teaching ministry, we will focus on the religious education movement, even though the issues between the two movements overlap in many ways.[49] Representatives of both movements articulated a much stronger role for theory and research in the practical theological disciplines. At the same time, they developed a far more dynamic understanding of the theory-practice relationship than was present during the theological encyclopedia period.

The religious education movement began to emerge around the turn of the century and was deeply influenced by liberal theology, the Social Gospel Movement, research in the psychology of religion, and philosophical pragmatism. George Albert Coe, frequently referred to as the dean of the religious education movement, is representative of the way this movement viewed its work.[50] Coe did not use the term "practical theology" to refer to his work, even though he occupied a chair in practical theology for much of his career at Union Theological Seminary in New York.

While Coe did not comment directly on why he rejected practical theology as a means of self-understanding, his various writings make it clear why he would have been uneasy with this category as it came to him through the theological encyclopedia period.[51] First, he was unwilling to allow theology in any form to dictate the norms of religious education, even in the manner suggested by liberal theology. Schleiermacher's notion that real knowledge is generated by philosophical and historical theologies and that practical theology is left with the task of formulating rules of art by which this knowledge is applied would have been completely untenable for him. Second, he believed that religious education theory stands in an extremely close relationship to forms of practice oriented toward personal and social reconstruction.

Coe was far more theological than is generally recognized and drew on liberal theology and the Social Gospel Movement throughout his career to formulate many of his ideas about the nature and purpose of Christianity. He was not inherently against making use of the insights of the other theological disciplines in his work. He was against the "sovereignty" of theology in religious education, the view that it alone sets the parameters within which religious education does its work.

In his own thought, Coe used a method that was deeply correlational, in the sense that the norms of religious education were formed through a conversation between theology and other—nontheological—disciplines. Religious education, he believed, will make its greatest contribution when it brings theology into dialogue with disciplines that are closely related to its own area of research and practice. It cannot and should not depend on other theological disciplines to carry out theoretical reflection on its behalf. Coe himself drew extensively on and was an original contributor to the philosophy of education, the psychology of religion, and philosophical value theory. He formed his norms for religious education by correlating the insights gained from these disciplines with theology.[52] Practical theology, as it previously had been defined, simply did not give enough impetus to the kind of high-level interdisciplinary reflection that lay at the heart of his work.

At the same time, he advocated a much more dynamic understanding of the theory-practice relationship than was present in practical theology as it was defined during the period of the theological encyclopedia. During the first and middle phases of his thought, Coe was strongly influenced by John Dewey in this regard. Religious education theory, he argued, must be grounded in and oriented toward the practice of religious education. Religious education practice, moreover, involves the ongoing reconstruction of personal values and the social order. Following Dewey, Coe believed that education is not primarily the transmission of the past or socialization into the present. It is the process by which society encourages individuals to appraise inherited personal and social values critically and to reconstruct them in an ongoing fashion. Education in general and religious education in particular are agencies of transformation in society. Theoretical reflection emerges out of the exigencies of this ongoing transformative practice—clarifying aims, criticizing means, and strengthening in any way possible education's reconstructive role.

The religious education movement, as embodied in Coe, offers us important clues about the nature and purpose of practical theology. We must go beyond the limitations placed on practical theology as it was defined in the period of theological encyclopedia in two important ways. First, practical theology has its own theoretical contribution to make. It is concerned with rules of art, but it also must carry out its own original theological and interdisciplinary reflection in order to locate these rules of art in broad understandings of the self, the church, and the contemporary social situation. Second, practical theology must be based on a more dynamic understanding of the theory-practice relationship than was present in its earlier formulations. Its theoretical reflection grows out of and is oriented toward some form of practice. This is the greatest contribution practical theology makes to the other theological disciplines: testing and revising their findings and generating new theological insights in the midst of practice itself. In a very real sense, then, practical theology is not merely the "crown" of theology, as Schleiermacher once put it, but one of its roots as well—a source from which theology draws its life.

The Rise of Neo-Orthodox Practical Theology

The contribution of the religious education movement and its representatives, however, must be viewed in light of the criticisms offered during the sixth stage of the emergence of practical theology—practical theology as formulated during the ascendancy of neo-orthodox theology. Karl Barth, the Niebuhrs, and other members of this movement rightfully pointed out the theological weaknesses of the Social Gospel Movement and theological liberalism which were appropriated by the religious education movement. These criticisms were incorporated by persons such as James Smart, H. Shelton Smith, and Sara Little. Coe and the religious education movement in general were criticized for not possessing sufficiently strong doctrines of sin, Christology, and eschatology. Nor was their understanding of the relationship between theology and the social sciences viewed as adequate, granting far too much authority to nontheological disciplines in the determination of norms for the church's life.

James Smart in particular mediated the insights of Karl Barth and his colleague Eduard Thurneysen to the church's teaching ministry.[53] In Smart's work, we are offered once more clues about what has been at stake in the emergence of practical theology. Following Barth and Thurneysen, Smart uses the term "practical theology" to understand his work. Neither Barth nor Thurneysen rejects the basic divisions of theology that were formulated during the period of theological encyclopedia.[54] What they do is alter drastically the foundations upon which theology in each of its forms is built. Theology is now seen as based on revelation or the Word of God. The Word in its primary form is Jesus Christ himself and secondarily is scripture as it witnesses to Jesus and contemporary proclamation by the church.

We now have entered once again the atmosphere of Luther and Calvin. The absolute priority of God's gracious action in Jesus Christ and a strong awareness of the radicality of human sin give rise to a very different understanding of theology and its proper method than was found in Coe and the religious education movement. Smart frequently describes this in terms of the image "watchman." Theology is to watch over the

church's proclamation and action to discern whether the
church is faithful in its hearing and obeying of the Word or has
given way to something else. As Smart puts it at one point,
theology is that part of our ministry "in which we deliberately
expose ourselves, our church, our preaching, to ruthless
searching criticism, first in the light of the Scriptures and then
in the light of what the church has said and done across the
ages."[55] In short, it is to "take the question of Christian truth
with complete seriousness."[56]

Smart believes that this self-critical search for the truth is
every Christian's task. Theologians, however, must ask this
question in a disciplined and systematic fashion. The specific
task of practical theology is "the study of the Church in action, the critique of its practices in the past, the determination
on principle of what should be its practices in the present, and
the training of its ministry to be guides into a right fulfillment
of its nature in response to God in the future."[57] It is crucial,
Smart believes, that practical theology remain *theological*. It
can understand God, humanity, and the church as it looks to
God's revelation in Jesus Christ. Coe and the religious education movement, he argues, lost their bearings in allowing
nontheological resources to determine their fundamental assumptions. To the extent that they were theological, moreover, the liberal and Social Gospel theology upon which they
drew were overly determined by cultural presuppositions.
Theology must remain firmly tied to the Word, in Smart's
view, to Jesus Christ as he is witnessed to in scripture. Practical theology has the task of measuring the contemporary practices of the church against this norm.

Clearly, Smart rejects a correlational method in practical
theology. In its place, he puts a theological method that begins with biblical theology, moves to doctrinal formulations,
and then sets forth the implications of these doctrines for
Christian education. In *The Teaching Ministry of the Church*,
for example, he derives his theory of Christian education almost exclusively from an examination of the doctrines of the
church, humanity, and scripture.

The strength of this approach is the seriousness with which
Smart takes theology and the firm scriptural and doctrinal
foundation on which Christian education is based. Smart's arguments remain a good example of the sort of internal dialogue within theology that must take place if practical
theology is to retain its integrity. Two things are missing, however: (1) an understanding of the ways practical theology is
grounded in some form of ongoing practice and (2) reflection

on the role and proper method of interdisciplinary work in practical theology. Even if theology is to have the first and last words in the church's teaching ministry, at some point it must enter into a dialogue with other nontheological disciplines from which it can learn about human development, education, and the social context in which the church is carrying out its contemporary ministry. Smart's understanding of practical theology gives no indication of how this can be done in an appropriate manner. Moreover, his understanding of the theory-practice relationship is exceedingly weak. Proposals for practice are rational deductions from higher level norms and provide no insight into the role of "rules of art" that grow out of and are oriented toward some form of practice. The living interaction of thought and action is lost.[58]

Smart's position represents one in a series of attempts to sort out the nature and purpose of practical theology. Those who discuss this theological category today can learn much of a positive and negative nature from the history of its gradual emergence. We would do well to remember that practical theology's concern with the practical is not its sole prerogative, that every branch of theology ultimately is concerned with helping persons "live to God." We should recall its close relationship historically to theological ethics and the way that the cases of conscience literature attempted to assist every Christian in engaging in practical moral reasoning. A struggle with the ambiguities inherent in its gradual focus on church functions and the eventual "clericalization" of practical theology would be worthwhile. "Clericalization" allowed practical theology to be viewed as providing rules of art for the professional practitioner, while transforming it into a specialized discipline that was not accessible to the ordinary believer.

From the insights of the religious education and pastoral care and counseling movements, we must remember that practical theology is not practical merely in the sense of providing a congeries of techniques and methods but has its own theoretical base, which it forms in dialogue with the other branches of theology and nontheological resources. From neo-Reformation theology, we must learn that practical theology should remain solidly theological in light of its grounding in the revelation of God in Jesus Christ.

Practical Theology: A Constructive Proposal

This brief outline of the history of practical theology provides us with insight into what was at stake in the gradual emergence of this category to describe a distinctive form of theological reflection. This history is complex and does not lead to a clear and simple understanding of what practical theology has been and what it should be today. It does, however, provide us with important clues about the special focus of practical theology, clues that must be taken into account if we are to rehabilitate this term with any integrity. I will begin with a constructive definition of practical theology and then explore the ways it attempts to build on the history that has just been outlined. Throughout, I will draw on the current discussion of practical theology, a discussion that represents a new stage in its development.

Practical theological reflection is disciplined and self-conscious moral reasoning undertaken by individual Christians and congregations in light of their theological convictions about God and the world in relation to God. It is an inherent dimension of the piety of every Christian, representing an attempt to love God with the mind as well as the heart. The central focus of practical theology is three-fold: (1) the practical moral reasoning taking place both in and about the various social practices that structure persons' lives and serve as the context for their vocations, involving (2) the interpretation of particular situations in order to discern what God is enabling and requiring persons to do and be, and (3) the enactment of concrete responses that shape and are shaped by these situations as they unfold through time. In short, the heart of practical theology is reflection that takes place in the midst of unfolding situations emerging out of social practices in an attempt to shape actional responses that are appropriate to what can be discerned of God's purposes for the world as they are brought to bear on unique contexts of experience.

While practical theological reflection is an inherent dimension of the piety of every Christian, it is best viewed as part of a larger conversation within and between various communities. The congregation is the primary locus of practical theological reflection, for it is there that persons are taught the requisite theological and ethical knowledge and nurtured in their use of this knowledge to reflect on their lives in the world. The congregation itself is a community of practical theological discourse. Its leadership, both lay and ordained, plays an important role in the quality of practical theological reflection that is carried on throughout its life. The congregation's capacity to teach and nurture this sort of reflection, however, is dependent on its participation in a dialogue with other institutional expressions of the church's teaching office: seminaries, ecumenical organizations, and denominational boards, agencies, and leaders, to name but a few. These various communities bring to the conversation different modes of theological reflection that can deepen, expand, and criticize the practical theological reflection of individuals and congregations.

At the heart of this definition of practical theology is an attempt to place it in a close relationship to the lives of ordinary Christians and congregations. From the beginning, the hallmark of Protestant theology has been its focus on the practical reasoning of existing persons and not the speculative interests of a detached mind, as Niebuhr pointed out above. It has been concerned with helping Christians "live to God." As theology began to focus on specialized forms of inquiry, practical theology attempted to make sure that this link with the practical was not lost, providing aids to the moral reasoning of ordinary Christians and ministers and attempting to mediate the findings of other theological disciplines to congregational life.

We have attempted to retain this primary focus on congregations and individuals in our definition by viewing practical theological reflection as an inherent dimension of the piety of every Christian. Piety is our deepest response to the divine and is composed of the basic attitudes and dispositions that flow from our relationship to God.[59] An important dimension of Christian piety is the attempt to live in ways that are consistent with what can be discerned of God's purposes for the world. This involves a reflective process, an attempt to grasp cognitively the meanings of scripture and tradition and use them to guide one's life in the world. Reflection is necessary in order to prevent the Christian life from becoming a matter of random intuition or mechanical repetition. The life of faith involves loving God with the whole self, including the mind.

This definition also places practical theology in a close relationship to the social practices that govern everyday life. As defined in chapter 2, "social practice" is a pattern of human interaction that structures action and its meaning in socially shared ways. Communities cannot exist without social practices that regulate their members' behavior and relations with one another. Practical theological reflection is closely related to social practices in this sense. It is here that persons live out their vocations, responding to God's call as it comes to them in and through the various duties and obligations that emerge in the midst of their life.

The concept "social practice" also can be used in a narrower and more specialized sense when linked to an understanding of the professions.[60] A professional performs a singular and essential social service that can only be carried out after a lengthy period of general and specialized education. The skills the practitioners of a profession employ are subject to rational analysis and emerge from a theoretical and research base. Often, standards of competence and moral propriety are defined by a professional organization that oversees the behavior of its members.

Professionals in this sense carry out certain social practices characterized by a high degree of intentionality based on the specialized theoretical knowledge underlying their work. The diagnoses doctors arrive at in the course of their work, for example, are dependent on the knowledge basis generated by research in medicine and related areas. Such specialized knowledge allows them to do their work in a disciplined and coherent manner. It is not unusual for a doctor's or lawyer's work to be referred to as a "practice."

Social practices in a broader and more specialized sense involve both action and understanding. Humans are constantly engaged in a process of interpreting the actions of others, the demands of particular contexts, and forming responses that are deemed appropriate. One of the most important dimensions of this interpretive process is the pattern of moral meaning by which persons judge the rightness and wrongness of their own actions and those of others. Inevitably, this also includes a "faith" dimension, if by faith we mean persons' trust in and loyalty to centers of value and meaning.[61] An evaluation of the goodness and badness of everyday life presupposes an interpretation of existence in relation to an ultimate context in which value judgments are made.[62] Our understandings of the virtuous life rest on these comprehensive interpretive schemes. Even persons who do not participate in organized religion construct comprehensive interpretive schemes to ground their moral reasoning. All persons have faith in this sense.

One of the most important tasks of congregational education is the ongoing formation and transformation of the comprehensive interpretive schemes and moral principles by which ordinary Christians make sense out of their everyday lives. It is here, in the struggle of Christians to interpret their lives in light of what can be discerned of God's pur-

poses for the world, that we locate practical theological reflection. It is not the special province of academic
specialists. It is the reflective dimension of piety. It is the
theological and moral reasoning persons undertake as they
seek to live out their vocations in the world. This does not
mean that ordinary Christians carry out theological reflection with the kind of coherence and systemization of an academic treatise. Practical theology is a different sort of
theological reflection, taking place in conjunction with
unique occasions calling for an actional response.

Typically, as persons make their way through the social practices of everyday life, they are not self-conscious about the
patterns of action and moral reasoning they are using. Social
practices provide continuity in communities from one context
of experience to another. However, there always is a unique
dimension to every context of experience, even the taken-for-
granted experience of everyday life. This is a function of the
historical or temporal character of existence. Even social practices that seem to establish a great deal of continuity from one
occasion to another are really participating in shifting patterns
of interaction.[63] The same greeting may be exchanged by the
same two persons every morning, but in a very real sense it is
different on each occasion.

When the uniqueness of experience comes to the fore, social practices are transformed into *situations*. Situations are
contexts that stand out from the ordinary flow of experience
because of their heightened particularity. They are delimited
by certain temporal boundaries: that is, they unfold through
time with a specific beginning and ending.[64]

Social practices that provide continuity to our lives and situations that stand out from everyday experience are not totally
unrelated. Situations do not emerge in a completely random
fashion. They develop out of the preexistent patterns that social practices structure. Moreover, persons do not approach
situations empty handed. They come with the styles of moral
reasoning they typically use to make sense out of their lives. It
is the task of practical theology to deepen our awareness of
and reasoning about the situations that emerge in the course
of the social practices that structure our lives. It is reflection
that grows out of and is oriented toward the guidance of
Christian vocation in the world, in an attempt to discern what
God is enabling and requiring persons to do and be.

As we have noted, social practices involve complex acts of
knowing and doing that are undertaken with little or no re
flection. Michael Polanyi uses the expression "tacit knowing"

to point to the fact that we know more than we can say.[65] We may not be able to articulate all of the mental and physical processes involved in driving a car, for example, even though we can drive quite skillfully. Much of our knowing remains tacit, especially in our everyday lives. At times, however, we are forced to come to terms with this dimension of knowing and explicitly reflect upon what we take for granted.

When social practices that allow us to move through life on the basis of habit and social convention are confronted with a situation in which the particularity of experience comes to the fore, a reflective process is set in motion. A child is supposed to get home from school at a certain time, but is over half an hour late. The parent begins to reflect on where the child might be, how this could be ascertained, what sort of help should be gotten, and other concerns. Accepted social practices are brought up short and a situation is encountered, setting in motion a reflective process.

Precisely this sort of reflection constitutes the heart of practical theology. But reflection is prompted by situations all the time. When is it properly characterized as practical theological reflection? The disposal is stopped up and help is needed. The dog next door has been barking for the last forty-five minutes. Such situations may or may not serve as occasions for practical theological reflection. They do so only when they elicit moral reasoning that is carried out in light of a person's convictions about God. One of the most important goals of congregational education is the nurture of our capacity to carry out this sort of reflection in a disciplined and self-conscious manner. What does this involve?

At an earlier point, we noted that situations are bounded temporally. They stand out from the flow of everyday life with a beginning and an ending. These temporal boundaries may be of short or long duration. A person may confront a situation that lasts many months: the decision to change jobs, for example, or to get a divorce. Or a situation may last only a few minutes. Regardless of the length of its duration, a situation is something that unfolds through time. The reflective style of practical theology is largely determined by the role it plays in situations as they unfold. It does not stand outside of the situation as would a researcher carrying out an experiment under controlled conditions. Nor does it follow the logic of applied theology in which axioms derived from other disciplines are applied to particular cases.

Rather, practical theological reflection *functions as part of the situation,* helping the participant enact concrete responses that shape and are shaped by the situation as it unfolds.[66] We can identify several stages in this reflective process: (1) identification of what is going on, (2) an evaluative description of why it is going on, including locating the situation in terms of the relevant "whole" of which it is a part and forming causal explanations of the situation, (3) determination of the relevant theological and ethical concepts and principles, (4) formation of possible courses of action based on accrued practical wisdom, and (5) enactment of a concrete response and continued reflection on the effects that it has.

Identification

When a situation is first encountered, it must be identified.[67] The flow of normal social practices has been interrupted, and a sense that something is amiss has emerged. The person now must attempt to answer the question, "What is going on?" This is by no means a simple and straightforward task. It involves the formation of an initial interpretation of what is amiss that frames the way the emerging situation is construed. This interpretation can be corrected, confirmed, or nuanced at a later point, but it is important in that it serves as the starting point of the reflective process. This initial interpretive activity is rooted in the accrued practical wisdom, education, and even moral character of the interpreter and is not devoid of theological and ethical implications.

A key element in this initial process of interpretation is framing the situation as being like other situations that have been encountered in the past. A friend who has come for a weekend visit, for example, repeatedly grows tearful. Her sadness is seen as being like that of other depressed persons that the interpreter has known. Persons bring a repertoire of interpretive schemas to the situations they confront. Recent research on memory suggests that short-term memory is quite limited with regard to the number of items it can store at any given time.[68] New information must be processed quickly in terms of schemas that reside in long-term memory. Indeed, persons frequently assimilate new information to schemas they already possess, even when this means distorting that information in certain ways. Research also reveals that people use "middle categories" to interpret their experience, classifications that are neither overly specific nor overly abstract.[69] One of the most important tasks facing congregational education and professional theologians in their nurture of practical theological reflection is the construction of middle categories of a theological and ethical nature that persons can use to interpret the "living text" of their lives.

Evaluative Description

The second stage of practical theological reflection focuses on the formation of an evaluative description of what is going on and why.[70] Information of two sorts is particularly important. One involves the gathering of further information about exactly what is going on. If we begin to interpret the sadness of our friend as a sign of depression, we can follow this up with questions about the length and severity of her sadness. We can focus our attention more closely on her behavior and the tone of her conversation. We can ask others if they have noticed signs of depression in the way that she behaves.

It is important to move beyond a notion of research as something that is done only under controlled conditions. Perhaps this should be called "praxis research": inquiry that focuses on the gathering of information affording an accurate reading of the situation at hand in order to determine possible courses of action.[71] Skill in judging what sort of information is relevant to the situation and worthy of this sort of investigation is especially important to practical theological reflection, for frequently there is not enough time to explore every facet of the situation.

Perhaps even more important is the ability to judge the relevant "whole" in which the particular situation should be understood.[72] Both temporally and spatially, the situation stands out from the flow of ordinary experience. Its demarcation, however, is always somewhat artificial, for boundaries always stretch backward and forward in time and outward in an interconnected network of relationships. An important part of understanding what is occurring in any situation is locating it in relation to the larger whole of which it is a part. It is one thing to reflect upon the fact that a person appears to be sad. It is quite another to grasp this sadness in terms of relevant wholes in which the person participates: family, work, health, and so forth.

A second type of information that is important to an evaluative description of the situation is the formation of causal explanations by which we attempt to determine the significant factors that have contributed to making the situation what it is. This kind of information is important for two reasons. First, it frequently helps us locate the situation in a longer history. Causal explanations reveal the underlying factors working to-

gether to make the situation what it is. Second, causal explanations frequently are closely related to the development of
possible courses of action. It makes a difference if we discover
that our friend's sadness is the result of recent marital difficulties and not the expression of a long-term chronic personality
disorder that has led her to the verge of suicide in the past.
"What is going on?" must deepen into "Why is this going
on?" in the second stage of practical theological reflection.

Relevant Theological and Moral Issues

The third stage in this sort of situational reflection involves
a determination of the theological and moral issues of relevance to the situation at hand. If moral reasoning in light of
our theological convictions is the heart of practical theology,
it might seem odd that issues explicitly moral and theological
do not emerge until this point. This is not completely the case,
however. What we choose to attend to in the first stage of
practical theological reflection and our identification of what
is worthy of investigation in the second stage are at least in
part determined by the religious beliefs, ethical principles,
and moral character that compose our religious identity. I
may choose to ignore my friend's tearfulness, for example, not
wanting her problems to ruin my weekend.

During the third stage, however, explicit theological and
moral reflection comes to the fore. It is important to recall
that our focus is on the practical theological reflection of ordinary Christians. Is it too much to expect average church members to have a basic network of theological beliefs and a
theological ethic by which to interpret the situations that confront them? I think not. In chapter 10 we will use James
Fowler's faith development theory in order to explore the
ways that our theological generalizations about God and our
moral reasoning emerge during the course of human development. Even children, we will argue, can engage in moral reasoning in light of their understandings of God. What persons
desperately need in most mainline churches today is help in
gaining the kind of knowledge and skill that is necessary to
allow them to make moral and religious meaning out of their
everyday lives. The problem is not so much that ordinary
Christians are incapable of this sort of reflection as that they
have not been given the opportunity to learn how to do it.

It is not my task to recommend a particular theological and
ethical position as the only one adequate for this sort of practical theological reflection. Clearly, there is a range of viable

theological options that persons can draw on. In the recent discussion of practical theology, two styles of theological and moral reflection emerged as particularly important: the neo-Kantian approach of Don Browning and the Niebuhrian approach of Charles Gerkin. In contrast to either of these, I prefer a position closer to the work of James Gustafson. All three are viable approaches to theological and ethical reflection in the face of concrete situations.

Browning draws heavily on the neo-Kantian moral philosophies of John Rawls and Ronald Green.[73] He argues that our notions of what we ought to do should not be formed from an evaluation of the perceived consequences of our projected actions in a given situation, but on the basis of a universal moral principle—justice. In the face of particular situations, persons must strive to do what is just. Building on Rawls's work, justice is presented as impartial fairness. Persons should pass behind a "veil of ignorance" that brackets out their own stake in the situation and attempt to view it from the perspective of all relevant parties. The just thing to do is that to which all parties would agree if they approached the situation with this kind of impartiality. In short, the moral ends we ought to pursue must be universalizable, that to which all rational persons would give consent.

While Browning acknowledges a role for situational reasoning by which concrete rules and roles are formulated and the immediate context grasped, his commitment to a neo-Kantian ethic leads him to argue in favor of a single universal ethical principle to determine what persons ought to do in the face of concrete situations.[74] A very different approach is adopted by Charles Gerkin.[75] Gerkin's understanding of practical theology is grounded in the hermeneutic philosophy of Martin Heidegger, Hans-Georg Gadamer, and Paul Ricoeur. He also draws heavily on various currents of narrative theology to portray the shape that human understanding takes, arguing that humans inevitably interpret their experience in narrative forms. To put it somewhat simplistically, the basic goal of practical theological reflection is a bringing together of the Christian story and the stories by which particular people and groups structure their experience.

Gerkin adopts a Niebuhrian "responsibilist" ethic to describe this process: Persons are to attend to God's activity in the world and to form fitting responses to that activity.[76] What ought to be done in particular situations is determined not through the application of a universal moral principle but by using theological patterns to identify how God is acting in the situation at hand. Is God rendering judgment through these events? Is redemption being offered? In light of their interpretation of what God is doing, persons then attempt to form responses that are appropriate to God's prior action.

Both Browning and Gerkin articulate important ways of understanding how theological and ethical reflection can take place as a part of practical theology. I would advocate a third, which is closer to the work of James Gustafson: what might be called a discernment theory of ethical reflection.[77] Unlike Browning, this position does not advocate a single universal ethical principle that can be brought to bear on every situation. Rather, a number of ethical principles of equal importance are viewed as potentially relevant to any given situation. One of the tasks of discernment is to determine what principles and rules apply.

Unlike Gerkins, this position is more reticent about our ability to determine exactly what God is doing in any particular situation. Every effort to read God's actions directly from the contemporary situation is fraught with uncertainty. In contrast, Gustafson argues in favor of the formation of theological generalizations growing out of rational reflection on God's past actions as recorded in scripture and what can be understood about the limitations and possibilities of the created order.[78] Ethical principles and moral rules that are consistent with these generalizations are then formed.

Greater emphasis, moreover, is placed on human agency in the moral life.[79] Rather than passively conforming to God's prior actions, humans are viewed as participating in the ordering of life, albeit participating in ways that are limited by the constraints of the divine governance through the created order. The primary moral question in the face of any concrete situation is, "What is God enabling and requiring me to do and be?"[80] To answer this question, persons must attempt to discern what is going on in the situation and why (the first two steps just described) and what moral principles, rules, and values are relevant in light of their theological commitments and interpretations of the general patterns of life. This is a complex process and, indeed, a very human one. There is no guarantee that *the* right or good solution can be discerned. Indeed, discernment frequently reveals the moral ambiguity of a situation [81] Values and goods that are equally important cannot be harmonized in the modes of action available. Any line of action taken will have a tragic quality about it, fulfilling some goods and diminishing others.

It is important to see the range of theological and ethical

approaches that are available to persons as they attempt to make moral meaning of the situations confronting them. I am not advocating that every Christian become a professional ethicist. What I am saying is that persons invariably engage in moral reasoning in conjunction with the social practices structuring their lives and the various situations that emerge in the course of these social practices. Practical theology transforms this kind of reflection into a self-conscious, intentional process, one that is based on an explicit awareness of theological beliefs about God and interpretations of the nature of the world. Ordinary Christians can and should be equipped to carry out this sort of reflection in the pursuit of their vocations in the world. It is an inherent part of their attempt to live to God.

Projecting Possible Courses of Action

The fourth stage of practical theological reflection is the determination of possible courses of action. On the basis of an evaluative description of what is going on and a determination of what ought to be done on the basis of theological and ethical reflection, consideration of strategies and roles should take place. The formation of a clear understanding of what theological and moral issues are at stake in a particular situation does not tell us, in and of itself, *how* we should proceed. It is during this stage that practical theological reflection's close relationship to action becomes particularly evident.

This link to action brings into focus a distinctive kind of knowledge that is an important dimension of practical theological reflection, knowledge of "how to." It is not enough to have some idea of what ought to be done; an understanding of the best ways of achieving this goal must also come into play. It is one thing to recognize that a person is severely depressed, for example, and the moral imperative is to see that she receives psychiatric treatment as quickly as possible. It is quite another to have the knowledge and skill necessary to get her to accept treatment or have her committed.

The importance of this sort of knowledge should not be underestimated. It represents a form of practical wisdom. Much of it can only be learned on the basis of trial and error or under the supervision of a more skilled practitioner. During this stage of practical theological reflection, it takes the form of reflection on possible courses of action. This serves as a link between the earlier stages of thought and the enacted response, affording intentionality regarding the actual actions that are undertaken

Enacted Responses and Ongoing Reflection

The fifth and final stage is really a series of substages. The enacted response growing out of this reflective process brings about certain changes in the situation. Reflection continues as the situation unfolds. For example, it is determined that the best course of action for getting your depressed friend some help is to draw her out about the amount of pain that she seems to be feeling and her past suicide attempts to determine whether or not she is willing to seek help with your gentle prompting. But suppose she is not? Reflection giving rise to other courses of action must continue to take place. You know that many depressed people have a diminished capacity to accept responsibility for their lives. You also know that this particular woman has never asked for help in the past. How much are you willing to trust her judgment? How forcefully should you intervene on her behalf?

John Dewey frequently described the relationship between reflection and action as being like an experiment.[82] Reflection proposes certain courses of action, which are then put into effect. Once they are actually enacted, observation determines whether the anticipated effects take place. An attitude of tentativeness and openness must permeate the courses of action being proposed. They are like hypotheses that must be tested in action and are subject to correction. Schön captures the essence of this well when he describes it as a reflective conversation.[83] Reflection participates in a kind of dialogue with the situation as it unfolds through time.

It is quite possible that different persons in the community of faith might be more proficient at one of the stages of practical theological reflection than others. A church-school teacher might be particularly skillful in knowing just the right approach to use with children who have a history of being difficult to teach. Her knowledge of "how to" emerges intuitively from years of experience. At the same time, she might be quite limited in her ability to articulate what is at stake ethically or theologically in the congregation's refusal to give up on these children and its continued struggle to find the right way of getting through to them. It may well be that someone else will offer theological and ethical reasons that inform the church's response to this situation.

It is important to acknowledge the variety of gifts that persons bring to the congregation as a community of practical theological discourse. While every Christian has the task of reflecting on his or her life in light of what can be discerned of

God's purposes for the world, there is no doubt that this sort of reflection is best pursued within a community of faith. Not only is an individual's reflection enriched, he or she also is given the opportunity to learn new competencies that will deepen his or her capacity to reflect in the future. In this way an individual will gradually achieve greater balance in the ability to carry out practical theological reflection.

Perhaps, for this reason, practical theological reflection is best thought of along the lines of a dialogue. It is an internal dialogue, to be sure, involving an inner discussion of the what, why, and how of the Christian life. But even more important, it is an external dialogue. It is a conversation among members of a concrete community of faith—a community that has enough trust and mutual respect to sustain, deepen, and even correct the reflection of each member. Just as surely as the capacity for individuals to engage in practical theological reflection must be nurtured, so too must the requisite communal structures and attitudes for practical theological discourse be nurtured in the congregation.

This ongoing dialogue within a congregation is itself part of a larger conversation. While the congregation plays a crucial role in church life as the center of practical theological discourse, its work must be sustained, deepened, and even corrected by other centers of teaching authority in the church. It is to this broader dialogue of the teaching office that we now turn.

9

Centers of Authority in the Teaching Office:
A Contemporary Proposal

To a great extent, the many problems that are besetting the mainline churches today stem from the fact that churches do not seem to be able to offer their members a compelling vision of the Christian life. The Bible and theology seem remote from the realities of everyday life and do not function as sources of guidance in the pursuit of Christian vocation. It is increasingly clear that denominational loyalty and congregational commitment no longer can be based primarily on such social factors as ethnicity, parental affiliation, or upward mobility. These factors were not particularly worthy foundations of church membership in the first place. Their diminishment has made it clear that denominations and congregations are increasingly dependent on their ability to project a vision that supports and transforms persons in their attempt to live to God in their own time and place

A Protestant Teaching Office

In large measure, this task is carried out on the congregational level of life. Church membership takes on real meaning for most persons in the concrete relationships, projects, worship, and service that congregations offer. If Christians do not gain a sense of the transforming, dynamic quality of the Christian life at this level, it is highly unlikely that they will gain it from denominational leaders or professional theologians. One of the most important tasks before mainline congregations in this regard is the linking of theology and ethics to life. Only as the Bible and church doctrine make contact with the tangible realities that impinge upon persons' lives in the world will their faith become meaningful. In the conceptual framework of chapter 8, the congregation must become a center of practical theological discourse. It must be a place where scripture and theology are taught in such a manner that they become an important part of the interpretive framework that persons use to make sense of their lives and the surrounding world. Theology must not be remote from everyday life but must imbue it with a deeper and richer meaning as the arena in which persons live out their vocations before God.

While congregations, as centers of practical theological discourse, have a key role in facilitating this kind of linkage of theology and life, they cannot do so in isolation from other centers of teaching authority in the church. The unrecognized genius of the mainline churches' Reformation heritage is the way that congregations are located within a constellation of teaching authorities, each contributing to the creation of a vision of Christian life in the contemporary world. Congregations all too easily can lapse into provincialism, appropriating only those dimensions of scripture and tradition that confirm their prior values and commitments. Similarly, charismatic leaders can rally followers to versions of Christianity that distort its doctrinal and ethical integrity.

Mainline Protestantism is blessed with a heritage that recognizes the dangers inherent in extreme forms of congregationalism and individualism. It brings these dimensions of the Christian life into dialogue with centers of teaching authority that can sustain, moderate, and even correct them. The model of the teaching office that emerges from the great Reformers' thought is one in which multiple institutional structures and roles play distinctive functions within the church's overall teaching ministry. Let us recall the central themes of the Reformers' thought that serve as the foundation of their understanding of the teaching office.

As we have seen, the great Reformers confronted the issues that have surrounded the teaching office from the very beginning of the church's life. How can the church maintain continuity with the original message of Jesus and preserve unity in the face of false teachings? What communal processes and agencies best help the church reinterpret the faith from age to age, confronting believers with the gospel and helping them discern the shape of an obedient life in the face of the particular demands of their own time and place? Is it possible to formulate ecclesiastical structures that can help the church make up its collective mind about matters of faith and morality without quenching the freedom of the Spirit of God? In spite of the differences that separate Luther and Calvin, the general lines of their response to these questions go in a common direction.

At the heart of the great Reformers' theologies was an affirmation of the absolute priority of the gospel. The good news of God's gratuitous mercy revealed in Jesus Christ stands at the beginning and the end of the Christian life. Human beings exist in rebellion against God and can only be restored to a relationship with their Maker through the forgiveness won in the life, death, and resurrection of the Mediator, Jesus Christ. The foundation of the Christian life, thus, is the unmerited, alien righteousness that is freely given to a sinful humanity in Jesus Christ. It is the gospel that authoritatively teaches us who God is and who human beings are in relation to God and one another. The gospel is the authority above all authorities in the church, the foundation upon which all others rest.

Second in importance in the Reformers' thought is the authority of scripture, which contains the accounts of the original apostolic witness to Jesus Christ. As such, scripture stands in a closer relationship to the source of faith than any other authority in the church. All matters of faith and morality that are necessary to salvation are contained in its teachings. Moreover, the Holy Spirit is bound to scripture. Those who claim to speak on the Spirit's behalf must appeal to the written word.

Does the authority of the gospel and scripture mean that the teaching office of the church is reduced to repeating the words of the Bible in a mechanical fashion? Does this rule out a role for church tradition and ecclesiastical authorities in the ongoing interpretation of scripture from age to age? The answer to these questions is an unequivocal "No!" There is a legitimate place for teaching authority in the church's life. The Reformers' emphasis on the authority of the gospel and scripture, however, does mean that the authorities who carry out the church's teaching ministry are *humanized.* No authority in the church can claim the status that belongs to the gospel and scripture alone. All church authority is human and, as such, is fallible and subject to correction.

Moreover, the Reformers' strong affirmation of the authority of the gospel and scripture led them to advocate a particular form of the teaching office. Highly centralized, hierarchical structures of teaching authority inevitably tempt the leaders of the church to substitute their own teachings for those of Christ, as Luther and Calvin said of the *magisterium* of their day. The form of the teaching office they advocated was one in which multiple offices and agencies at various levels of church life were granted important roles. Representative bodies, theologians, ministers, congregations, and individual conscience all were seen as having an important role to play. It is out of the ongoing conversation between these very human teaching authorities that the normative beliefs and practices of the church are determined and reinterpreted.

There is no question that the institutional form of the teaching office during the Reformation period and the subsequent period of Protestant orthodoxy was deeply influenced by the established pattern of church life. The church's ability to establish normative beliefs and practices was frequently dependent on its privileged relationship to the civil authorities. The congregation and the individual were not always given their proper due as centers of teaching authority in their own right. At their best, however, the Reformers pointed toward a dialogical model of the teaching office that locates authority in a number of institutions and roles in the church's life.

Contemporary mainline Protestantism has a great deal to learn from this understanding of the teaching office. It points toward a third way beyond modern individualism and counter-modern authoritarianism as they influence American religion. Undoubtedly, the mainline churches must reconstruct the thought of the Reformers in conjunction with the possibilities and limitations of the voluntary pattern of American denominationalism. They cannot and should not strive to reestablish patterns of teaching authority that unwittingly lapse into coercion on the basis of an unholy alliance with the civil powers. The dialogical, dispersed nature of teaching authority in the Reformers' thought, however, points beyond the institutional forms that initially evolved in conjunction with the established pattern of church life. It is possible that certain aspects of the Reformers' thought can be actualized more fully within the context of contemporary denominationalism.

Three centers of teaching authority can be identified in the teaching office on the basis of the Reformers' thought: (1) centers of scholarly theological inquiry and clergy education, (2) centers of practical theological reflection and lay education, and (3) centers of teaching and education on behalf of the denomination as a whole.

In the contemporary mainline churches, the first of these centers is largely focused on seminaries and universities and the professional theologians on their faculties. They represent the intellectual center of the church, the seat of scholarly inquiry that deepens and challenges congregational and denominational life. They are also centers of clergy education, providing congregations and denominations with leaders who are solidly grounded in scripture and theology and can relate them to everyday life.

The second center of teaching authority focuses on practical theological reflection. This takes place primarily in congregations. Here, concrete communities and individuals are given the opportunity to appropriate the Christian faith in deeply particular ways. The faith once delivered comes alive as it is linked to the concrete histories and circumstances of persons and local churches. The linking of faith and life unleashes sources of vitality, giving birth to new forms of church life that are fitting to the contemporary world.

The third center of teaching authority is found in denominational bodies and leaders who represent the church as a whole. Frequently, their most important function is to broaden the perspective of congregations by maintaining the catholicity of the faith and addressing contemporary socioethical issues in light of the insight and wisdom of the entire church. This center of teaching authority is greatly undervalued in most mainline Protestant churches. A major task before these churches is to reestablish a healthy dialogue between its representatives and other centers of the teaching office.

The interrelation of these three centers of the teaching office is illustrated in the following diagram.

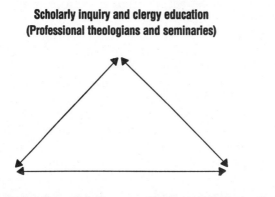

Scholarly inquiry and clergy education
(Professional theologians and seminaries)

Teaching and education on behalf
of the denomination as a whole
(Representative leaders and bodies)

Practical theological reflection
and lay education
(Congregations)

Each of these centers of teaching authority has a distinct contribution to make to the three tasks of the teaching office discussed in chapter 1: (1) the determination of the church's normative beliefs and practices, (2) the reinterpretation of these beliefs and practices in shifting cultural and historical contexts, and (3) the formation and sustenance of educational institutions, processes, and curricula by which the church's beliefs and practices are taught, allowing them to be appropriated meaningfully by each new generation and grasped with deeper understanding over the course of individuals' lives.

As we have seen, the first task is largely transmissive-preservative, focusing on forming and preserving communal identity. The second task is reinterpretive-transformational, focusing on relating the faith to new historical contexts and reconstructing it in light of these contexts. The third task is primarily educational, focusing on the formation of institutions and resources that support the activity of teaching in the church. It is important to reiterate that all three tasks are carried out by each of the centers of the teaching office. The teaching office becomes distorted if one of its centers focuses exclusively on only one task, leaving the others to be carried out by other parts of the church. Representative leaders, for example, may legitimately focus on transmitting and preserving the teachings constitutive of a denomination's communal identity, but if they are never willing to take the risks inherent in relating their teaching to contemporary issues, their contribution to the teaching office is likely to become skewed. Likewise, seminaries that abdicate their transmissive-preservative function in an exclusive preoccupation with contemporary scholarly issues do not carry out a key task in a voluntary pattern of church life: the preservation of the "far" tradition in the face of pressures toward individualism and localism.

Each center of teaching authority has a unique contribution to make to the church's overall educational ministry. Paul's image of the church as the body of Christ is helpful at this point. While every part contributes to the overall health of the body, each has a distinctive function to play. The hand cannot do the eye's work; nor can the mouth perform the task of the legs. If one part does not function properly, the entire organism suffers. Other parts of the body can sometimes pick up the tasks of a dysfunctional part, as enhanced hearing sometimes is able to compensate for blindness. This sort of compensatory work, however, cannot really replace the healthy functioning of the original organ. Each center of the teaching office has a distinctive contribution to make to the life of the church. This chapter is devoted to identifying these contributions and pointing out ways of improving lines of communication between the various centers of the teaching office.

A final word must be offered before turning to this task. In the face of the many pressures of individualism and fragmentation in modern life, it seems virtually impossible to hope for some sort of consensus to emerge in mainline denominations. Only tightly knit, authoritarian communities seem able to achieve a high degree of common accord. They do so, however, at a great cost, sacrificing the capacity for self-criticism and demanding a high degree of conformity. Is it too much to believe that the mainline churches might represent a third way, a form of community able to achieve some measure of consensus about the Christian life without resorting to coercion?

A dialogical teaching office may very well represent the best hope for such a possibility. Consensus is not uniformity; nor is teaching coercion. True consensus rests on the consent of the parties involved. True teaching seeks to enhance the understanding of the learner. Consensus will only emerge in mainline Protestant denominations out of an educational process, a process by which persons are given the opportunity to understand and appropriate for themselves the beliefs and practices that guide congregational and denominational life.

If mainline Protestantism were to create an educational ecology in which various centers carry out vital teaching informed by an ongoing dialogue between the academy, congregations, and representative bodies and leaders, it might well be that genuine consensus would emerge. A compelling vision of the Christian life might begin to take shape, a vision of what it means to be a Christian and a community of faith in the contemporary world. Teaching and consensus go hand in hand. Only with the recovery of the teaching vocation of various centers of church life will the realization of common accord in the mainline churches be a possibility.

Centers of Practical Theological Reflection and Lay Education: Congregations

Throughout Christian history, the congregation and the individual have been afforded various kinds of authority in the teaching office. Frequently, the role of the laity has been viewed under the label "the sense of the faithful," the ability of ordinary Christians to recognize and receive true teaching by its leaders.[1] The Protestant church developed its thought on this matter in a highly polemical situation.

As we saw in chapter 6, Luther changed his position somewhat over the years as to the authority of congregations in the teaching office. During the early part of the Reformation, when Roman Catholic priests continued to hold jurisdiction in areas in which Reformation churches were beginning to appear, he argued strongly for the right and ability of congregations to judge the teaching of their leaders. A leader's official position in the church hierarchy was no guarantee that he was faithful in teaching and preaching the gospel. Later on, Luther's conflict with Karlstadt and his observation of the Peasants' War made him more cautious in this regard. Governing bodies and offices beyond the congregation, representative of the church as a whole, were viewed as playing an important role in preserving the preaching of the gospel and proper interpretation of scripture.

The tension here is also found in the thought of Calvin. On the one hand, congregations are seen as holding a position of unique importance in the Christian life. It is here that the preaching and teaching of the gospel take place in ways that call persons to faith and sustain them as they attempt to live out their vocations before God.[2] The congregation can never be seen as a mere subdivision or cell of the real church. In its own particular situation, it is the church in its fullness, containing all that is necessary for salvation: the preaching and teaching of the gospel, baptism, the Lord's supper, and different ministries. On the other hand, congregations are located within a constellation of church structures and roles that represent the church as a whole. These structures and roles play an important part in maintaining the catholicity of the faith, stretching congregations beyond their own particular embodiment of the Christian life to a broader vision of the church and God.

This tension between congregational particularity and the catholicity of the faith is important to keep in mind while examining the congregation's role as a center of teaching authority. The congregation makes a crucial contribution to each of the three tasks of the teaching office. It must pursue these tasks, however, in a way that honors not only its own particularity but also the catholicity of the faith as that is given expression by other centers of teaching authority in the church's life.

Research in the newly emerging field of congregational analysis gives special credence to the importance of taking congregational life seriously in all its particularity.[3] In this research each congregation is seen as having its own culture based on unique social practices, language, sacred symbols, sense of time, sacred space, and norms.[4] These bind the congregation together as a community and are the foundation of its identity. Charles Gerkin and James Hopewell in particular call attention to the narrative structure of congregational culture.[5] Like every community, the congregation knits together the unique events and circumstances of its past and present into a coherent narrative whole, projecting a sense of the future that it is living toward. The culture of a congregation tells a story that reflects and shapes the community's unique appropriation of the gospel, giving particular expression to its understanding of what it means to be God's people in its own concrete time and place.

One of the most important tasks facing ministers who would help their congregations become centers of practical theological reflection is to understand this culture. Until it is grasped, they will be like a person who does not understand the lay of the land but must run across it in the middle of the night. They will be unaware of the pitfalls ahead and the already established roads. They will not know the best places to forge new paths. Understanding the culture of a congregation is a crucial part of leading that community in practical theological reflection. This culture reflects the history of that particular community of faith, providing a language, a range of biblical and theological images, stories, and concepts, and a set of social practices by which that congregation attempts to live before God. Members of the community reflect *within* the linguistic and conceptual parameters of this culture. Once they understand this framework, ministers will be far more adept at using the material it provides to help the congregation reflect upon the situations that confront it. Moreover, they will have a greater chance of facilitating change within the culture itself, deepening and broadening the vision of the Christian life that it projects.

This affirmation of congregational particularity, however, must be balanced by an equal affirmation of catholicity at this level of church life. Congregational culture can distort as well as particularize the gospel. Congregations need to be supported, challenged, and even corrected by a more catholic vision of Christianity, a vision that frequently is articulated by other centers of the teaching office. Much of popular American religion, for example, is highly Arminian in its understanding of the relationship between human agency and divine forgiveness. Denominations that historically have rejected Arminianism must find ways of assisting congregational education in teaching doctrinal positions that are more consistent with its heritage.

Congregations, moreover, are not always willing to struggle with socioethical imperatives that call prevailing norms into question. Attitudes of racism and sexism, for example, are frequently interwoven into the congregation's culture. The catholic sense of the church, as articulated by representative bodies and leaders, may call these attitudes into question, inviting the congregation to reconstruct its culture. In short, there should be an interplay between particularity and catholicity in the congregation's educational ministry, an interplay that influences the way it carries out each of the three tasks of the teaching office.

Transmission

This is especially evident in the first task, the determination of the church's normative beliefs and practices. On the one hand, the congregation is *the* sphere where the teaching of Christian doctrine and morality is oriented toward personal understanding, taking into account the particularity of individuals and the church community. The foundations of practical theological reflection are laid here or not at all. This commitment to particularity in congregational education, on the other hand, must be balanced by an affirmation of the catholicity of the faith. The foundational teachings of congregational education are not the creative invention of each congregation or minister. They should reflect what the church as a whole believes and practices.

Catechetical instruction serves as an excellent example of the need for balance between catholicity and particularity. Historically, catechisms have been formed by representative bodies and function as a summary of the essential Christian doctrines found in scripture. Instruction in the catechism has been seen as playing two important roles in church life: (1) It affords individuals the opportunity to appropriate the vows made on their behalf at baptism, confessing their faith before the congregation, and (2) it provides every member of the church with a common set of beliefs.

If it is genuine, an individual's confession of the faith must be deeply personal, emerging out of the unique history and circumstances of his or her life. At its best, catechetical instruction involves a living dialogue between the minister and the catechumen by which the seed of faith planted at baptism is nurtured in the life of each individual.[6] At the same time, the individual is asked to confess the faith of the whole church. He or she is asked not only to memorize the normative beliefs of the church but also to understand them as they are given expression in the questions and answers of the catechism.

Catechetical instruction is an excellent example of the congregation's role in the determination of the church's normative beliefs and practices. In large measure, its role is one of reception and transmission. It does not write the catechism but sees to it that the beliefs the catechism articulates take hold in the lives of those receiving instruction. Its task is to hand on the faith, channeling its creativity into forming teaching approaches that allow personal appropriation to take place, not into the invention of the theological substance of what is being taught.

The transmissive function of congregational education extends beyond catechetical instruction, but it follows the same general pattern. The teaching of scripture, for example, should be informed by the normative beliefs of the church. How often are children taught the Bible in a manner that is highly moralistic, communicating the message that they will win God's favor only if they are good in school or at home? How frequently are adults taught that their material prosperity is a sign of God's blessing? In a very real sense, the congregation has the responsibility of teaching its children, youth, and adults the normative beliefs and moral perspectives of its denominational heritage, making sure that all church members understand the difference between sound Christian doctrine and popular culture.

Does the congregation play a more active role in the determination of the church's normative beliefs and practices? It does so in one of two ways: (1) in judging the teachings of other centers of teaching authority, and (2) in forming persons grounded in Bible and doctrine who are capable of serving on representative bodies of the denomination. The latter represents a fairly direct way that congregations influence the church's normative beliefs and practices. Almost all mainline Protestant denominations involve laypersons in governing bodies that are responsible for working on behalf of the denomination as a whole. In their education of these persons, congregations exert an important influence on the beliefs and practices that are offered by the denomination.

Congregations, moreover, have the responsibility of judging the teachings of other centers of the teaching office. They are not to assent passively to the social teachings of the denomination, for example. They are to judge them according to the catholic sense that is in them. In a similar fashion, they are to judge the theologies coming out of seminaries and universities. Ideally a circular process takes place. Centers of teaching authority beyond the congregation help shape a catholic sense of the faith that congregations, in turn, bring to bear on the ongoing work of these centers.

Transmission of the faith, as such, is not a unidirectional process, coming from the other centers of teaching authority down to congregations. It is the outgrowth of a dialogical process. Congregations have a proper role in giving consent to the normative beliefs and practices of the church, handing them on to their members, and, in the process, educating persons capable of serving on bodies charged with determining the teachings of the whole church. Without congregations that are engaged in the process of transmitting the faith in this way, the teaching office in each of its centers is gravely diminished.

Reinterpretation

The transmissive task of education is not the only one undertaken by the congregation, however. The congregation also carries out the task of reinterpreting the normative beliefs and practices of the church in shifting cultural and historical contexts. One of the major sources of innovation in the congregation is something that we have pointed to already: the need to relate the teachings of scripture and tradition to the particular culture of each congregation. Congregations and individual believers are not Christian in general. They are Christian in terms of the concrete language and practices by which they live out the faith in their own time and place.

This activity of particularizing the gospel is one of the most important sources of innovation in the church. In the conjunction of the faith universal and the congregation in its particularity, new forms of Christian life emerge and old issues reappear that once were alive in scripture or church tradition. Christianity takes on new life as congregations discover language, conceptualization, and practices appropriate to their own context. It is here that Christianity becomes a living tradition or lapses into forms of dead traditionalism.

Many examples of innovation in congregational life reverberating back through the teaching office as a whole can be pointed out. One of the best illustrations is found in contemporary African Christianity. Forced to give up African singing and dancing in church worship by the first generation of missionaries, many congregations began to introduce these expressions of traditional African culture into their worship during the past decade. Representative leaders and theologians have been forced to ask a number of questions as they take a new look at the relationship between traditional African culture and the gospel: Is it possible that non-Western understandings of nature that are less domineering provide better models of how Christians should relate to the created order? Is polygamy ruled out in all cases, even though it clearly is present in the Old Testament? What role should dance and other forms of expressivity play in worship?

Congregations have long been sources of church renewal in ways that anticipate the work of scholars and denominational leaders. The base communities in Latin America, the sanctuary movement in the United States, and the lay-led Sunday school movement of the eighteenth and nineteenth centuries are all examples of grass roots movements that bring into focus ideas and practices that are not being addressed by church leaders and professional theologians. It is especially important that this innovative spirit among the laity be encouraged in mainline Protestant churches today. It is a travesty that parachurch organizations often do a far better job of tapping into the creativity and leadership of the laity of mainline churches than those churches do themselves. It is also a travesty that parachurch organizations seem to be far more creative in developing new forms of ministry than do the mainline churches. Even a cursory examination of youth ministry over the past decade underscores this point.

If congregational innovation emerges out of a firm foundation in scripture and church tradition and is co-sponsored by ministers who are not afraid to share leadership with the laity, it has the potential of breathing new life into mainline Protestantism. Both representative bodies and seminaries have a role to play in judging the propriety of such congregational innovation, to be sure. There is no way, however, that mainline denominations will rekindle a dynamic spirit in their midst on the basis of innovation taking place in theological education or denominational programming alone. This dynamism will only emerge from a revitalized laity that has caught a compelling vision of the Christian life. The laity has much to teach the other centers of teaching authority.

Educational Institutionalization

Congregational education also carries out the third task of the teaching office: the formation and sustenance of institutions, processes, and resources that allow teaching to take place. It is important to recall the distinction between education and teaching made in chapter 1. Education is the broader process by which a community systematically and intentionally transmits and evokes knowledge, attitudes, values, and skills that are deemed worthwhile. Teaching is an occasion that attempts to foster deepened understanding of the subject matter on the part of students. Education is much broader than teaching. It includes administration, the production of teaching resources (e.g., written material, desks, drawing implements, and space appropriate for teaching), and opportunities for discussion and debate over the ends of education. Education should enable teaching to take place.

Almost from the beginning of this country's existence, the Protestant churches have been denominated by a Sunday school pattern of education. Congregational education has been thought of almost exclusively in terms of the church school on Sunday morning. Administration, resources, and debate over the appropriate goals of church education have largely assumed this pattern. Congregational leadership has spent much of its energy on developing teachers for the church school, purchasing the best curriculum for their classes, making sure that the space is adequate for the number of persons participating, and so forth. It is a remarkable fact that in spite of the major differences separating the evangelical Sunday school movement, the religious education movement, and the neo-orthodox response, all focused much of their energy on the Sunday school pattern of education.

This pattern has been called into serious question during the past two decades by advocates of the religious socialization approach to Christian education.[7] As they have pointed out, we can no longer assume the sort of educational ecology that existed when the Sunday school first came into existence. It is simply no longer the case that the public schools, the media, and the family reinforce the same values and beliefs being taught in the church school. Rather than focusing on the church school pattern of education, they argue that the congregation's life in its entirety should be viewed in terms of its educational potential.

While accepting their analysis of the breakdown of the educational ecology, I do not believe that this should lead to an overemphasis on congregational education in isolation from other centers of teaching authority in the church. What is necessary is the rehabilitation of an ecology of education within the church, something that is more consistent with the teaching office as it is found in classical Protestantism. Moreover, an unfortunate by-product of the religious socialization approach has been a diminished emphasis on teaching in formal contexts in the church. Teaching does not take place solely in formal contexts, to be sure, but unless it takes place in such contexts it is highly unlikely that teaching will take place in informal contexts or, if it does, that it will be of a high quality.[8] In a congregation's institutional support of its educational ministry, it must assess how it can strengthen the already existing patterns of teaching that are present in the church. The church school remains the single largest focus of teaching in most congregations, and nothing should be done to undercut this important agency of congregational education. Questions of appropriate curriculum, space, and teacher recruitment and training remain important.

It is crucial, however, that congregational education broaden its sights beyond the church school and begin to institutionalize its educational program along somewhat different lines. The church school as an agency of education has shown itself to be weak in certain important respects. It frequently does not offer enough time or continuity of participation to deal with issues in great depth, especially those involving sustained intellectual discussion or personal self-disclosure. Congregations must augment this pattern of education with others that are not linked to Sunday morning. Two such patterns are particularly important.

The first centers on transitional moments in personal and corporate status in the lives of church members. Congregations would do well to view these as "teachable moments" full of potential for deepening persons' appropriation of the faith. The ritual components of these transitional events should be undergirded by systematic and intentional teaching. Baptism of infants, for example, should serve as the occasion for real instruction on parenting responsibilities from a Christian perspective. Catechetical instruction, marriage, death of a spouse, election to a church office, leaving home, and divorce are all examples of special moments of transition in persons' lives. They should be nurtured by special educational programs that tap into the vast educational potential already present. It is precisely at such times of transition that many persons are most ready to learn.

The second pattern focuses on the creation of opportunities to go deeper into a subject matter than typically is possible in the church school. This involves the formation of highly committed groups that meet together for a designated period of time in order to pursue a particular educational goal. Many nondenominational Bible study programs that have emerged during the past decade are excellent examples of this sort of educational pattern.[9] Persons are told in advance what sort of commitments they will have to make if they are to be a part of the group. Attendance will be expected, reading between sessions will be required, and they may even have to memorize certain key biblical texts or concepts. Other groups may focus more on personal growth in faith. Such groups typically form a covenant by which they set forth the kind of participation expected of each member and develop structures of accountability to see to it that this covenant is kept.

The congregation must discover ways of institutionalizing its educational ministry in each of these areas. It must find curriculum, develop teachers, and perform the administrative tasks necessary to enable teaching to take place through these agencies on a regular basis. Perhaps most important of all, it must find a way of creating a climate of expectation in the congregation that makes participation in these sorts of educational activities highly desirable.

In addition to this sort of formal teaching, the minister and other officers of the church also should view the congregation's educational program as taking place in informal contexts. Ministers who are solidly grounded in scripture and tradition and are adept in using these resources in practical theological reflection have a special role to play in teaching the congregation whenever "teachable moments" arise in its life. Committee meetings can serve as excellent opportunities for the minister to invite persons to reflect upon the issue at hand in light of the relevant ethical and theological issues.

Pastoral conversations are another area in which teaching can take place in an informal way. It is frequently here that persons reveal personal beliefs or practices that are at variance with the church's norms. Belief in reincarnation, for example, or that baptism "saves" infants from hell is illustrative of the kinds of misunderstandings that often come to light during pastoral conversation. It is important that ministers use such moments as opportunities to teach persons what the proper beliefs and practices of the church are. Such teaching can be done in a highly personal manner that respects the individual while communicating important elements of church teaching.

The congregation's relation to two other contexts of education also needs mention: the family and schools providing general education. It is ironic that mainline Protestantism gives so much lip-service to the importance of the nuclear family but provides so little support for the family's teaching ministry.

Without question, some of the most important teaching about God and the Christian life takes place in the family, especially during childhood. If the images and stories by which the child forms its sense of self and world are solidly grounded in scripture and church tradition, a foundation for later growth in faith has been laid. If this foundation is not formed during this period, however, it will be difficult to compensate for it later in life. Congregations must find ways of providing institutional support for the nurture of faith in the home. Material should be developed and classes offered that help parents appropriate their responsibilities as teachers. Links should be formed between the teaching that takes place in the congregation and that which occurs in the home.

The congregation's relation to schools of general education is deeply problematic at present. The strong connection between the public school and the church that existed in years past is no longer present. While the difficulties this creates for the church must be acknowledged, it does not make sense to yearn nostalgically for days gone by. The more appropriate response is for the church to begin to struggle forthrightly with the important questions surrounding its relation to general education. Is the common school the only way of educating the public? Should the mainline churches begin to consider more seriously whether private Christian schools are a legitimate alternative to public education? What stake, theologically, does the church have in a common school that brings together persons from all parts of American society? If no religion can be established in American society, does this mean that religion must be banished altogether from public schools?

These are important questions that congregations are only beginning to struggle with on a theological level. On issues like these they will benefit greatly from a sustained dialogue with other centers of teaching authority in the church. Seminaries, professional theologians, and denominational task forces have important roles to play in helping congregations discern with depth and breadth their relationship to general education.

To summarize, congregational education plays a crucial role in the teaching office. It is here that the normative beliefs and practices of the church must be transmitted in such a fashion as to take root in the minds and hearts of individuals and communities. In the act of particularizing these teachings in the unique culture and circumstances of each congregation, powerful forces of reinterpretation are unleashed that may lead to

important innovations in the church as a whole. Congregations must institutionalize their educational ministries by
forming ongoing patterns of teaching that are supported by
administration, finances, curriculum, space, and well-trained
teachers. Only if congregational education is carrying out all
three tasks of the teaching office will the other centers of
teaching authority be able to function properly. If persons
come to seminary without a deep grounding in scripture and
tradition and a vital Christian piety, theological education will
be forced to spend an inordinate amount of time laying foundations that it should be able to presuppose. Without congregations that can judge the teachings of representative bodies
and leaders on the basis of a deep knowledge of scripture and
tradition, the teachings of such bodies and leaders will gain
only a superficial hearing on the basis of popular culture.

The congregation plays a crucial role in the teaching office.
It is not the only center of teaching authority, however. It
stands in need of the support, challenge, and correction of
other centers. It is part of a broader dialogue by which the
church hands on and reinterprets its central teachings.

Centers of Teaching and Education on Behalf
of the Denomination as a Whole:
Representative Bodies and Leaders

As we have seen, the Reformers opposed all claims to infallibility in the church, for this was to put some aspect of the
church in God's place.[10] They also were skeptical of centraliz-
ing authority in the hands of a few institutional offices or agencies because of their awareness of the reality of sin, preferring
that the teaching function be dispersed throughout the
church. Nevertheless, there is an important role for a center
of teaching authority by which denominations carry out the
three tasks of the teaching office on behalf of the church as a
whole. Growing out of the conciliarism of the Reformers,
these important agencies of the teaching office are representative in nature. They gather up the wisdom that is dispersed
throughout the church at any given time—including that of
theologians, congregations, church leaders, and individuals—
and attempt to confess what the church believes in its own
time and place. One of their most important functions is to
represent the catholic sense of the church, mediating the
"far" tradition to congregations and raising up contemporary
socioethical issues that congregations may attempt to ignore.

Traditionally, bodies and offices that are representative of

the church as a whole have been considered under two head-
ings: the *quid* of the teaching office (the "what," its official
teachings) and the *quo* of the teaching office (the "who," the
body or office that formulates such teachings). Protestants
typically have been more willing to acknowledge the importance of the *quid* of the teaching office, the significance of
confessions, creeds, and social teachings important to denominational identity and mission. They have not always been as
clear about the status of the *quo*, the legitimate teaching authority of representative leaders and bodies who work on behalf of the denomination as a whole.

This center of teaching authority cannot exist without concrete institutional roles and structures that are acknowledged
as making an important contribution to the teaching office. All
too often, rampant individualism and a generalized alienation
from large-scale organizations undercut the authority of this
center of the teaching office. Representative bodies and leaders, however, are not properly understood if they are seen
solely in terms of their administrative and legislative tasks.
They have an important role to play in each of the three tasks
of the teaching office. Frequently, it is the teaching of such
bodies and leaders that enables congregations to move beyond the provincialism of their local culture and raises the
pressing issues facing the denomination that call for inquiry by
seminaries and professional theologians.

Transmission

Historically, this center of teaching authority has played an
extremely important role in determining the church's normative beliefs and practices. Such things as confessional statements, creeds, and catechisms—formed under the auspices of
representative bodies—have served as the clearest statement
of the core elements of a denomination's identity at any given
time. In the Protestant tradition, such denominational official
teachings are viewed as authoritative interpretations of scripture, bringing into focus and prioritizing the various parts of
the Bible and summarizing its essential teachings. The *Book of
Order* of the Presbyterian Church (U.S.A.) explicitly acknowledges the role of official teachings in the church:

> In these confessional statements the church declares to its
> members and to the world who and what it is, what it believes,
> what it resolves to do.
> These statements identify the church as a community of peo-

ple known by its convictions as well as by its actions. They guide the church in its study and interpretation of the Scriptures; they summarize the essence of Christian tradition; they direct the church in maintaining sound doctrines; they equip the church for its work of proclamation.[11]

The Evangelical Lutheran Church acknowledges a similar role for its confessional or "symbolic" statements of faith in *The Book of Concord*.[12]

The United Methodist Church represents an interesting case, for it is explicitly "nonconfessional." While it has never required subscription to an official confession by its clergy, it has maintained throughout its history certain doctrinal standards that represent the core of its theological convictions.[13] John Wesley formulated the *Articles of Religion* as an appendix to his abridgment of the *Book of Common Prayer* and the earliest *Discipline* of the church. The *Articles* later were moved to the front of the *Discipline*, where they have remained ever since. The first restrictive rule of the *Discipline* states: "The General Conference shall not revoke, alter, or change our *Articles of Religion* or establish any new standards or rules of doctrine contrary to our present existing and established standards of doctrine."[14] In addition to the *Articles of Religion*, Wesley also published four volumes of sermons in *Sermons on Several Occasions* and notes on the New Testament and church doctrine in *Explanatory Notes Upon the New Testament*. These were to serve as guidelines in determining standards of doctrine, especially in cases of dispute. While the Methodist tradition has not engaged in the writing of confessions, it does possess certain official teachings that identify a "marrow of Christian truth," as the *Discipline* puts it, that can bind the church together and guide it in its interpretation of scripture.[15]

The official teachings of denominations have two important functions. First, in cases of dispute they help determine whether the thought of a minister or theologian falls within the limits accepted by the church. Many of the confessions were formulated in the face of doctrinal controversy and attempted to set forth the boundaries of theological acceptability. Second, and more important, they bring into focus essential tenets of denominational identity by which that faith community understands its life before God, serving as the basis of its educational ministry. Their theological concepts provide a language in terms of which contemporary issues can be discussed and debated. They serve as a lens through which scripture can be read, bringing into focus and clarifying its various parts.

Without a core of theological convictions and a common memory by which it can articulate who it is and where it has come from, no group can sustain a strong enough sense of identity to survive as a viable community. This is as true of congregations and denominations as any other group. It is not necessary to have uniformity of belief and practice to the point that all variety is eliminated, but it is necessary to have a normative core on the basis of which pluralism can be sustained within genuine community. Too frequently in mainline Protestantism, the importance of normative beliefs and practices that can provide a common foundation for individual and communal identity has been overlooked. A fear of authoritarianism or the unwitting embrace of individualism has undercut the church's willingness to identify and teach those beliefs and practices by which it is sustained as a community.

In almost all mainline denominations, representative bodies by which the church can determine such teachings are already in place. These represent one form the *quo* of the teaching office takes in these churches and are acknowledged as such in most official statements of denominational polity. In the Presbyterian Church (U.S.A.), for example, additions to the *Book of Confessions* take place under the direction of the highest governing body, the General Assembly, composed of representatives of various presbyteries. New confessions, statements of faith, and catechisms only become official teachings of the church if they have been approved by the General Assembly on two consecutive occasions and by two thirds of all presbyteries.[16] Similarly, in the United Methodist Church, it is the General Conference that is invested with the authority to teach on matters of doctrine and morality for the denomination as a whole. This goes back to Wesley's earliest conferences, which focused on three basic questions: (1) What to teach (the substance of the gospel)? (2) How to teach (the proclamation of the gospel)? and (3) What to do (the gospel in action)?[17]

The authority of denominational leaders and bodies is primarily persuasive, not juridical. They do not set down doctrines and moral norms that must be obeyed as a condition of salvation. The teaching office is not conceptualized along the lines of a tight, clearly ordered hierarchy, with the most authority concentrated at the top. This can be seen in the status accorded the official teachings formulated by the highest governing bodies of the mainline denominations. At the lower levels of denominational life—the level of presbyteries, annual conferences, synods, and the various agencies by which these bodies carry out their work—their authority largely is indirect. They have the greatest influence when they have shaped the actual identities of persons who lead the church, functioning in the background to provide a common language and set of convictions by which these persons carry out their work. In general they do not function as tests of orthodoxy.

At key points, however, the official teachings of the denomination play a determinative role in a more direct fashion. This is especially the case in the educational formation of the leadership of the church. Conferences, presbyteries, and synods all have ways of examining those persons who are candidates for the ordained ministry to make sure that their theological convictions fall within the range of acceptability. This rests on the recognition that much of the work of the teaching office in Protestantism is carried out by ministers who mediate the theological tradition of the denomination to their congregations.

In the Presbyterian Church (U.S.A.), for example, presbyteries are charged with the task of examining the theological position of each person who is a candidate for ministry or is transferring from another presbytery. Candidates cannot be ordained unless they express "theological views compatible with the confessional documents of the church."[18] Moreover, ministers of the word and officers of congregations (elders and deacons) must be able to give an affirmative response to the following question: "Do you sincerely receive and adopt the essential tenets of the Reformed faith as expressed in the confessions of our church as authentic and reliable expositions of what Scripture leads us to believe and do, and will you be instructed and led by those confessions as you lead the people of God?"[19]

How could persons respond affirmatively to this question with any integrity if they had not been afforded the opportunity to learn the "essential tenets of the Reformed faith"? Here, acceptance of the official teachings of the church is viewed as a prerequisite of responsible church leadership. The United Methodist and Lutheran denominations likewise assume normative doctrinal positions in their examination of those seeking to enter the ministry. United Methodists ask those who are candidates for ministry if they believe that the denomination's doctrines are "in harmony" with scripture and if they will "preach and maintain them" in their ministry.[20] Questions about Christian perfection, which have a distinctively Methodist ring, are a part of the ordination service.

Thus in the examination of those seeking to enter the ordained ministry, the official teachings of the church play an important role in determining the theological competence and acceptability of the church's leaders. Almost nowhere else in church life is the authority of official teachings this direct. Even at this point, moreover, most bodies charged with overseeing the candidacy process use such teachings to establish a range of theological acceptability and not as a literal standard of orthodoxy to which candidates must subscribe.

Reinterpretation

In general the most important role played by the official teachings of a denomination is an educational one. They serve as summaries of the essential elements of denominational identity that should be handed on from generation to generation, laying a common foundation on the basis of which community can be formed and sustained. This center of teaching authority also plays an important role in the second task of the teaching office: the ongoing reinterpretation of the church's beliefs and practices in shifting cultural contexts. As we have noted, mainline denominations already have in place mechanisms by which this takes place with regard to official denominational teaching. This kind of reinterpretative activity is relatively rare. More frequent is that undertaken in conjunction with ongoing teaching on socioethical issues offered by representative bodies and leaders. This sort of teaching represents a legitimate effort to relate the faith once delivered to the contemporary context. Frequently, it plays an important role in inviting congregations to confront dimensions of the Christian faith that are not an important part of their own local culture. While socioethical teachings on contemporary issues do not possess the same kind of status as long-standing normative beliefs and practices of the church, they do have special significance.

For example, the recent statement by the United Methodist Bishops on nuclear disarmament, *In Defense of Creation,* was to be taught from every pulpit, and special material for study in congregations was developed. This teaching was not viewed as binding on conferences, congregations, or individuals, but it carried special weight as the teaching of leaders representative of the church as a whole. These leaders play a special role in guiding the church on matters of social import. They have the prerogative of raising questions and focusing issues with which the denomination as a whole should struggle. Why then is it that this sort of teaching is so frequently met with disdain in congregations or ignored altogether? What will it take for the ongoing teaching of denominational leaders and bodies to regain a place of authority in congregational life?

Without question, one of the most important reasons that this kind of teaching is so easily disregarded in the contemporary church is the widespread prevalence of the sort of individualism we have referred to throughout this book. The self is viewed as the final arbiter of its own beliefs and practices, and any sense of the church's teachings as having priority over individual preference is rejected. The mainline churches must recognize this attitude in their midst and not allow it to undermine the legitimate role this sort of teaching should play in the congregation's life. The leaders of congregations have a special role. They should draw on the normative beliefs and practices of the church in the educational ministry of their congregations and use them to guide their ongoing life. They must attempt to foster a teachable spirit in their congregations.

More than this is necessary, however, to reestablish the authority of ongoing teaching by representative bodies and leaders. Teaching authority, it will be recalled, depends on the freely given respect granted to a teacher on the basis of the recognition of his or her superior wisdom or competence. For representative bodies and leaders to have teaching authority, they will have to demonstrate competence and wisdom on issues of importance to the Christian life. Moreover, they will have to set up a process by which their teachings are communicated to individual Christians and congregations in a manner that is genuinely educational: that is, engages the persons and groups being addressed and attempts to facilitate deeper understanding.

Why is it that representative bodies so frequently fail in this regard? In large part, it is because these bodies often only attempt to exercise their teaching ministry when theological and ethical issues have become a legislative matter. An explosive issue such as homosexuality or nuclear disarmament that is currently in the public eye becomes an object of study in preparation for legislative action. The discussion of such issues tends to become highly politicized, with ideological perspectives far more determinative than theological and ethical considerations. Frequently a number of such issues are considered in a single meeting, far surpassing the ability of the group to deal with them sensitively and in depth.

Moreover, the persons who compose representative bodies often do not have the theological competence necessary to raise the more complex dimensions of such issues in terms of present scholarly research. Discussion and debate under the constraints of limited time in a highly charged, politicized atmosphere simply are not conducive to the formation of teachings that possess sufficient theological depth and scholarly understanding to command the respect of the members of congregations. Even when commissions or committees are appointed to study an issue over a period of time, the fact that they are serving as consultants of a legislative process tends to diminish their role as teachers with special competence.

One concrete step that the mainline churches might take to rectify this situation is to establish bodies at national and regional levels charged with the tasks of studying contemporary issues on an ongoing basis.[21] These bodies could influence legislative action, but only indirectly, removing the church's teaching from highly politicized legislative processes. They would be charged with the task of addressing theological or ethical issues of central importance to the life of the church. They would study such issues over a period of time, drawing on the best scholarship and research that is available. Only gradually, as consensus emerged within the group, would they attempt to develop their findings into teachings that address the church as a whole.

Important issues facing the contemporary church lend themselves to this kind of ongoing reflective process. World hunger, nuclear disarmament, and threats to the ecology, for example, are not issues that are going to be resolved quickly. They are going to be with us well into the next century. The church has been far more effective in American history when it has mobilized its energy in an ongoing, sustained fashion around a small number of issues—like slavery or civil rights— than when it has dispersed itself around every issue that happens to become the object of the media's attention.

Such bodies could be composed of seminary faculty, denominational leaders, and members of congregations who have special gifts or expertise pertinent to the issue under study. It is crucial that the teachings formulated by these groups be offered to the church in a manner that is truly educational. The task of teaching is to deepen the understanding of those being addressed, not to offer prophetic utterance. Ideological pronouncements from afar are far less likely to have authority than teachings that attempt to take their audience seriously, including an opportunity for congregations and seminaries to dialogue with and even criticize the teaching being offered.

Educational Institutionalization

The third task of the teaching office also is pursued by representative bodies and leaders. There are many important ways that the denomination as an institution supports the educational ministries of congregations and seminaries. Denominational publishing houses, for example, produce curricula that no single congregation could devise on its own. They also facilitate an exchange of ideas between the scholarly community and congregations in the books they publish. Specific denominational agencies, moreover, provide support for the development of the educational ministries of congregations. Presbyteries, annual conferences, and synods frequently appoint staff persons who give support to ministries for specific groups like youth, singles, or the elderly. National denominational agencies often provide financial support for seminaries and for ministries on college campuses.

In these and many other ways, the denomination gives institutional support to the educational ministry of the church as a whole. In an era of dwindling finances and declining church membership, it is imperative that the mainline churches continue to uphold their teaching ministry. If denominational publishing houses are dominated solely by a profit motive, for example, the publication of scholarly research vital to the long-term health of the church will be severely diminished. Similarly, if support for college chaplains continues to be cut back, the mainline churches' ministry to a group that is the most likely to switch to the unaffiliated segment of the population will be undercut.

In short, there are many ways that mainline denominations give institutional support to the teaching ministry of the church. As crucial as continued financial support of these things are, even more important is a renewed sense of the importance of the denomination's contribution to the teaching office. A wide range of institutional roles and structures is already in place that have potentially important contributions to make to the denomination's teaching ministry but fail to do so because of uncertainty about the shape their contribution should take. The mainline churches would benefit greatly from a wide-ranging discussion of patterns of teaching authority appropriate to bishops, moderators, task forces, ecumenical councils, publishing houses, denominational boards, and other institutional forms of denominational life. It is important that these churches attempt to overcome the alienation that many church members feel toward levels of denominational life beyond the congregation. More objective forms of authority in the teaching office that can represent the catholic sense of the church are necessary to the healthy functioning of congregations. They deserve and should work to procure the respect of those located in other centers of the teaching office.

Centers of Scholarly Inquiry and Clergy Education: Seminaries and Professional Theologians

In the modern church, theology has been understood primarily in terms of the highly specialized work carried out by the theological faculties of universities and seminaries. This has resulted in the loss of understandings of theology that were important at earlier points in the church's life, particularly an understanding of theology as the reflective dimension of piety. The restoration of the teaching office that is being called for in this book is closely related to a broader restoration of theology to the actual life of congregations and denominations.

This does not mean, however, that theological reflection and discourse are identical at every level of the church's life. This was not the case even when theology remained relatively unified as a science and its close relationship to piety was maintained. During the Middle Ages, the rise of cathedral and monastery schools led to a distinction between the pastoral teaching office and the doctoral teaching office.[22] The former referred to the teaching ministry as exercised by the pope, the bishops, and the representative bodies they convened. The latter referred to the teachings of theologians situated in centers of higher education.

It gradually became clear that these two groups had distinct but interrelated roles to play in the church's teaching ministry. Just what these roles were and how they were to be related was a matter of debate and political conflict. To this day, very real tensions exist in the Roman Catholic Church between those who would view the teaching role of theologians as operating within the pastoral *magisterium* and those who view theology's task as the free pursuit of truth along scientific lines unconstrained by the official teachings of the pastoral leadership.[23]

Protestantism does not escape this same tension. In recent years, it has been felt directly by faculty members of seminaries affiliated with the Southern Baptist Church who are being subjected to strict doctrinal tests by the fundamentalist faction that has been in control of the Convention in recent years. At the opposite end of the spectrum, the seminaries of many mainline denominations often seem to allow their faculty members to operate as free agents with no responsibility whatsoever to their denomination's theological heritage or pastoral leaders.

A series of questions emerges from the tension between seminaries and professional theologians and the pastoral leadership of denominations: What claim do the normative beliefs and practices of a denomination, as they are given expression in its official teachings, have on theologians who teach in denominational seminaries?[24] What role should professional theologians play in shaping, criticizing, and reinterpreting the normative beliefs and practices of the church? How close a relationship should exist between centers of scholarly inquiry, especially those that educate clergy, and denominations that provide financial assistance to these institutions? What is the primary audience of academic theology, members of the theological guild, ordinary Christians, clergy, denominational leaders, or the non-Christian world? What sort of relationship should exist between the kind of theological reflection taking place in congregations and that which occurs in centers of higher education? Clearly, centers of scholarly inquiry have an important role to play in the teaching office, but these questions are indicative of the confusion permeating contemporary mainline Protestantism about what this role should be.

Tensions Between Transmission and Reinterpretation

H. Richard Niebuhr provides us with a helpful starting point for reflection on these questions in the following description of the two tasks of the seminary:

> As center of the Church's intellectual activity, animated by the Church's motivation and directed by its purpose, the theological school is charged with a double function. On the one hand it is that place or occasion where the Church exercises its intellectual love of God and neighbor; on the other hand it is the community that serves the Church's other activities by bringing reflection and criticism to bear on worship, preaching, teaching and the care of souls.[25]

In describing the seminary as the center of the church's intellectual activity, Niebuhr does not mean to imply that the use of intellect in the community of faith is confined to this setting alone. Rather, the seminary brings into focus and pursues with greater depth something that is an inherent part of every Christian's life: the intellectual love of God with the entirety of one's mind. Faith, Niebuhr points out, must seek to understand its divine object and all of life in relation to that object. To do otherwise would limit the scope of faith in one of two ways. It would limit the understanding of faith to the apprehensions of only one part of the self—the emotions, for example. Or it would limit God's activity to certain spheres of life—the personal morality of the private sphere, for instance. In contrast, persons are to love God with their whole selves, including the mind, in the attempt to bring their faith to bear on every aspect of life.[26] The seminary is the institutional center of this activity, not its sole agent.

This is not to say, however, that seminaries and professional theologians do not have a special role to play in the intellectual love of God. In their scholarly research and writing, they raise the cognitive apprehension of God to a level of abstraction and depth that is not typically achieved in the thought of ordinary Christians. It is precisely for this reason that Niebuhr goes on to describe the seminary in terms of a second function: theoretical reflection on and criticism of the various activities by which the church responds to God. Professional theologians have acquired a knowledge base and research competencies that can be of special help to the church as it attempts to discern whether or not it is being faithful to God in its worship, witness, fellowship, and service. As Niebuhr puts it, "The worshipping Church needs a theology of worship not as preliminary or as addition to, but as accompaniment of, its action. So also in the case of preaching and teaching."[27]

The two functions of the seminary that Niebuhr describes stand in a very real tension. As an expression of the intellectual love of God, scholarly theological inquiry must be free to pursue truth for its own sake.[28] It must not be under the control of the pastoral leadership of denominations and congregations, pursuing only those questions and issues they deem important. Frequently, scholarly inquiry that does not seem immediately relevant to the life of denominations and congregations will raise issues of great import to the church in the long run. A respectful distance must exist between centers of scholarly inquiry and other centers of the teaching office. On the other hand the second task, which Niebuhr identifies also, is a part of the calling of seminaries and professional theologians. If they do not reflect in a systematic fashion on the patterns of ministry that are constitutive of the contemporary church, who will? They and they alone have the specialized knowledge and research competencies to construct theoretical models of ministry that can guide the work of congregations and denominations.

It is important to explore what is at stake in both sides of this tension and how it affects the contribution of seminaries and professional theologians to the teaching office. Scholarly commitment to truth for its own sake has been expressed in a variety of ways in church history. Luther's initial criticisms of the pastoral leadership emerged out of his understanding of what it meant to be a doctor of the church. Across the centuries, other theologians have followed in his footsteps, posing the question of truth in terms of their commitment to the witness of scripture. On behalf of the Bible, they have called the church and its pastoral leadership into question, reminding them of moral and theological imperatives that have been forgotten.

Theologians standing in the liberal tradition have posed the question of truth somewhat differently. In their view, it is imperative that theologians be free to pursue lines of thought raised by contemporary forms of historical and scientific investigation. For example, in spite of the difficulties posed to dogmatic theology by historical critical approaches to the Bible, seminary scholars must be free to carry out research that is not encumbered by official denominational doctrinal positions. A prior commitment to denominational standards can predetermine research findings and lead to circular forms of reasoning.

In both cases, the doctors of the church are seen as living in the tension between the scholarly community and the church community, struggling with unanswered questions, formulating tentative hypotheses, and, in general, serving as the center of the church's intellectual life. There can be no question that many times it has been theologians situated in centers of learning who have forced the church to confront difficult questions it would otherwise have avoided.

It is no accident, thus, that theologians and seminaries frequently view themselves in terms of the second task of the teaching office, the reinterpretation of the church's normative beliefs and practices in shifting cultural and historical contexts. They are the cutting edge of the church's attempt to incorporate the insights of contemporary scholarship. Modern exegesis, for example, has incorporated the methods and theoretical base of historical and literary criticism and, more recently, the sociology of knowledge. This has led to a dramatic transformation in the way the Bible is approached by pastors and laypersons. Similarly, preaching, pastoral care, and Christian education all have been enriched by the findings of the social sciences. The emergence of developmentally appropriate curricula in the church, for example, is a direct result of research in developmental psychology and education. In a wide variety of ways, centers of scholarly inquiry have been responsible for important shifts in the church's normative beliefs and practices through a process of reinterpretation that attempts to take into account contemporary intellectual inquiry.

This reinterpretive role, however, is not the only one played by this center of the teaching office. Almost as frequently, seminaries and professional theologians are involved in the preservation and transmission of the inherited traditions of the church. This is an especially important task in American denominationalism in which voluntarism has consistently worked in favor of congregational and individualistic understandings of the faith. Historically, theologians and seminaries have played an important role in handing on the inherited beliefs and practices of their theological tradition in an attempt to preserve and deepen communal identity and counteract the local theologies of popular culture. They have attempted to convince their students and the denomination in general that the church must reclaim certain aspects of its heritage or stand firm in maintaining doctrinal standards.[29]

The question of truth that professional theologians pursue out of an intellectual love of God is thus not without impact on the church, even though this may not be its immediate motivation. At some point, however, theologians and seminaries must turn their energies more directly to the life and work of the church, the second task that Niebuhr identified. They are directly involved in congregational and denominational life in a wide variety of ways. Seminary faculty members frequently serve on denominational task forces responsible for formulating theological or ethical teachings for the church. They often are asked to lead workshops in congregations or continuing-education events for ministers and laity. In these and other ways, they contribute directly to the teaching ministry of the church.

Educational Institutionalization

Without question, the single most important direct contribution seminaries make to congregations and denominations is their education of clergy. As we have seen, there is some debate at present about whether the seminaries are carrying out this task in an adequate fashion. Farley's work has brought into focus what many consider to be the greatest difficulty facing the seminaries in this regard: the modern dispersal of theology into a series of unrelated disciplines. Seminary students experience the problem this creates on a firsthand basis: They pass through a series of courses that seem to lack an integrating center and appear to be remote from the actual work of the parish minister.

It is worth asking whether seminaries fall into the same trap characterizing virtually all of professional graduate education today: educating persons in the knowledge and skills appropriate to pursuing research programs in university settings but not in ways that are directly related to the actual practices of professionals.[30] Questions about the relationship between seminary education and the practice of ministry mirror questions being raised in a number of fields. Professionals, it is argued, carry out their practices in the face of unfolding, indeterminant situations. A major part of their work involves defining the emergent problems they encounter and forging actual responses in the midst of situations that are still unfolding. The approaches to knowledge and research appropriate to highly specialized academic research programs simply do not match those used by professionals in their actual practices.

In terms of seminary education, this means that a distinction must be maintained between the requirements of scholarly inquiry and the pedagogics of clergy education. The former should inform the latter but not determine its basic structure. Several recent proposals of reform in theological education have adopted the rubric of practical theology to describe the kind of reflection appropriate to clergy.[31] They argue that clergy should be educated in ways that enable them to carry out practices guided by practical theological reflection, precisely the sort of theological reflection appropriate to their role as professionals. They also should be educated in how to facilitate practical theological reflection in their congregations, something that is essentially a teaching function. In short, the pedagogical requirements of the seminary should not be dominated by the inherited divisions of the theological encyclopedia, which mirrors modern, academic specialization.[32] Rather, they should be organized around the kind of knowledge and skills that are necessary to the education of practical theologians.[33]

Does theological education prepare persons for this kind of reflective practice? At present, most seminaries remain trapped in the patterns emerging out of the period of theological encyclopedia. It is increasingly clear that these patterns make it difficult for them to balance the two tasks of the seminary that Niebuhr identified, serving as the intellectual center of the church's life and providing direct assistance to the church in carrying out its various ministries. The education of pastoral leadership—undoubtedly the heart of the seminary's second task—stands in real tension with how it carries out its research and inquiry. Until a way is found beyond the hyperspecialization of scholarly theological inquiry, it will be difficult for the seminary to develop a curriculum that provides persons preparing for the ministry with the knowledge and skills appropriate to their work in congregations. Without leaders competent in practical theological reflection and apt at facilitating theological reflection in others, congregations and denominations will suffer. Once more, we see the interdependence of the various centers of the teaching office. Strength in one part is dependent on strength in the others. Without seminaries capable of uniting the intellectual love of God, the educational of clergy, and service of the church, the teaching office as a whole will be diminished.

The Special Role of Ordained Ministers in the Teaching Office

At various points, reference has been made to the special role of ordained ministers in the teaching office. Because of their education and special relationship to the denomination, they are uniquely qualified to facilitate dialogue between the various centers of teaching authority in the church. Their seminary education and ongoing participation in continuing education events put them in a position of being able to mediate the findings of scholarly research and writing to congregations. Similarly, they often are the persons in their congregations most knowledgeable of denominational policies, programs, and teachings. In short, they occupy a critical position amid the three centers of teaching authority. If they are unwilling or unable to foster dialogue between these centers, it is highly unlikely to take place. It is crucial that ministers in mainline Protestantism begin to recover the importance of teaching in their own ministries and to recognize the all-important role they play in the teaching office as a whole. How is this role best conceptualized?

Historically, one of the most important ways of understanding the special status of the ordained ministry has been in terms of its *representative* nature. Ministers are representative in a twofold manner. On the one hand, in their preaching, teaching, and care, *they represent the congregation's ministry.* Clergy are not the ministers of the church; they represent the ministry, which all Christians share. On the other hand, *they represent the gospel*, which exists prior to any congregation and calls it into being. Their office is defined primarily in terms of the preaching of the gospel and its proper representation in the sacraments, without which a congregation cannot really be a church of God. As such, ministers are never mere functionaries of their congregations but are representatives of the truth of God. At times, they must align themselves with scripture or church authorities beyond the congregation in order to protect the gospel in its fullness.

This twofold understanding of the representational nature of the ordained ministry points us to the special role that ministers play in the teaching office of the church. On the one hand, they are first among equals in the pursuit of the teaching ministry. The purpose of their teaching is to enable others to read the Bible for themselves and to carry out practical theological reflection in their own lives. They teach that others might minister with greater understanding. On the other hand, they are bound in a special way to the gospel and must teach on its behalf. Their task is to ensure that its truth is heard in their congregations, a truth that may well be articulated by centers of teaching authority lying beyond the local church. On behalf of the gospel, they may have to represent the teaching of the denomination or the seminary as it lifts up some part of the Christian life that has been overlooked or even willfully opposed by the congregation.

Transmission

We see this tension reflected in ministers' contribution to each of the three tasks of the teaching office. They are specially situated amid the three centers of the teaching office and are uniquely qualified to facilitate dialogue between them. This is especially evident in their contribution to the transmission function of the teaching office. On the basis of their seminary education and their knowledge of the denomination's official teachings, they should play an especially important role in the handing on of the core convictions by which the denomination is constituted as a community. At key points in the congregation's life, ministers have the opportunity to be directly involved in teaching in order to make sure that a firm foundation in scripture and church tradition is laid. Officer training, catechetical instruction, new members' classes, Bible studies, and teacher training are all opportunities for ministers to hand on the normative beliefs and practices of the church.

Their task at this point is no different from that of any other teacher in the church: They are to lay a solid foundation of Christian doctrine upon which the life and ministry of all members of the congregation can be built. However, they are uniquely qualified to represent the "far" tradition in the transmission of the faith on the basis of their knowledge of theology and church history. This is not the place for ministers to become preoccupied with their own originality or creativity, but to represent scripture and church tradition accurately and to discover efficacious ways of teaching it to the members of their congregations.

Reinterpretation

Ministers also have a special contribution to make to the reinterpretive task of the teaching office. Perhaps the most important role ministers play in this regard emerges in relation to the congregation's ability to engage in practical theological reflection. It is here that the faith once delivered is related to a congregation's culture in its particularity and the unique situations that confront its members.

Once more, there is a twofold tension in ministers' pursuit of this task. They should be *the* practical theologians in the congregation on the basis of their special knowledge of scripture and theology and their competence in linking both to life. As such, they represent the gospel's claim on every part of a Christian's life, including the mind, and its demand that piety become reflective in the attempt to view all things in their proper relation to God. However, ministers are not merely to carry out practical theological reflection on the congregation's behalf. They are to teach all members of the congregation how to reflect upon their lives theologically. They are to be midwives in the process by which others give birth to meaning.

It is important to note that as ministers assist their congregations in carrying out the interpretive task they are once again in a special position to facilitate dialogue among the various centers of the teaching office. By and large, it is ministers who have the ability in a given congregation to move back and forth between the highly abstract language of scholarly theology and the concrete circumstances of the congregation and individuals. It is they who are aware of denominational policies and resources that can support and challenge their congregations in their attempt to relate the faith to their own particular situation. Moreover, they typically are far more knowledgeable than the laity of the kind of reinterpretations of the faith that are being discussed and debated in other centers of teaching authority and are capable of communicating them to congregations. The impact of biblical criticism on congregational life, for example, has largely been mediated by ministers who have helped laypersons move beyond a precritical reading of the Bible. In general, ministers have a tremendous impact on the way that reinterpretive activity in the denomination or seminary is received in congregations—whether it is supported, opposed, or ignored altogether.

Educational Institutionalization

Ministers also play a key role in the third task of the teaching office, the institutionalization of the church's educational ministry. At the congregational level, unless ministers give their support to this ministry in terms of administrative commitment, staff relations, financial allocations, and the creation of an overall ethos in which congregational education is viewed as important, the congregation's teaching ministry is likely to languish. Their commitment to this ministry should represent the commitment of the congregation as a whole. Indeed, their own commitment is likely to engender such a commitment among others. Moreover, they represent the claims of the gospel when they call their congregations to take seriously their responsibilities in handing on the faith and deepening the understanding of their members over the course of their lives. Congregations that do not teach are susceptible to false teachings or a sense of complacency in which ideas formed early in life are never challenged or deepened.

In their commitment to the teaching ministry of the church, thus, ministers enact both sides of their representative calling. They must be committed to the teaching ministry of the whole congregation, teaching themselves and seeing to it that others are equipped to teach. At the same time, they must remind their congregations that they cannot be the church of Jesus Christ unless they carry on his teaching ministry. They must see to it that their congregations allocate resources and expend energy on this ministry of the gospel. They must facilitate dialogue between the various centers of teaching authority in the church. Only the commitment of ministers to a vision of what the teaching office might be will allow this ministry of the church to regain a position of importance in mainline Protestantism today.

10

Congregational Education and the Nurture of Practical Theological Reflection: A Faith Development Perspective

Throughout this book, the argument has been made that the teaching office of the church is broader than the congregation. Multiple offices and agencies at various levels of church life make important contributions to the church's overall teaching ministry. The congregation is situated in a mutually expansive conversation between a variety of teaching authorities, past and present. Locating the congregation in this constellation of authorities broadens the horizon of the church's teaching ministry as it has been understood in recent years.[1] It invites us to view the church's teaching ministry ecologically, holding in mind the important contributions and interdependence of a wide variety of educational institutions.

Congregational Education in the Teaching Office

This chapter focuses on congregational education. We have described the congregation as playing a unique role in the teaching office: It is the center of practical theological discourse in church life. It is to be a community in which the cognitive apprehension of all things in relation to God is seen as an inherent part of the vocation of every Christian and, accordingly, is nurtured throughout the congregation's educational ministry. By identifying the congregation as a community of practical theological discourse and locating it within a broader understanding of the teaching office, two questions of importance are raised. First, are special qualities of congregational life and individual faith necessary for full participation in the ongoing dialogue of the teaching office? Second, how do congregations nurture the development of practical theological reflection in their members over the course of their lives?

These questions represent two issues that are important dimensions of every educational theory. The first focuses on the ideal community and its mature members toward which the educational process is attempting to move persons.[2] Whether it articulates it explicitly or not, every educational theory projects a social ideal and a concomitant understanding of human maturity that undergirds its determination of the sorts of attitudes, values, skills, and capacities it deems worthwhile and worthy of inclusion in the educational process. In terms of our purpose, this focuses on understanding what a congregation looks like if it is truly participating in a dialogical teaching office.

The second question brings into focus an equally important issue: the description of persons' styles of knowing and learning and the ways that these shift across the course of human life. Every educational curriculum assumes some sort of understanding of persons' learning capacities at different points in their lives and attempts to set up a course of study that teaches them those values, attitudes, skills, and knowledge they are capable of appropriating as they grow. In terms of our interests, this focuses on describing how a congregation can nurture practical theological reflection in its children, youth, and adults in ways that are appropriate to their present capacities.

The work of James Fowler is extremely helpful in addressing both of these issues. Fowler's work in faith development theory describes a series of stages that persons move through in the ways they structure the world in relation to their centers of value and meaning. His theory does not describe patterns of faith found solely in the Christian community. Nevertheless, his research is an important dialogue partner in the attempt to describe the kind of congregation that is a full partner in the teaching office and that nurtures practical theological reflection across the course of its members' lives through its educational ministry.

Fowler's work is particularly helpful with regard to the second issue, the need to understand how persons grow and develop in order to design an educational curriculum that is consistent with their capacities to learn. Faith development theory projects a series of stages that provide insight into persons' abilities to undertake practical theological reflection in qualitatively different ways over the course of their lives. At any given point, a congregation will have persons at several different stages of faith and, accordingly, must design an educational curriculum that is sensitive to the possibilities and limitations of each stage.

Just as importantly, faith development theory helps us grasp certain qualities a congregation must possess if its members are to function as full partners in a dialogical teaching office. While faith development theory describes styles of faith knowing in individuals, it has been extended by Fowler in his recent work to describe the "modal level" of a community. Modal level describes the average expected level of development a community projects. In its leadership styles, its quality of congregational interaction, and its substantive images of the Christian life, a community projects understandings of mature faith. Persons are encouraged to grow to a certain stage of faith, but if they move beyond that stage, they run the risk of being labeled as deviant.

For the congregation to participate as a full partner in the teaching office as it has been described in this book, it would need to have as its modal level the fifth stage Fowler describes, conjunctive faith. In ways that will be described more fully, this stage of faith is characterized by a *committed or principled openness.* Persons at this stage can assume the individuation of the previous stage and now are willing to acknowledge the limitations of their own faith perspective. They are deeply conscious of their need for dialogue with other perspectives on truth that can expand and correct their own. They are capable of holding in tension multiple truths that cannot be integrated easily into a logically coherent system of thought. It is precisely this style of faith that is necessary for genuine participation by a congregation and its members in the teaching office. They must open themselves to the insights of multiple authorities at various levels of the church's life and be willing to live with the tensions generated by the interaction of differing perspectives, perspectives that cannot be easily reduced to a single ideology or theology.

Conjunctive faith thus provides us with a normative image of the congregation and individual faith when they are full partners in the teaching office of the church. This is not to say that congregations or individuals cannot participate in the teaching office of the church if they are not characterized by this modal level stage of faith development. In many ways, individuals and congregations need the formative and expansive input of the teaching office even more at other stages of faith. Conjunctive faith as an individual stage and a modal level is a *norm,* an ideal representation of what congregations and individuals would be capable of if they were entering into the tensive dialogue characterizing the teaching office at its best.

Moreover, Fowler's theory goes even further, reminding us that congregations and individuals need more than the committed openness characterizing conjunctive faith. The church as a whole, congregations, and individuals must keep before them images that are eschatological, images of a universal community that will only be fully actualized in the kingdom of God. They also must keep before them understandings of radical faith, faith that is oriented toward the kingdom of God, even within the vicissitudes of the present historical order.

This is the importance of Fowler's sixth and final stage in faith development theory, universalizing faith. In this stage, persons go beyond a readiness to dialogue with multiple perspectives. Out of an apprehension of what H. Richard Niebuhr calls the "principle of being"—the source and guiding influence of all that is—persons in this stage display a readiness to act on behalf of universalizing apprehensions that are not present in the previous stage. To describe this in terms of Christian theology, their vision of the future kingdom of God leads them to a proleptic actualization of the imperatives of that kingdom, already, today, in the confines of present existence.

Persons who embody this stage of faith are extremely rare. It is not realistic to imagine that a congregation would have this stage as its modal level of faith development. Even if conjunctive faith is normative for the congregation and the individual in the teaching office, however, it is extremely important that images and concepts consistent with universalizing faith be kept alive in the preaching and teaching of the church. This is not dependent on the immediate presence of a person in this stage of faith in the congregation. All that the congregation must do is allow the universalizing images and concepts of scripture and liturgy to speak with their own voice. Every time the church receives communion, it has the opportunity of bringing before it images of the messianic banquet in which persons from north and south, east and west will sit at the table of God. Every time portions of scripture are read that portray Jesus' proclamation of the kingdom of God, the church has the chance to hear of the universal reach of God's love and concern.

The teaching office in all of its various expressions must constantly feel the lure and the judgment of such universalizing apprehensions. They are what keep the dialogue of the teaching office ongoing, qualifying every teaching and every authority with a firm "not yet." They are what keep the conversation open, reminding the teaching office of the limited number of parties who are participating in that dialogue at any given time in light of the kingdom's inclusion of those who have no voice in this world. They are what keep the conversion humble, reminding the church that it is not the kingdom of God. They are what force the conversation to become more than words, pointing to the possibilities of the "already" of the universal community that can be worked for and lived toward even within the confines of the present age.

Even as congregational education holds up the norm of conjunctive faith as a partial description of the normative images of self and society that it is educating persons toward, it must also hold before it the insights of universalizing faith. In this way, the teaching office of the church is reminded of what it is: a finite, sinful function of the church that is used by God to communicate a universal message of forgiveness and hope that transcends the moral and epistemological limitations of every human form and every churchly expression.

Practical Theological Reflection in the Christian Life

Practical theological reflection is not the whole of the Christian life, and its education is not the sole aim of the congregation's educational ministry. The Christian life is broader than the intellect alone. Of special interest in recent years has been the important role of the religious affections, the imagination, and moral action in the life of faith.[3] A truly comprehensive theory of congregational education would need to address each of these in their relationship to one another and the teaching ministry of the church.

The religious affections focus on those enduring patterns of emotion that direct human energies in habitual directions. One of the most important tasks facing congregational education today is gaining a deeper understanding of the various ways that the congregation and the family can attend to the formation of the affectional dimensions of the religious life, focusing on the heart as well as the mind. The imagination also plays an important role in the life of faith. In recent years, various philosophers have drawn attention to the ways that human reason always assumes certain generative metaphors and images that guide its work.[4] In crucial ways, the life of the mind is opened or closed by the richness of the imagination that informs its reasoning. In recognition of the importance of the imagination, the role of the aesthetic in the church's teaching ministry has recently begun to draw more attention.[5]

Ways of nurturing the imagination and transforming it are viewed as fundamental to the educational program of the congregation. Likewise, moral endeavor recently has been brought into focus as an important dimension of the Christian life. The increased prominence of praxis epistemologies in Christian education and theology is based on the awareness that Christian truth must be acted on and not merely thought or felt.[6] Styles of congregational education have begun to emerge that focus on engaging church members in transforming action in the world and reflecting on scripture and theology out of that actional context.

The Christian life, thus, is a multifaceted and complex reality, including patterns of emotion, the images and metaphors of the imagination, and moral commitments and actions. The cognitive apprehension of all things in relation to God is only *one* dimension of this life, and its nurture is only one aim in a comprehensive theory of congregational education. The importance of practical theological reflection in the Christian life, however, should not be underestimated.

While the religious affections are the motivating force behind human thought and action, our patterns of emotion can deceive us as well as lead us to God. More than we care to admit, our affectional patterns are tied to our earliest childhood relationships. The capacity to stand outside of our experience and gain some theological and personal insight into the ways that our emotions lead us to form distorted understandings of God is an aim worthy of pursuit in congregational education. Similarly, while reason never rises above the imagination, it can become self-conscious, reflecting back upon itself and the images and metaphors it uses. It can test their adequacy against scripture and contemporary human insights. Furthermore, moral action without reflection is mindless. Our actions must be imbued with purpose and intention or else they will fall below our deepest convictions. Practical theological reflection that guides our actions can save us from the dangers of the habitual and conventional.

The capacity to engage in practical theological reflection is not the entirety of the Christian life, but it is an important dimension of it. Its nurture is not the sole aim of congregational education, but it certainly is one of them. This recognition of the limited but important role of practical theological reflection in congregational education helps us grasp the limited but important contribution of Fowler's work to Christian education.

Faith development theory does not represent a comprehensive theory of the self. It does not tell us everything we need to know about the human affections, especially the ways that the forces of the unconscious shape our emotional and cognitive patterns. Nor does it provide us with a complete account of the human imagination and the important role it plays in creativity and religious experience in adulthood. Nor is it a theory of human action and interaction, describing the various structures and roles that shape our enacted responses to the external world.

By itself, faith development theory does not describe exhaustively any of these things, although it can throw some light on all of them. Its focus is on the ego's development and the various stages it passes through as it structures itself and the world in relation to centers of value and meaning. It describes a process by which various functions of the ego become increasingly differentiated and reintegrated in the achievement of more complex patterns of knowing. Faith development theory does not describe all that can or should be said about the life of faith. It does bring into focus, however, dimensions of faith knowing that undergird our capacity to engage in practical theological reasoning.

Practical theology, we can recall, is the moral discernment that Christians undertake in light of their theological convictions as they encounter situations in the midst of their vocations in the world. Fowler's work is helpful in gaining insight into how this sort of reflective process can be nurtured over the course of a person's life. It throws light on the ways that congregational education can help children, youth, and adults form generalizations about God that are grounded in scripture and church tradition. It points to the different styles of moral reasoning that emerge from stage to stage and the ways parents and teachers can tap into and expand these styles. The ability to engage in practical theological reflection does not develop automatically in every Christian. It only emerges in conjunction with a congregation that is a community of practical theological discourse, one that teaches its members over the course of many years how to think theologically about God, how to formulate moral norms and principles in conjunction with their theology, and how to use these things to discern what God is enabling and requiring them to do in particular situations. Faith development theory does not tell us everything that is important in the life of faith or the human personality, but it does throw important light on how the congregation can devise an educational program that nurtures this sort of practical theological reflection.

Congregational Education in a Developmental Perspective

One of the most common misunderstandings of Fowler's work is the view that it is a simple extension of the Piaget-Kohlberg school of structural developmental psychology. Criticisms that are made of Piaget's and Kohlberg's work are automatically applied to Fowler. This is a mistake. There actually are three important sources of faith development theory: Piagetian structuralism, Erik Erikson's ego psychology, and the theological ethics of H. Richard Niebuhr. Of these three, Niebuhr's work is by far the most important. I have traced the interrelation of these three sources of Fowler's thought elsewhere, and there is no need to repeat it here.[7] More important for our purposes are the ways that faith development theory can help us conceptualize the nurture of practical theological reflection in the educational program of a congregation that is participating in a dialogical teaching office. Three broad principles of congregational education emerge out of a faith development perspective: (1) Ongoing patterns of communal life and intentional contexts of teaching are *both* important in the congregation's educational ministry, (2) congregational education should formulate teaching goals and styles that are sensitive to where people are in the developmental process, and (3) the material that congregations and denominations deem worthy of handing on to their members should be organized so that its content is appropriate to the present stage of faith knowing and its form appropriate to the next stage of development. Each of these principles can be described more fully.

1. Ongoing patterns of communal life and intentional contexts of teaching are both important in the congregation's educational ministry. Too often, contemporary Christian education theories have viewed socialization and teaching in formal contexts as antithetical.[8] A faith development perspective helps us to recognize that it is misleading to cast their relationship in either-or terms. Development is a function of both patterns of communal life and intentional contexts of teaching.

The modal level of a community—its average expected level of development—is an important dimension of a congregation's culture. It has a great deal to do with the quality of support that persons receive in their ongoing development. The church teaches indirectly through its life: the leadership styles that are employed, the images of Christian maturity that are projected, and the ongoing styles of interaction used in various group settings. To ignore or overlook this in congregational education would be to miss one of the most important factors that affect whether persons grow in faith during their lives.

A faith development perspective, however, also brings into focus the importance of intentional contexts of teaching and learning that are specifically designed to increase understanding of a particular subject matter on the part of the learner. Research has shown repeatedly that one of the single most important factors in ongoing development is education. This should not be surprising, for education, if it is done well, provides an opportunity for persons to develop their capacity to reason, to take the perspective of other persons and groups, and to broaden the amount and kind of information they take into account.

A faith development perspective thus makes us sensitive to the ways that ongoing patterns of communal life and intentional contexts of teaching and learning both are important facets of congregational education. This leads to a second general educational principle that this perspective affords.

2. Congregational education should formulate teaching goals and styles that are sensitive to where people are in the developmental process. This educational principle has three implications for congregational education: (1) It must meet people where they are in terms of their present structures of faith knowing, (2) it must recognize signs of readiness for stage transition that have not been generated by education per se and provide assistance in making this transition, and (3) it must encourage faith development within formal contexts of teaching and learning.

The first of these is a direct implication of Piaget's understanding of knowledge: Persons must construct knowledge if they are to make it their own. New information must be actively integrated into patterns of knowing and existing information they already possess. Otherwise, it remains inert, an inactive bit of material that is not used in the person's knowing of the world.

It is also important that teachers and leaders of educational programs be sensitive to signs of stage transition, the second implication of this educational principle. They should recognize that such periods frequently involve uncertainty and doubt, as old ways of thinking about God and self no longer are meaningful but new ones have not yet emerged. A faith development perspective allows us to see that transitional periods are a necessary part of growth in faith. It allows us to accept and affirm persons in such times, communicating to them that doubt and struggle can be a legitimate part of faith and not necessarily its antithesis. It provides congregational teachers and leaders with insight into the sorts of issues that persons in transition from one stage to another typically face.

Congregational education also must attempt to foster development in and through the church's teaching ministry, the third implication of this principle. To make development a direct aim of education is controversial. Fowler himself has explicitly rejected this in his most recent writings. As he puts it, "It probably is not helpful to think of stage transition or development from one stage to another as the direct goal of pastoral care, preaching, or Christian education"[9] There are good reasons for Fowler's reticence about making development a direct aim of education. Critics of faith development theory frequently have charged Fowler with furthering a view of education and religion as a matter of moving people "onward and upward."

This criticism cannot be sustained, however. It flies directly in the face of the contributions of prominent members of the structural developmental tradition to public education in recent years. Persons like David Elkind and Kieran Egan, operating out of a Piagetian perspective, have eloquently called into question the ways that American culture tries to hurry its children to grow up too fast, too soon, moving them as quickly as possible from one stage to the next.[10] They build on Piaget's insight that certain kinds of information can only be learned at certain stages and it does not make sense to try to force children to learn something beyond their present capacities. The charge that Fowler and other structural developmentalists lend themselves to an "onward and upward" approach is unfounded.

In light of this strong warning against trying to accelerate development unduly, does it make sense to have development as a direct aim of education at all? I believe that it does, for two reasons. Much important work in the field of moral development has indicated that education can undertake certain kinds of activities that directly contribute to the likelihood that persons will develop more adequate forms of moral reasoning.[11] Congregational education has much to learn from this body of research. Just as importantly, there seems to be an optimal correlation between stages of faith and different phases of the life cycle. Fowler has projected this correlation as follows:[12]

Infancy	Primal faith
Preschool	Intuitive projective faith
Mid childhood	Mythic literal faith
Adolescence	Synthetic conventional faith
Young adulthood	Individuative reflective faith
Middle adulthood	Conjunctive faith
Middle adulthood and beyond	Universalizing faith

There is a kind of natural fit between transitions from one stage to another and the various psychosocial tasks persons face during the life cycle "seasons" listed on the left side of this chart. It is important that the church recognize this fit and formulate educational programs that are explicitly designed to encourage development at appropriate times. During young adulthood, for example, persons are facing decisions in which they are having to take responsibility for their lives as never before: choice of career, choice of marital partner (or whether to marry at all), military service, establishment of own home. With proper care and restraint, it is not unreasonable for the church to project an expectation that young adults should begin to undertake the kind of work involved in making the transition toward a more individuative style of faith and designing programs to this end. Why is it that college and seminary classes are far less afraid than most congregations of challenging students' assumptions and literally forcing them, by way of papers and exams, to begin to think for themselves? The absence of such dynamic educational programs in the church frequently has more to do with the poor quality of educational leadership and the general flaccidity of mainline Christianity than with an inappropriate use of developmental theory. Properly understood, development can be a legitimate aim of congregational education. This brings us to the final educational principle that a faith development perspective affords.

3. **The material the congregation and denomination deem worthy of handing on to their members should be organized so that its content is appropriate to the present stage of faith knowing and its form appropriate to the next stage of development.** This principle is not easy to understand, especially if the stages that Fowler describes are not understood. What is meant by this principle is likely to become clearer as we move

through the stage descriptions that follow. The first part of this principle was pointed to in our discussion of the need to present material to students in a manner that allows them to construct it within their present structures of faith knowing. If a child constructs knowledge primarily in terms of narratives, for example, it does not make sense to present material that makes use of abstract thought. The content should match the child's present structure of faith knowing.

The second part of this principle is more complex. It can best be explained in terms of an illustration. During the first stage of faith, intuitive projective faith, children form generalizations of God in terms of images—a gestalt of feeling and cognition by which the divine is pictured. Children at this stage cannot spontaneously form narratives to describe their experience, nor can they follow complex stories. The capacity to narratize experience only emerges during the next stage. However, this is precisely the larger pattern of coherence or form that teachers should use to organize the various images of God that children are forming during this stage. The biblical material presented to children should be organized in terms of the larger narrative pattern of the Bible. The story of creation gives way to the story of Adam and Eve, and so forth.

The formation of a larger narrative in terms of which the different images of God are nestled must be done by the teacher or the curriculum, for children cannot do it themselves. In this way, the deep structure of the content of the material anticipates the form of coherence of the next stage. Images are organized in terms of narratives; narratives, in terms of beliefs; beliefs, in terms of theology; and theology, in terms of dialogue. The content of the subject matter is presented in terms of the learner's present capacities, while the form of this material anticipates the next stage of development.

To summarize, three broad principles of congregational education emerge from a faith development perspective. First, the importance of both ongoing patterns of communal life and intentional contexts of teaching and learning are underscored as important features of the congregation's teaching ministry. Second, congregational education should formulate teaching goals that are sensitive to where people are in the developmental process, meeting people where they are by working within their present structures of faith knowing, looking for signs of stage transition and providing support based on the particular issues being faced, and attempting to encourage the development of new structures of faith knowing at certain key points in persons' lives. Third, material the congregation deems worthy of handing on to its members should be organized as follows: Its content should be organized according to the capacities of the present stage of faith and its form according to the next highest stage. We will attempt to explicate each of these principles as we move through the different stages of faith.

Childhood Stages of Faith: Becoming Members of the Tradition

Primal Faith

Fowler refers to primal faith as a "pre-stage" in faith development theory, for it exists prior to language and is not really open to the kind of empirical research that faith development theory pursues. It might seem odd to view infancy as a time in which faith is being born. The infant cannot even speak, much less understand who God is. Psychology makes it clear, however, that some of the most important aspects of the human personality are formed during the first years of life. From a faith development perspective, the parents and others involved in the care of the infant are laying important foundations for the understandings of God that will emerge later in childhood. In a very real sense, parents are participants in congregational education, charged with the awesome task of communicating to the infant a message of love and acceptance that can sustain him or her beyond the times of anxiety and hardship that are an inevitable part of early life.

During the first months of life, the infant and caretaker must negotiate a series of separations that the infant passes through. Each of these separations is the culmination of growth on the infant's part as he or she moves from a state of total dependency and symbiosis with the caretaker. Such times of separation, however, are also filled with anxiety and vulnerability. Though the infant is physically separated from the mother at birth, cognitively and emotionally an awareness of that separation only emerges gradually.[13] The psychologist Margaret Mahler refers to this as a process of separation-individuation.[14]

Developmental advances of this sort are times of special vulnerability. The caretakers must find a way of balancing two needs. On the one hand, infants must be allowed to endure the times of anxiety that are an inevitable part of the achievement of independence. On the other hand, they must continue to receive assurance of the parent's love and concern.

They must be given the opportunity to form strong bonds of attachment to the caretakers.[15]

What does this have to do with faith development and the nurture of practical theological reflection? Faith development theory believes that how parents respond to the dialectic of attachment and independence that characterizes the first years of life communicates a great deal to the infant about the sort of world this is. As infants first begin to become aware of themselves as separate beings, with all the anxiety that this induces, primal others are present who communicate empathetic trust and acceptance or mistrust and uncertainty. It is out of these earliest childhood relationships that our first inklings of God are born, for better or for worse. In a very real sense, the caretakers serve as representatives of the ultimate context of the infant's existence.[16]

The quality of attachment bonds and support of the ego's initial moves toward independence also profoundly affect persons' ability to engage in practical theological reflection at later stages of life, affecting their ability to learn, to interact with peers, and to take the perspective of other persons and groups.[17] Unless infants have experienced empathy, it is unlikely that they will enter empathetically into the perspectives of others. Without the confidence that is born in early attachment relationships, they are less likely to take the risks that attend future growth.

What does this mean for the congregation in its efforts to nurture practical theological reflection? Most importantly, it means that congregations must take far more seriously their support of the parents of newborns. The congregation nurtures the faith of the infant indirectly, through the parents. Parents can be supported in a wide variety of ways: special groups for mothers and fathers of newborns, classes that provide health care information and examine different approaches to parenting, and the intentional linking of mothers and fathers of newborns with persons who have passed through this stage of life recently.

A second important emphasis of congregational education during this period is the formation of classes that help prospective parents struggle with the complex questions surrounding the care of the infant. With the advent of dual-career families, the issue of the primary parenting of newborns has become increasingly complex and difficult. If the faith development perspective is correct, however, important foundations of faith are being laid during this period of life. There are no simple answers to the many complex issues involved in balancing a nonsexist commitment to two careers and the need of newborns for quality care. The congregation as a community of practical theological discourse is uniquely suited to helping couples work on these issues prior to having a baby and providing a reflective context for renegotiation of their different roles following the infant's arrival. To the extent that their congregation is a community in which such a reflective process takes place on a regular basis, the parents of newborns are far more likely to gain the kind of perspective that will help them carry out their roles as mediators of God's love to their child.

A final issue raised by a faith development perspective is the quality of care the congregation provides in its own programs on Sunday morning and during the week. For many infants, their first extended times of separation from parents will be at church. The congregation has a responsibility to ensure quality care of infants in an attempt to make this initial time of separation a positive experience. Even during this period the infant can be sent the message that he or she is welcome in the family of God.

Intuitive Projective Faith

This stage of faith typically emerges at around two and a half or three years of age, as the child begins to use language to communicate with the surrounding world. In American culture, it lasts through the preschool years, until ages five through seven.[18] Central to Fowler's description of this stage is his reconstruction of Piaget's understanding of preoperational modes of thought.

By "preoperational," Piaget means that children in this stage do not yet possess the capacity to order their experience in logical categories, even relatively simple ones. The world of the preoperational child is still quite fluid, for he or she is not able clearly to sort out the differences between fact and fantasy, being unable to draw on categories of causality and temporality to organize the world into an orderly, lawful place. Consequently, children understand events in an episodic fashion, as relatively independent episodes whose meaning is dominated by a single outstanding feature.

Robert Selman's work is a particularly important extension of Piaget's theoretical approach.[19] Selman traces the development of persons' perspective-taking ability: the capacity to construct the point of view of another individual or group. During the period identified by Fowler's first stage, Selman describes children as egocentric. They are unable to separate cognitively their own point of view from that of others. They can empathetically intuit what others are thinking and feeling but lack the cognitive capacity to construct others' perspectives in a consistent fashion.

Like Selman, Fowler builds on Piaget's understanding of the preoperational stage of cognition. However, he does not describe this stage in terms of what it is not (preoperational: i.e., prior to logical reasoning) but in terms of what it is: a time in which the imagination is in the process of constructing deep and long-lasting images of the ultimate context of existence. An image is a gestalt of feeling and cognition that coalesces into a relatively static internal representation.

Another way of grasping the style of faith knowing that begins to emerge during the intuitive projective stage of faith is to view it as a time of metaphorical knowing. A metaphor is the use of something that is familiar to understand something else that is not as well known. This is implied in the etymology of the word: *meta* coming from the Latin "across" and *phora* from "to carry." A metaphor carries meaning across from one domain that is familiar to another that is not. Religious language is full of metaphors. Relationships that are a part of the fabric of everyday life are carried across to describe the unseen God: father, mother, lord, and king. The metaphorical nature of the images being formed during this stage of faith provides insight into the ways that the congregation and family directly and indirectly educate the imagination of children. Out of the actual experience of concrete relationships and events, children construct meanings that are carried across to describe God. They begin with immediate experience and move across to form imagistic meaning.[20]

In a very real sense, the congregation, as the gathered community, is not itself the place where the most important education occurs during this stage. The family continues to make the most significant impact on the images of God and religious values that the child constructs.[21] Parents and family members remain the significant authorities, and the child's social awareness is largely confined to family life and playmates. Congregational education, however, does have a contribution to make during this period.

A great deal is communicated indirectly to children during this stage. Children will identify with the values and beliefs that are lived out in the significant relationships of which they are a part. They will know at a deep if unconscious level if they are a meaningful part of the family of God. It makes a real difference whether they are welcomed into the worship service, for example, by the use of songs, sermon stories, and rituals that take their level of understanding into account. Whenever the congregation gathers, it would do well to remember the children in its midst and not exclusively orient itself to the adults who are present.

It is very important, however, that the congregation take seriously the intentional contexts of teaching and learning by which it attempts to hand on central understandings of the faith. An overreliance on tacit messages communicated indirectly through the community's ongoing life can be dangerous, for children during this stage do not always grasp the message that is intended. It is not unusual for a child to focus on one feature of a story in the sermon, for example, and come away with a distorted understanding of the point that was being made. Teachers of children in this stage must strive to communicate in a clear and simple fashion the basic teachings that they are trying to convey.

For this reason, teachers of children in this stage must be able to function as practical theologians, persons who are clear about the basic tenets of the Christian faith. In a very real sense, they must begin the process of inviting children to participate in the larger dialogue of the teaching office by interpreting to them the normative beliefs and practices of the church in ways that are accessible to the intuitive projective style of faith knowing. How should this take place?

In general, the most important content of teaching during this stage should be the stories of the Bible. Scripture not only takes its rightful position of primacy in the life of faith as the authoritative witness to God, it also lends itself to styles of teaching that are appropriate to this stage. Many of its stories can be geared to the imaginative capacities of children, providing powerful material on the basis of which children can construct their images of God.

Much care should be given to the overall organization of the cycle of Bible stories used in congregational education during this stage and the way the stories are interpreted by the teacher to the children. Teachers should be given much assistance by the curriculum and by the pastoral leadership of the congregation in thinking through the important, normative beliefs of the church that are brought to expression in the biblical material being taught. They must be given the opportunity to think through issues of selection and interpretation in light of the denomination's own doctrinal standards.

Children in the intuitive projective stage of faith are becoming members of a tradition. What tradition is the congregation handing on to them? Much teaching of the Bible to children never surpasses moralism. By every doctrinal standard of import in the Protestant tradition, moralism is inadequate theologically, representing the attempt to secure righteousness before God through human works. Yet children's sermons and church school classes frequently focus their attention almost exclusively on children's moral behavior. The gospel message of God's forgiveness and justifying work in Christ is buried beneath a heavy overlay of moral exhortation. Teachers must think through what the central beliefs of the faith are and allow these beliefs to serve as hermeneutical guides in their presentation of biblical material to children.

The overall organization of biblical material should follow the principle set forth in the first part of this chapter: The content should be aimed at intuitive projective faith while the form should be consistent with the next stage of faith, mythic literal faith. For the moment, let us focus on the form of the material. What is the larger pattern that is used to structure the various Bible stories that are taught? In my view, it should take the form of the next stage, mythic literal faith, in which narrative is important. The overall cycle of individual Bible stories used on different occasions should be woven together into a larger narrative that the teacher constructs on the child's behalf. This prestructures the child's own construction of a narrative on the basis of scripture that becomes a possibility during the next stage. The Bible as canon tells a story. Teachers or church school curriculum should arrange individual Bible stories in a manner that makes this larger narrative evident.

How should the content of the material be presented to the child during this stage? It should focus on teaching approaches that are largely experiential, something that is consistent with the metaphorical knowing of intuitive projective faith. Teaching should start with concrete experiences on the basis of which generalizations about God are formed. It should use experientially oriented methods like drama, storytelling, and dance to present biblical material to children and create concrete experiences they can carry across to form images of God.[22]

When biblical content is presented directly to children, several general rules should be kept in mind. This content should be organized in a simple story form in which a relatively few characters are involved in a plot that is clear and easy to follow. As Kieran Egan points out, the story should be organized in terms of binary opposites, bold contrasts that are unambiguous to the child: good and evil, happy and sad, bad and forgiven, and so forth.[23] To a large extent, these contrasts should be framed in terms of feelings that constitute connecting points between the story and the child's own experience.[24] It is no accident that stories like David and Goliath, which lend themselves to this kind of interpretation, frequently become so powerfully embedded in the imagination during this stage that they are remembered for life.

As we have already mentioned, the congregation is not the primary agent of education during this stage. Of great importance is the role of parents as teachers of the faith in the home. Faith is caught as well as taught during this stage. Many of a child's deepest understandings of God are formed out of the beliefs and values that are communicated indirectly through the everyday life of the family. But parents can strive to be intentional about what they are teaching their children. What are some of the important things that they can do?

First, parents can intentionally form family rituals that embody concretely the meanings of the gospel across the course of the day and the year.[25] The morning meal, for example, can be used as a time for the family to remind itself of the presence of God at the beginning of the day, pausing to recite together a special prayer and offering spontaneous expressions of concern about the day ahead. The end of the day can serve as a time of daily reconciliation, during which parents help children understand relationships or events that are troubling them but which they have difficulty grasping because of cognitive limitations.

Second, parents can self-consciously teach their children those values they believe are consistent with the Christian faith. It is here that the seeds of adult ethical reflection and action are planted. This means that parents need to be clear in their own minds about the values they think are important. They must serve as practical theologians in the home. Surely, values like forgiveness, honesty, humility, love, fairness, and the courage to stand against the crowd are worthy candidates. While these values are largely caught as children see their parents embody them in their own lives, there also is a role for lifting them up in conversation and special times of teaching. Many children's books, for example, can be helpful tools for teaching values, describing situations and characters that embody certain moral attributes.[26] Children's television programs also can be used to teach values, especially when viewed by the parent and child together and discussed.

A third thing families can do is adopt a style of parenting that encourages practical theological reasoning as a part of the ongoing give and take of family life. Children do not wait until they are grown up to begin making moral sense of the situations that impinge on them in light of their understandings of God. It is important for parents to have a clear idea of the kind of moral reasoning children typically employ during this stage and attempt to work within it, meeting children where they are. At the same time, they can be sensitive to signs of stage transition and stretch their children's thinking toward the next stage of faith.[27]

In large measure, children's moral reasoning during this stage is dominated by a fear of punishment and a desire for reward, especially from their parents. In light of their egocentrism, morality seems to move in only one direction: Children obey adults with little sense of why they should obey certain rules or the effects that their actions have on others. Frequently, they follow rules only when an adult is present or when they think there is a good possibility of getting caught.

How can parents meet their children where they are during this stage? In large measure, they can do so by being the authority their children need, appealing to their children's desire to obey.[28] They should explicitly and self-consciously place certain limits on their children, set certain standards of what is right and wrong behavior, and not be afraid to hand out rewards and punishments. This is precisely how their children are learning moral meaning.

At the same time, however, it is crucial that parental authority not be exercised in an arbitrary manner. Martin Hoffman has identified a style of parenting he calls "power assertion."[29] It is a style in which parents issue commands to their children but do not offer reasons as to why the children are being asked to behave in a certain way. Even though children during this stage have difficulty understanding the point of rules because of their cognitive egocentrism, they can begin to develop a sense that rules are not grounded arbitrarily in a parent's own whims but are the outgrowth of certain religious values that the parent prizes. It is important to communicate directly the religious values that underlie the expectations the parent has for the child, modeling the importance of reason-giving in the face of moral situations.

While direct moral instruction of their children is important during this stage, parents should resist the temptation to fall into moralism, giving their children the impression that the heart of the Christian life is trying to do what is right in order to avoid God's punishment and win God's favor. Perhaps the most important way of ensuring that this does not happen is the creation of an atmosphere in the family based on the capacity to give and receive forgiveness. Parents not only need to offer forgiveness to the child, they also need to ask for forgiveness. This should be interpreted to the child as a sign of ways that all of us are dependent upon God's forgiveness, allowing us to keep trying to do our best out of gratitude for God's continuing love in spite of our moral failures.

Mythic Literal Faith

The second stage of faith is called mythic literal faith. This stage begins to emerge between five and seven years and frequently lasts until early adolescence, eleven to thirteen. Some adults, however, are best characterized by this stage. One of the most important aspects of this stage of faith is what Piaget calls "concrete operations": the use of inductive and deductive forms of reasoning on concrete material. This cognitive advance brings about shifts in three important areas.

First, concrete operations affords an understanding of causality that allows the child to distinguish fact from fantasy and to begin constructing a world "out there" that follows laws not of the child's own making. As Egan points out, this newly constructed external world can be quite threatening, and one of the tasks facing congregational education is to provide the child with a narrative by which this reality is named and negotiated.[30] A second thing that concrete operations affords is what Selman calls simple perspective-taking: the ability to view objects and events from another person's point of view.

While the interiority of others—their inner feelings, motives, and personality dynamics—remains relatively undeveloped, this advance in perspective-taking brings about a third important dimension of this stage: reciprocal understanding in the interpersonal domain. Other persons are acknowledged as having a point of view that they bring to relationships and that must be taken into account. Kohlberg identifies the style of moral reasoning that is based on this sort of reciprocity as "tit for tat" or "you scratch my back and I'll scratch yours."[31] Fairness is viewed as the process of making agreements between different parties. This kind of reciprocity in social interaction and moral reasoning spills over into the religious domain. During this stage, it is common for children to view God along the lines of a quid pro quo: "If I follow God's rules and do what God wants me to do, God will take care of me and things will go well; if I do not, God will be angry with me and things will not go well.''`

Concrete operations and the various advances it brings serve as the basis of the central element of mythic literal faith: the rise of the ability to *narratize* experience. Persons in this stage are now able to organize the flow of their experience into an orderly series of events. They possess a new readiness to hear and appropriate the stories of the faith community. In large part, congregational education during this stage focuses on the importance of providing a narrative to children by which they can interpret the newly constructed external world. Perhaps a better way of putting this would be to say that the Christian "myth" should be constitutive of the external world that the child constructs during this stage.

By "myth" we do not mean a statement that is false (e.g., the story about George Washington cutting down a cherry tree is a myth—that is, it is not true). Rather, "myth" here is being used in the fashion of recent cultural anthropology and comparative religion: a narrative by which a community describes ultimate reality and defines everyday patterns of life in relation to that reality. Mircea Eliade, Victor Turner, and others have described the dialectic between sacred times, when the myth is rehearsed in song, ritual, dance, and storytelling, and profane times, in which the roles and relationships of everyday life are lived out.[32] The community's myth names the social and even physical world, providing an interpretive framework by which it is understood. It binds the community together and creates a common identity.[33]

At the heart of a congregation's culture is a myth in this sense, a common story shaping the identities of its members and teaching them to view the world in relation to God. Without question, one of the most important tasks of congregational education during this stage is providing opportunities for children to hear and see this story rehearsed with such power that they begin to identify with it and the community that lives by its meanings. The Christian myth should help them to name the external world, leading them to view it in ways that stand in tension with other social definitions to which they are exposed.[34] But where in contemporary congregational life is met the yearning of mythic literal faith for communal stories that can help it name reality? Where are found the moments of ritual and spoken word that truly have the power to influence the child's understanding of life? What are some of the ways that the congregation can lift up its story for persons in mythic literal faith and for the community as a whole?

Ideally, in its weekly worship the congregation narrates in song, ritual, and sermon the story by which it lives as a community, a story that has the power to name the external world and transform the roles and relationships of secularized life into opportunities for vocation. The recent interest in the liturgical seasons of the Christian year that can structure preaching and liturgy represents an important step toward rehearsing the Christian story as a whole over the course of the year. Many Protestant churches would do well to recover other facets of their liturgical heritage that would allow them to dramatize this story more directly in ritual in ways that can capture the imagination of children.

Sunday morning worship is not the only time when the mythic dimensions of the community can be rehearsed. Special transitional moments in the life cycle (birth of a child, marriage, moving, retirement) or marker events in congregational participation (confirmation, first communion, election as a church officer, becoming a teacher) also can provide powerful opportunities for the linkage of the Christian story and the individual as he or she moves through the life cycle.[35] One of the most important of these sorts of rituals explicitly linked to this stage of faith during the classic period of the Reformation was catechetical instruction, called confirmation in the modern church. While the timing of this rite has been the subject of some debate, a strong case can be made for continuing to link it with mythic literal faith.

The discontinuation of instruction in a catechism by most mainline denominations has left a major void in congregational education during this stage of faith. This was one of the primary means of initiating all members into the Christian story. While much of the content of classical catechisms was far too difficult for children in this stage to understand (requiring abstract reasoning not yet achieved), there was real genius in the basic intent of teaching a common catechism. It served as a way of mediating normative beliefs to every church member, beliefs that possess the authority of representative bodies and not merely that of individual ministers or church educators. It also was a way of mediating the teachings of other centers of teaching authority to the congregation.

Mainline Protestant churches would do well to reestablish the functional equivalent of catechetical instruction during this stage of faith. They should do so, however, in a way that embodies the educational principle that the content of teaching should be accessible to a given stage but the form should point to the next stage. The catechisms worked best when they came the closest to embodying this principle. They told the story of the Christian faith in the flow of their questions and answers but articulated this story in terms of explicit theological beliefs that are more appropriate to the next stage. Both the Larger and Shorter Westminster catechisms, for example, place the story of Adam and Eve near the beginning and formulate questions about sin within the context of the story of the Fall. A modern catechism should carry out this principle even more explicitly. The outline of the Christian story as given in scripture should determine the basic flow of the catechism, with questions about issues like sin, the law, and the atonement emerging within the context of this story.[36] Narrative should constitute the basic content of the catechism, while the doctrinal beliefs of the question-and-answer format should constitute its basic form.

Thus far, we have focused our attention on the congregation. The family's role during this stage should also be highlighted. Almost everything that was said about the family in the previous stages continues to be operative. Families can do much to influence the child's understanding of God and to encourage practical theological reasoning that is appropriate to this stage of faith. With regard to the latter, it is important that parents work within the present structures of mythic literal reasoning while attempting to stretch them toward the next stage.

At an earlier point, we described the kind of reciprocity that characterizes social and moral reasoning during this stage. There are many situations in which parents would do well to draw on the logic of reciprocal reasoning in relating to their child. In light of an argument with a friend at school, a ten-year-old might say, "Why should I try to set things right? He started it. Why should I be nice to him if he's not going to be nice to me?" Parents can work within this style of reasoning in an attempt to communicate something of their religious values: "If you are not willing to forgive others who have done something bad to you, how can you expect others to forgive you when you hurt them? Jesus told us to forgive one another again and again."

Parents need a light touch in linking religious values to moral reasoning in order not to fall into moralism. Nevertheless, they should teach such values to their children directly and in conjunction with real-life situations. The kinds of values that children use to carry out reciprocal reasoning make a real difference. Contrast these two statements, both of which employ reciprocal reasoning: "Shoot the ball whenever you get a chance because everybody else is going to do the same thing" and "Try to do your part as a member of the team so others will want to do their part too." Very different values are being communicated, though both are appealing to reciprocal reasoning.

These illustrations are indicative, however, of the reasons that parents need to stretch their children beyond this stage of moral reasoning and point to the important role of religious values and beliefs in helping them do so.[37] Reciprocal moral reasoning—tit for tat—falls short of the kind of love that lies at the heart of the gospel: While we were yet sinners, Christ Jesus died for us. As recipients of this love, Christians are to love others, even when there is nothing in it for them. Parents must appeal to and enact this sort of love in their interaction with their children. It is also important that they involve their children in family activities in which this love is acted out: helping an elderly neighbor, participating in a soup kitchen, befriending a family that is in need of help.

In short, the parent as practical theologian must walk a tightrope between working within the styles of reasoning that come naturally to the child and stretching this reasoning by introducing religious themes that are not reducible to the logic of reciprocity. An overemphasis on the former leaves the child within a moral world of tradeoffs. A premature concentration on the latter can push the child beyond what he or she can really understand and end up reinforcing a kind of moralism. Judgment and balance are called for in the effort to accept the child where he or she is and plant the seeds of future faith development.

Youth and Adult Stages of Faith: Becoming Participants in the Tradition

Synthetic Conventional Faith

The transition from mythic literal faith to this stage is closely related to the advent of what Piaget calls formal operations: the ability to engage in hypothetico-deductive reasoning. Typically, near the beginning of adolescence in American culture, children begin to use general concepts and hypotheses in the service of abstract reasoning. The single most important item, which the advent of formal operations makes possible, is a major shift in perspective-taking. Persons can now engage in mutual interpersonal perspective-taking: the ability to construct another individual's perspective, not just on an object or event but on them. (I see you seeing me.)

This is based on a deeper awareness of the interiority of others: their thoughts, feelings, and expectations. This ability to take another's perspective on one's self gradually becomes mutual, as persons in this stage become aware that other people recognize that they too are forming a perspective on them. (I see you seeing me seeing you.) Suddenly, the interpersonal world comes alive, as persons become highly sensitive to the thoughts and feelings of others. Closely related to this is the construction of a composite of perspectives from the interpersonal domain, forming what George Herbert Mead called the "generalized other." This is a general group norm representing what "they" think and not just the perspective of another individual.

The advent of mutual interpersonal perspective-taking and the generalized other lead to what Sharon Parks calls a "mirror self."[38] With a heightened sensitivity to the thoughts and feelings of others and to social norms (especially those of the peer group), persons begin to define themselves in terms of the reflected appraisals of significant others and primary reference groups. Their moral reasoning is closely related to this mirroring process, drawing on conventional expectations of what a nice person is supposed to do and be. Being a "good" daughter, for example, means fulfilling parental expectations or substituting for them a different set of expectations derived from the peer group.

These general cognitive and perspective-taking advances set the stage for the style of faith knowing that characterizes synthetic conventional faith. This is a stage in which persons form their centers of value and meaning in terms of the values and beliefs of significant others and primary reference groups.[39] While persons can stand outside of the flow of experience and form abstract generalizations by which to describe it, the generalizations they construct to form their basic values and beliefs are deeply dependent on the important persons and groups with which they identify. They key off others in the construction of their own beliefs and values. Moreover, their faith is tacit in the sense that it has not been critically examined and self-consciously chosen. Another way of putting this is to describe synthetic conventional faith as a stage of conformity.[40] It is a time in which persons look to the expectations of significant others and primary reference groups, accepting the roles, beliefs, and values that they prize.

In light of this understanding of the way persons construct their centers of value and meaning during this stage, what shape should congregational education take? In answering this question, it is important to point out that many adults do not move beyond this stage of faith. While we will describe the forms of congregational education that are important to this stage in terms of ministry with youth, virtually everything that is said about the importance of relational forms of ministry and the need to project a clear set of theological and moral norms is also applicable to adult forms of synthetic conventional faith.

Persons in this stage are now ready to become full participants in the Christian tradition. They can play a more active role in using the beliefs and moral values of the Christian faith to construct an understanding of who they are and to engage the various life situations that confront them. The accent of congregational education begins to shift from socialization to a more critical appropriation of the tradition, something that is more fully taken up in the following stage. Persons come to the dialogue of the teaching office with an ability to articulate their own beliefs and values and the general norms of the faith community in which they participate.

It is precisely because of the tendency of persons in this stage to limit themselves to the conventions of their immediate communities that the need for participation in broader forms of the teaching office is so important. Exposure to perspectives that go beyond and expand those of the local community can enrich the tacitly held beliefs and values that persons in this stage are constructing. Those who work closely with young people have long known the importance of educational opportunities that can stretch them: regional youth retreats, multi-church service projects that take young people into a different community, summer leadership seminars, and cross-cultural exchanges. All these have tremendous educational potential and represent important opportunities to initiate youth into the broader conversation of the teaching office by which the church struggles together to determine what it believes about God and how it can best serve God in the contemporary world. Young people during this stage are looking to others to help them construct their central values and beliefs. It is crucial that the circle of those who count is expanded through participation in a dialogical teaching office.

Even in a viable teaching office, however, this stage is characterized by conformity, and the heart of congregational education for youth can be summarized as follows: Provide a clear set of theological and moral conventions to which young people can conform. The question is not whether they will conform; it is what they will conform to. It makes a tremendous difference whether they appropriate the more materialistic or nihilistic sides of youth culture or whether they are offered a clear alternative that is based on a Christian social conscience and a fuller sense of the problems, needs, and perspectives of others as mediated through the teaching office. In both cases, social conventions will be internalized and tacitly held, but the quality of moral and religious commitment will be drastically different.

How are these conventions best communicated during this stage? It is not surprising in light of mutual interpersonal perspective-taking that what have come to be called relational forms of youth ministry are extremely important. This style of congregational education is based on a recognition of the need to develop strong relationships, not only with adult leaders but also between young people themselves. This acknowledges synthetic conventional faith's orientation toward the values and expectations of significant others and primary reference groups and matches it with adults and a youth peer group that places a great deal of emphasis on relationships.

Adult leaders must be willing to meet young people on their own turf. Activities that are not explicitly religious (e.g., attending ball games, eating lunch together, sponsoring a social event) are crucial ways of building relationships. Only to the extent that an adult leader truly becomes a significant other will he or she be taken seriously. Young people will begin to identify themselves in terms of those values and beliefs that the leader prizes. Similarly, great importance should be attached to the group atmosphere that permeates the classroom or the youth group. In light of their sensitivity to the interpersonal realm, most young people are vulnerable to the negative messages that so often emerge from the natural cliquishness characterizing this stage. It is crucial that the church youth peer group do more than merely reflect this cliquishness; it must become a place where young people experience a sense of belonging that is grounded in their common loyalty to Jesus Christ.[41]

In addition to relational forms of ministry, congregational education should also attempt to nurture the practical theological reflection of those in this stage. Young people are now capable of engaging in practical theological reasoning at a depth that was not possible at previous stages. The ability to engage in abstract reasoning, to construct the interiority of others, and to form a general perspective on social realities makes possible a qualitatively new level of theological and moral reflection. Youth leaders can nurture this sort of reflection in several important ways.

First, they should be intentional about projecting a clear set of conventions that are couched in interpersonal terms. As we have seen, persons in this stage view morality in terms of living up to their understanding of what a "good boy" or "good girl" should be and do. This set of internal expectations is a composite of the values and beliefs of significant others and peer groups with which they identify. It is extremely important that the congregation in its work with youth project a clear image of those qualities that characterize a good Christian. These qualities should be portrayed in interpersonal terms: that is, as qualities of relationship. For example: Good Christians are honest with one another and with their friends. They don't always think just about themselves but try to take the needs of others into account. They are especially sensitive to those who don't fit in—the newcomer, the person who is overweight, the quiet one. Christians can think for themselves. They don't always go along with the group just because everybody else is doing something.

This same emphasis on the interpersonal should influence the way that youth leaders present God to persons in this stage. Many young people yearn for a deeper, more personal relationship with God, based on a richer sense of God's interiority that is comparable to the interiority of other persons. Charles Shelton has developed a friendship model of spirituality that is especially appropriate to this stage, focusing on Jesus as a friend with whom time should be spent and honest communication developed, and who can provide support and guidance in times of need.[42] Small-group Bible studies that allow for personal sharing and attempt to build community also can play an important role during this stage.[43] Projecting this sort of understanding of God and a clear image of what a good Christian is like meets synthetic conventional youth where they are and provides them with an internal set of beliefs and values that they can use to negotiate the various relationships in which they are involved.

While this emphasis on the interpersonal is not fully adequate to the totality of the Christian faith (Jesus is not just a friend but is also our judge, Lord, and redeemer), it is appropriate for persons in this stage. The congregation would do well, however, to balance this emphasis with a second approach to the education of practical theological reflection: the cultivation of the capacity to reflect critically on personal experience and the surrounding world.

Michael Warren and Thomas Groome point to what I have in mind here in their concepts of politicization and shared praxis.[44] Both men call attention to the ways that young people can now step outside of their experience and reflect upon it critically. While this is not to be confused with full-scale individuation, it does represent the ability to use abstract reasoning to form general concepts about the surrounding world, allowing persons to become aware of the ways that various social forces influence their lives.[45] Denominational curriculum material should be developed that uses this educational approach to expose young people to pressing concerns that the church has addressed in its social teachings (such as nuclear disarmament, the economy, and religion in public life). In this way, it would be an accepted convention for young people to reflect critically on social issues the church as a whole has deemed important.

An important part of the capacity to reflect critically on personal experience and the surrounding world is the construction of a set of beliefs and values affording a perspective by which the various items that are the focus of critical reflection can be evaluated.[46] For this reason, it is crucial that young people be given an opportunity to engage in serious intellectual study of the teachings that constituted the basis of their catechetical instruction. They are now ready to appropriate intellectually the beliefs and values that they were taught in conjunction with the Christian story as it was told during the previous stage.

The relationship between content and form that we examined in each of the earlier stages continues to hold true. Persons in synthetic conventional faith have beliefs and values in the sense of constructing abstract concepts about God and the Christian life. But they do not yet "have" the larger theological or ideological system of which these beliefs and values are a part. This will only emerge during the next stage of faith. It is important, however, that teachers and leaders articulate the theology that undergirds the beliefs and moral values they are attempting to communicate. In this way, young people will gain a glimpse of the kind of issues they will have to grapple with in constructing their own theological perspective.

Congregational education during this stage has been described in terms of ministry with youth. As was pointed out above, many adults do not move out of this stage of faith. It is not hard to see the relationship between what we have already described in conjunction with youth ministry and much ministry to adults in the congregation. It is relationally oriented, focusing on visitation, fellowship, and pastoral care. It assumes a tacitly held set of beliefs and values that permeate the congregation as a whole or certain groups within the congregation (a church school class, a Bible study, or the like). Rational justification of committee decisions on the basis of an explicit theology or ethic is rarely called for. While it is important for congregational leaders to understand and work within the style of faith knowing that characterizes synthetic conventional faith, it is also important that they have a clear idea of the next stage of faith development in order to help individuals and the congregation as a whole to face the challenges and opportunities of individuation.

Individuative Reflective Faith

While individuation is not the *telos* of faith development theory, it is one of several important aims that it brings into focus for congregational education. All too frequently, congregations content themselves with a style of faith that is primarily conventional, emphasizing understandings of God and the Christian life that have a highly interpersonal flavor. The central achievement of individuative reflective faith is the ability to stand outside of those beliefs and values that were tacitly held at the previous stage, to locate them in a general theological and ideological system, to compare and contrast that system with others, and then self-consciously to construct a theological perspective that is thought to be true.

In short, a full-scale process of individuation takes place. Persons "own" their beliefs and values in ways that were not possible during the previous stage. They become *participants* in the Christian tradition in a qualitatively new way, drawing on its storehouse of theological and ethical understandings to form an explicit and self-chosen set of ideas by which to interpret the various situations that confront them in life. They now have a theological perspective on the basis of which they can undertake practical theological reflection in a disciplined and self-conscious fashion.

There are two closely related but distinguishable aspects of the process of individuation characterizing this stage of faith: the emergence of what Fowler calls an "executive ego" and the formation of a clear ideology. These two tasks do not necessarily take place at the same time.

The emergence of an executive ego focuses on the development of a sense of self that is not strictly a function of the reflected appraisals of significant others and primary reference groups. The person now has a self that is independent of and can be expressed through the various roles and relationships in which he or she participates. As the term "executive" implies, the person has internalized authority that previously was granted to others. There is an "I" that is in charge of and negotiates the different choices and commitments that a person makes.

As a part of constructing and sustaining this newfound sense of self, persons in individuative reflective faith carry out a second task: the formation of a clear ideology. By "ideology" is meant a system of ideas by which a person articulates his or her centers of value and meaning and the nature of the world in relation to these centers of value and meaning. The capacity for abstract thinking is now used to its fullest. Persons are not satisfied with beliefs and values they have taken over from others but strive to form a comprehensive conceptual framework in which these beliefs are defined and developed in a systematic fashion. An important part of forming an individuated self thus involves the ability to construct an explicit, self-chosen set of ideas by which a person can articulate what he or she holds to be true. A person may make the transition to this stage by leading with either the emergence of an executive ego or the construction of an ideology. It is not infrequent for persons to focus primarily on one of these tasks in the initial phase of stage transition and then build on the gains that have been made as the other central aspect of the transition is faced.

Many persons begin the transition to this stage during college years, for example, leading with the construction of an ideology and dealing with the tasks involved in forming an executive ego only after graduation as they are forced to accept responsibility for their lives in a variety of ways. Conversely, many persons only move to this stage as they confront mid-life and begin to struggle with the question of who they are when they are not defined by their job or their parenting role. They lead with the issues surrounding the emergence of an executive ego, and only later do they engage in the task of constructing a set of ideas by which to define their own beliefs. In my own research on a parachurch group that sponsors spiritual renewal retreats for long-time church members, still another pattern emerged. The only persons who began to make a stage transition as a result of the retreat were persons who had undergone emotional experiences in which they had come to realize God's love in a deeply personal fashion. This emotional renegotiation of internal images of God seemed to provide them with the permission to claim internal authority and gave them the motivation to figure out their own theological perspective.

Congregational education must be sensitive to the wide variety of ways by which persons make the transition into this stage of faith. Not only should leaders of the church be on the lookout for signs of stage transition, they also should design intentional contexts of education that are explicitly oriented toward helping persons grapple with the kinds of issues involved in making the transition to individuative reflective faith. One of the most important contexts is small high-commitment groups designed to combine study and personal sharing.

One such group could be geared primarily to young adults. All too often, Christian groups on college campuses are little more than extensions of the kind of youth ministry that is appropriate to synthetic conventional faith. The kind of group that would support persons in the transition to an individuative reflective style of faith is different in significant ways. Emphasis should not be placed on the communication of a clear set of conventions to the group. Indeed, almost the opposite is called for; persons would be encouraged and supported in their struggle to define their *own* values and beliefs. Ideally, a balance would be achieved between intimacy, which allows genuine sharing, and honest confrontation, which holds people accountable for their decisions and presses them to achieve greater clarity about the values and beliefs that they really prize. Small-group Bible study or vocation-clarification groups, designed to assist persons in discerning God's call in the various commitments they are making, would be especially appropriate in helping young adults deal with the issues involved in making the transition to a more individuated faith.

A second group of a similar nature could be geared toward persons who are entering mid-life. Research has shown that a number of men and women begin to undertake the work of individuation during this period of their life as they struggle to define themselves beyond their roles at work and at home. Such groups could strive to achieve the same combination of personal sharing and study. While their central focus would vary (e.g., deepening discipleship, women in transition, life beyond mid-life, reworking our vocations), they would all focus on assisting persons in examining critically the values and beliefs of their life to that point and providing them with support in taking responsibility for the next phases of their lives in a qualitatively new way.

Congregational education would do well to offer as a third setting ongoing church school classes that are primarily oriented toward individuative reflective issues. Congregational leaders should attempt to identify such classes already in existence or should try to organize a church school class or weekly Bible study that is geared toward this stage, if none already exists. It is important that new members or long-term members who seem to be moving into this stage find a context in the church that supports them in their struggle toward individuation. Too often, people feel compelled to go elsewhere to examine the values and beliefs they were socialized into or to raise hard theoretical questions about the church and theology.

These sorts of classes typically cannot foster the same level of personal sharing that small high-commitment groups achieve. They serve another purpose, however, providing persons with the kind of conceptual material that is needed to construct a full-fledged theology. They also provide opportunities for persons to test out their theology in dialogue and debate with others in the class. It is extremely important that this sort of class offer its members general concepts and principles and point to the ideological schemas that these concepts and principles are a part of. In this way persons construct not only beliefs about God and the world in relation to God but the theological frameworks in which these beliefs are located.

It is not enough, for example, for persons to understand intellectually basic beliefs of the Christian tradition like the atonement, salvation, the person and work of Christ, and providence. They now must be exposed to different theological perspectives on these beliefs and encouraged to determine for themselves which theological perspective is the most adequate. For example, it is one thing to know that the Reformed tradition has always placed great emphasis on God's electing power and quite another to recognize the major differences between Barth's and Calvin's understandings of this theological doctrine. Persons in this stage of faith are now capable of understanding what is at stake theologically in this matter.

Is it too much to expect church members to become this knowledgeable of scripture and theology? I think not. Many are hungering for classes that will challenge them to engage in serious theological reflection. What is missing are curricular resources and classes in the congregation that undertake this kind of reflection. Seminaries and denominational publishing houses would do well to work together in creating a literature that uses the critical findings of scholarship within an educational format that is accessible to persons who are just beginning to construct a full-scale theological perspective.

What persons who are moving into this stage cannot do, however, is simultaneously construct an ideational system as part of the process of individuation and recognize the limitations of the particular ideology that they are forming. Once more the educational form must point toward the next stage of faith, even as the content is geared toward present structures of faith knowing. During individuative reflective faith, this means the persons must be invited to construct ideologies in the midst of a dialogical form. What does this involve?

It is not infrequent for highly ideological, charismatic leaders to be adept at provoking the transition to this stage of faith. Persons do the work of individuative reflective faith in terms of the conceptual framework that the leader and the group provide. What is unfortunate about this way of moving into this stage is that it reinforces the tendency to engage in the sort of dichotomizing, reductionist reasoning that is an inevitable part of individuative reflective faith. The leader and the group are seen as having the truth, which is set against all other perspectives. The truth of others is not fully taken into account.

Congregational education during this stage can lay the foundation for a movement beyond this kind of ideological reductionism by helping persons develop higher-level conceptual frameworks in the midst of a dialogical setting. Persons are encouraged to form their own ideological perspective, but they are not offered a *single* perspective that is held by a dominant leader or by the congregation as a whole. They will define their beliefs over against other positions, but as they do so, they continue to relate to others who subscribe to positions that are different from their own. This can qualify the real narrowness of groups and persons who offer persons moving into this stage a monolithic framework. There is no encouragement from within such groups to move beyond the limitations of individuative reflective faith.

Once more, we are faced with the need for congregations to participate in the broader dialogue of the teaching office. To the extent that this dialogue is a living reality in the congregation, persons will be confronted on an ongoing basis with perspectives that are different from their own. There is no question that this can lead to the politicization of the church's teaching ministry, if the ideological style of faith that characterizes this stage is allowed to determine the tone of this dialogue. Several denominations are engaged in such highly charged ideological struggles at the present time. Questions of truth are defined in either/or terms. The position of opponents is ridiculed. The determination of the church's normative beliefs and practices becomes more a matter of power than of teaching authority resting on perceived competence and wisdom. The individuative reflective stage of faith cannot sustain a dialogical model of the teaching office, for this office is dependent upon leaders who have transcended a narrowly ideological understanding of the faith and can articulate the theological grounds of a more inclusive understanding of the church's teaching ministry.

Conjunctive Faith: Becoming Guardians of the Tradition

Conjunctive faith is characterized by the willingness to engage reality in a paradoxical and multileveled fashion that is absent from the previous stage. The focus of its attention is no longer on individuation and ideology formation. It can assume these things and allow them to move into the background. One of the major characteristics of conjunctive faith is its recognition of the limitations of its own ideological perspective and the need to engage the perspectives of others in order to discern the truth. It has moved beyond the previous stage's tendency toward reductionism in this regard and has the capacity to suspend its own perspective temporarily and enter into the "otherness" of different persons, groups, and causes. Its view of truth is paradoxical, holding in tension various perspectives that cannot be readily reduced to logical compatibility. This openness, however, is not to be confused with a synthetic conventional version of relativism. It is a principled openness, an openness grounded in the convictions of a particular tradition and the perspective on truth that it engenders.

Persons in this stage of faith have the capacity to be guardians of the faith tradition. At earlier stages, persons have been equipped by the congregation to become members of their tradition by incorporating its images and stories into their understanding of God and the world in relation to God. They have been encouraged to become participants in the tradition, using its beliefs and moral values in order to construct their personal identities and to engage the world around them. But now they must do more. They must serve as guardians of the tradition, handing on its central meanings and extending them into the present in light of the needs and issues of the contemporary situation. Only persons who know and love a tradition while recognizing its limitations can guard it against the dangers of both an overaccommodation to the surrounding world and a sterile protectionism of its past expressions.

Jaroslav Pelikan once pointed out that tradition is the living faith of the dead while traditionalism is the dead faith of the living.[47] Guardians of a tradition know what is at stake in this distinction and are concerned to use their tradition as a foundation for living faith in the present. It is not infrequent for persons in the previous stage to view themselves as the guardians of Christian truth and the true protectors of its genuine meaning. In their hands, the teaching office can become a club to beat into submission those who disagree or to ward off every challenge to the "true" perspective. This is why persons become the real guardians of the faith only when they have the capacity to view their own particular theological position as part of a much richer and broader religious tradition, as the finite expression of a truth that transcends any human formulation. To guard the tradition means more than defensively protecting it. It is to preserve its function as a medium of truth, not the truth itself, as a womb of living faith.

Both individuals and congregations can serve as guardians of their tradition in this sense. At an earlier point, we pointed out that conjunctive faith represents the ideal modal level of a congregation that is a full participant in the teaching office. Persons are invited to take into account the perspectives of multiple teaching authorities located at different levels of the church's life. They are asked to hold in tension the different perspectives and truths these authorities articulate. Both directly through congregational education and indirectly through the ongoing patterns of congregational life they are taught that they are part of a much larger dialogue through which their own perspective and that of the congregation as a whole are broadened and enriched.

Persons in this stage are especially ready for this dialogue among various centers of teaching authority, and it is not difficult to imagine some of the ways they might be supported in their participation. Materials written by theologians working in seminary contexts could be particularly helpful in deepening persons' understanding of their own religious heritage and the way it is part of the broader Christian tradition. Such material could also articulate important theological issues in their complexity and the different stances that have developed in the past and are emerging in the present. The special competence of theological scholars is used to help persons move beyond reductionistic, monolithic stances on complex issues.

Preaching about and study of the various social policy statements the denomination has produced also could serve as a way of encouraging persons to move beyond their own perspectives. Frequently, these teachings invite them to take into account groups and moral issues that are not a part of their ongoing life. Participation in the teaching office encourages them to acknowledge the limitations of their own perspective and the moral relevance of that of others. In a similar fashion, ecumenical and interfaith dialogue between the congregation and other religious communities can help persons move beyond the reductionistic stereotypes so frequently present in religious communities. It also can afford them the opportunity to see themselves through others' eyes, opening them to the strengths and limitations of their own faith tradition.

These examples could be multiplied many times over. The point is relatively simple: Congregations through their ongoing interaction with multiple sources of truth in the teaching office can engage their members in the kind of expansive dialogue that encourages them to move toward conjunctive faith. This does not negate the need to form a strong Christian identity at earlier stages based on the normative beliefs and practices of the church. It presupposes this process of identity formation. But it also recognizes the importance of a genuinely dialogical style of faith knowing in individuals, congregations, and the teaching office as a whole. Without leaders who embody the kind of principled openness that characterizes this stage of faith, it will not be possible for the church to sustain itself as a community of communities, a community in which a wide range of institutions and offices are seen as important.

Intentional contexts of teaching and learning also have something of great significance to offer to the congregation's formation of an educational program that assists persons in moving toward this stage. Styles of teaching can be employed that help persons break open the tight, systematic ideologies they constructed at the previous stage and become more open to the truth claims of other perspectives. Egan is helpful at this point in describing the intentional introduction of anomalies in teaching.[48] In helping persons consolidate individuative reflective faith, teachers should offer students general categories by which they can construct higher-level theoretical perspectives. To help them move beyond that stage, however, they should introduce anomalies that challenge the adequacy of these categories as definitive accounts of reality. An anomaly is knowledge that cannot be explained or understood from within a particular theoretical perspective. It simply does not fit. When taken seriously, an anomaly forces those who subscribe to a particular theoretical perspective to acknowledge its limitations and to open themselves to the truth of alternatives.

An especially important way of introducing anomalies in congregational (and seminary) education is by inviting persons to bring their theological or ethical perspective into dialogue with those portions of scripture that cannot be reduced to its formulations without remainder. Theologies that place a strong accent on God's transcedence, for example, could be asked to come to grips with the heavy emphasis on God's providential care and participation in historical processes pointed to at various places in scripture. Such anomalies can help persons recognize the partiality of their own theology and begin to open them to the need for the corrective influence of other perspectives.

Moreover, a congregation that provides opportunities for its members to engage in practical theological reflection in the course of its church work and in conjunction with their own lives provides an important context for the emergence of conjunctive faith. At its best, practical theological reflection comes to grips with the particularity inherent in every situation that it is interpreting and responding to. General categories of understanding are helpful in orienting persons to the important issues at stake in the situation, but they ultimately cannot tell a person what to do in *this* particular situation.

In a sense, this brings us full circle. Congregations as communities of practical theological discourse have an important responsibility to teach their members the basic theological and moral concepts by which they, as individuals, are enabled to carry out practical theological reflection. Individual members, in the midst of the various social practices that structure their everyday lives, constantly confront situations that bring them up short and elicit practical theological reflection. Such reflection can deepen social life into an opportunity for vocation, forcing them to ask: In the face of this concrete situation, what is God requiring and enabling me to do and be? Individual Christians will only be able to answer this question if they are part of a congregation whose educational ministry equips them with the tools to carry out practical theological reflection. In so doing, a congregation also will be encouraging its members to become guardians of the faith tradition, mastering its normative expressions and extending them into the present in conjunction with the unique problems and possibilities of the day.

Congregations will only be able to teach this kind of practical theological reflection if they themselves are participants in a dialogical teaching office, a teaching office in which the congregation is constantly conversing with other centers of teaching authority: seminaries, professional theologians, denominational agencies and leaders, representative bodies, and other congregations. Paul's description of the church as the body of Christ is apt. The congregation cannot do the individual's work as a practical theologian. The denomination in its various forms cannot replace the congregation, nor can the congregation thrive without the broader expressions of church life that the denomination embodies. Seminaries as the intellectual center of the church's life can deepen the congregation's theological and ethical reflection.

Mainline Protestant Christianity is in need of persons who can grasp the vision of a teaching office that builds on the very best of the Reformation heritage. Such leaders and the congregations in their charge will recognize the importance of forming institutions and processes by which denominations can teach the normative beliefs and practices that are the basis of their common identity. They will also recognize, however, that such beliefs and practices remain finite, fallible expressions of the gospel and scripture at any given time and are subject to correction. Only this sort of critical affirmation of teaching authority is adequate to the vision the Reformers projected. For this reason, the mainline churches have a great deal at stake in the nurture of a conjunctive style of faith in their educational ministries.

Epilogue

Mainline Protestantism is at a crossroads. The path it chooses
to travel today will be of great consequence well into the next
century. Its continued diminishment cannot help but diminish
the whole of American life. The challenges before it are great,
to be sure. It must come to grips with the fact that it is now
one of many religious communities with influence and power
in American life. It must recognize its tendency to accommodate to the surrounding culture and confuse the Christian way
of life with the American way of life. It must realize that its
low birth rate points to the likelihood that it will not reproduce itself at the same rate as other religious communities. It
must form a new, more critical civic piety among its members.

These realities and others represent major challenges to the
way that the mainline Protestant churches historically have
viewed their role in American society. At the same time, they
represent opportunities. They represent the opportunity for
these churches to rediscover their heritage and to begin defining themselves less in terms of the surrounding culture and
more in terms of what it means to be the church of Jesus
Christ in the contemporary world. They represent a chance
for these churches to become clearer about their religious
identities and the normative beliefs and practices that sustain
these identities. They present the possibility of a new civic
faith that can sustain dialogue and openness in a pluralistic
society without sacrificing commitment to those beliefs and
values that are consistent with the biblical witness.

It will be unlikely, if not impossible, for any of these possibilities to come to pass without the emergence of a much
stronger teaching office in the Protestant main stream. Only as
these churches come to grips with their need to determine

their normative beliefs and practices, to reinterpret these beliefs and practices in shifting cultural and historical contexts, and to form institutions that give support to ongoing teaching at every level of church life will they develop the capacity to transform the problems that beset them today into new patterns of church life tomorrow.

The need for leaders with a clear understanding of the importance of the teaching office to the future of mainline Protestantism is present in each of the three centers of teaching authority. It is not merely the concern of those who teach Christian education in the seminaries. It embraces the very heart of what it means to serve as the intellectual center of the church's life, balancing a scholarly commitment to truth with a real concern for congregational and denominational life. Nor is it merely the issue of those who participate in agencies charged with overseeing the denomination's educational program. It goes to the very heart of the work of representative bodies and leaders. Nor is the importance of the congregation's educational ministry merely the concern of the church educator or a few committed laypersons working in this area. It is the heart and soul of a congregation's ability to form and transform persons with the capacity to link theology and life in the service of Christian vocation.

It is perhaps foolish to single out any group of leaders as especially important to the recovery of a stronger teaching office in mainline Protestantism. Honesty, however, forces me to conclude by doing so. The ordained ministers of the church are in the best position to facilitate the emergence of a revitalized teaching office in the contemporary church. It is they who can interpret the work of professional theologians and seminaries to the congregation. At the same time, it is they who can put pressure on this center of teaching authority to fulfill its role in the teaching office in terms of its scholarly work and its theological education. Ministers are best able to mediate denominational teaching to the congregation and to call the denomination at every level to take its teaching ministry seriously. But most important of all, the ministers of the church are in the best position to lead congregations to an understanding of themselves as centers of teaching and practical theological reflection and not just as places where personal needs are met and crises surmounted.

It will not do for the ministers of the church to wait for changes in other centers of the teaching office, important as these are. They must begin to rethink their own ministerial commitments, the way they do or do not reflect a commitment to the church's teaching ministry. Teaching ministers will give birth to teaching congregations. Teaching congregations will give rise to denominational leaders and bodies that can once again teach with authority. Denominations committed to teaching will give rise to seminaries that view themselves as contributors to the teaching office. Ideally, changes should take place simultaneously at all levels of church life, for each center of teaching authority has its own unique contribution to make. But the ministers of the church have a special opportunity and responsibility to take the lead. It is for them that the mainline Protestant churches are waiting.

Notes

Chapter 1: Mainline Churches in Crisis

1. Wade Clark Roof and William McKinney, *American Mainline Religion: Its Changing Shape and Future* (New Brunswick, N.J.: Rutgers University Press, 1987), pp. 33–39. They are drawing on Robert Handy's use of the term "disestablishment"; see *A Christian America* (New York: Oxford University Press, 1984), ch. 7. Handy argues that the changes going on today are the aftershocks of the second disestablishment of Protestantism, which took place during the 1920s and 1940s. Others, like Stephen Tipton, have argued that the sixties were a watershed in their own right. See Stephen Tipton, *Getting Saved from the Sixties* (Berkeley, Calif.: University of California Press, 1982).

2. In particular see the following works for the theological renewal of pastoral care and counseling: Charles Gerkin, *The Living Human Document: Revisioning Pastoral Counseling in a Hermeneutical Mode* (Nashville: Abingdon Press, 1984), and *Widening the Horizons: Pastoral Responses to a Fragmented Society* (Philadelphia: Westminster Press, 1986); Thomas Oden, "Recovering Lost Identity," in *Journal of Pastoral Care*, vol. 34, no. 1 (1980).

3. I am using "rediscovery" and "recovery" in Jaroslav Pelikan's sense. The former refers to a renewed historical awareness of something; the latter, to an appreciation of what has been rediscovered to the extent that it alters present values, attitudes, and practices. See his *The Vindication of Tradition* (New Haven, Conn.: Yale University Press, 1984), chs. 1 and 2.

4. Roof and McKinney, *American Mainline Religion*, ch. 3.

5. Ibid., ch. 5. The discussion that follows is deeply indebted to the demographic work and analysis in this book.

6. Ibid., p. 161.

7. Ibid.

8. Ibid., p. 165
9. Ibid., pp. 168–169.
10. Ibid., p. 177
11. Ibid.
12. Ibid., pp. 168–169.
13. Ibid., p. 170
14. Ibid., p. 16
15. Ibid.
16. See, for example, Parker J. Palmer's *The Company of Strangers: Christians and the Renewal of America's Public Life* (New York: Crossroad Publishing Co., 1981) and Jack Seymour, Robert O'Gorman, and Charles Foster, *The Church in the Education of the Public* (Nashville: Abingdon Press, 1984).
17. Richard Neuhaus, *The Naked Public Square: Religion and Democracy in America* (Grand Rapids: Wm. B. Eerdmans Publishing Co., 1984).
18. Roof and McKinney, *American Mainline Religion*, ch. 6.
19. H. Richard Niebuhr, "Back to Benedict?" *Christian Century*, vol. 42 (1925), pp. 860–861. Niebuhr argued this position in a different way under the influence of neo-orthodoxy when he wrote *The Church Against the World* (Chicago: Willett, Clark & Co., 1935) with Wilhelm Pauck and Francis Miller. Perhaps it is no accident that Alasdair MacIntyre has drawn on this same image near the end of his recent book *After Virtue* (Notre Dame, Ind.: University of Notre Dame Press, 1981), p. 245. Modern society, he writes, is waiting for a "new Benedict," a person and a community that can reestablish a narrative of the Good and the kinds of social practices by which the virtuous life is enacted. Like Niebuhr, MacIntyre sets forth the need for a temporary withdrawal from modern life in order for communities to overcome the individualism and moral relativism that are so prevalent in the contemporary world.
20. Niebuhr, "Back to Benedict?" p. 861.
21. *The Compact Edition of the Oxford English Dictionary* (Oxford: Oxford University Press, 1971), vol. 1, p. 1979.
22. Ibid.
23. C. H. Dodd, *The Apostolic Preaching and Its Developments* (New York: Harper & Brothers, 1936), ch. 1.
24. James Smart, *The Teaching Ministry of the Church* (Philadelphia: Westminster Press, 1954), pp. 19–20.
25. Robert Worley, *Preaching and Teaching in the Earliest Church* (Philadelphia: Westminster Press, 1967); Charles Melchert, "An Exploration of the Presuppositions of Objective Formation for Contemporary Protestant Christian Educational Ministry," Ph.D. dissertation, Yale University (1969), p. 198.
26. Here I locate myself in the "classical" sociological tradition of

Max Weber and, to a lesser extent, Emile Durkheim. See Max Weber, *The Protestant Ethic and the Spirit of Capitalism*, tr. Talcott Parsons (New York: Charles Scribner's Sons, 1958), *From Max Weber: Essays in Sociology*, ed. and tr. H. H. Gerth and C. Wright Mills (New York: Oxford University Press, 1947), and *The Theory of Social and Economic Organization* (New York: Oxford University Press, 1947); Emile Durkheim, *The Division of Labor in Society* (Glencoe, Ill.: Free Press, 1947), *The Elementary Forms of the Religious Life* (New York: Free Press, 1965), and *Moral Education* (New York: Free Press, 1961).

27. Clifford Geertz in *The Interpretation of Cultures* (New York: Basic Books, 1973) provides a particularly good description of the "is" and "ought" of culture and religion in chs. 4 and 5.

28. Werner Jaeger's classic study of Greek *paideia* remains the definitive discussion of this concept. See *Paideia: The Ideals of Greek Culture*, 3 vols. (New York: Oxford University Press, 1945). This concept has begun to reappear in recent discussions of theology and education. For example, see Edward Farley's use of it in *Theologia: The Fragmentation and Unity of Theological Education* (Philadelphia: Fortress Press, 1983), pp. 152–156, and James Fowler's in "Pluralism, Particularity, and Paideia," *Journal of Law and Religion*, vol. 2, no. 2 (1984), pp. 263–307.

29. J. N. D. Kelly, *Early Christian Creeds* (Essex, England: Longman Press, 1950), ch. 2.

30. These concepts are developed by Douglas Ottati to explicate the two tasks of theology in conjunction with the work of H. Richard Niebuhr. See his *Meaning and Method in H. Richard Niebuhr's Theology* (Washington, D.C.: American University Press, 1982), ch. 1.

31. Jaroslav Pelikan's account of this is particularly illuminating. See *The Christian Tradition: A History of the Development of Doctrine*, vol. 1, *The Emergence of the Catholic Tradition, 100–600* (Chicago: University of Chicago Press, 1971).

32. R. P. C. Hanson, *The Continuity of Christian Doctrine* (New York: Seabury Press, 1981), ch. 3.

33. This definition obviously is dependent on Lawrence Cremin's work. See, for example, the definition he offers in *Public Education* (New York: Basic Books, 1976), p. 27. However, it also is influenced by William Frankena's work on education, as will become apparent.

34. William Frankena has pointed out the philosophical horizon inherent in the normativity of every educational curriculum. Why should this knowledge, these skills, those attitudes, and these values be deemed "worthwhile" and the center of the educational curriculum? What determines whether something constitutes "learning" or not? To answer these questions, education must provide a theoretical justification for its selective focus. Ultimately, Frankena believes,

this justification is metaphysical, providing an account of why particular items are considered worthwhile and central to the educational
curriculum in light of the nature of ultimate reality. See his *Three
Historical Philosophies of Education* (Chicago: Scott, Foresman &
Co., 1965).

35. Thomas Groome, in particular, has drawn attention in recent
years to the political nature of education. As he writes, "The point is
that in all educational activity choices are made about the past to be
conserved and the future to be proposed. These are political
choices, and the activity arising from them is a political activity." To
a large extent, Groome seems to have the interaction between student and teacher in mind when he makes this observation. His comment, however, is equally applicable to the broader processes by
which a *community* decides what knowledge, skills, values, and attitudes are worthwhile and how these are best handed on to the next
generation and deepened across the course of the human life cycle.
This is inevitably a political process. See *Christian Religious Education: Sharing Our Story and Vision* (San Francisco: Harper & Row,
1980), p. 16.

36. My views on the importance of understanding in teaching
have been influenced greatly by the thought of Sara Little and
Charles Melchert. See Sara Little, *To Set One's Heart: Belief and
Teaching in the Church* (Atlanta: John Knox Press, 1983), pp. 23–25,
and "Religious Instruction," in *Contemporary Approaches to Christian Education*, ed. Jack Seymour and Donald Miller (Nashville: Abingdon Press, 1982), pp. 43–45; Charles Melchert, "Understanding
and Religious Education," in *Process and Relationship*, ed. Iris and
Kendig Cully (Birmingham, Ala.: Religious Education Press, 1978),
pp. 41–48.

37. Ronald Hyman, *Ways of Teaching* (Philadelphia: J. B. Lippin-
cott Co., 1974), pp. 10–11.

38. This distinction was mentioned to me by Sara Little, my former colleague at Union Theological Seminary. She first heard teaching authority and commanding authority contrasted by H. Richard
Niebuhr, with whom she did her doctoral studies at Yale.

Chapter 2: The Perils and Possibilities of Modernization

1. "Developmental" paradigms in particular have been especially
important in this century. These paradigms have a tendency to view
non-Western countries as "underdeveloped" and to hold up the historical movement from traditional to modern societies in the Western world as normative. Marxist accounts of modernity have also
been important, viewing the process in terms of the ownership of
the means of production. The advent of industrial capitalism and the

rise of the middle class are the key elements of a modernization that is itself a transitional phase to a socioeconomic system in which the means of production are collectively owned and the proletariat emerges as the dominant class.

2. See ch. 1, note 26.

3. Clifford Geertz, *The Interpretation of Cultures* (New York: Basic Books, 1973), p. 93. See Stephen Tipton's discussion of this in *Getting Saved from the Sixties* (Berkeley, Calif.: University of California Press, 1982), pp. 274–277.

4. Geertz, *Interpretation*, pp. 89–102.

5. Peter Berger et al., *The Homeless Mind: Modernization and Consciousness* (New York: Random House, 1973), p. 9.

6. James Davison Hunter, *American Evangelicalism: Conservative Religion and the Quandary of Modernity* (New Brunswick, N.J.: Rutgers University Press, 1983), p. 12.

7. For an excellent discussion of this see Berger et al., *Homeless Mind*, chs. 1–7.

8. *From Max Weber: Essays in Sociology*, ed. and tr. H. H. Gerth and C. Wright Mills (New York: Oxford University Press, 1974), pp. 51ff.

9. See James Gustafson's critique of a functional reductionism of God and religion in *Ethics from a Theocentric Perspective: Theology and Ethics*, vol. 1 (Chicago: University of Chicago Press, 1981), pp. 16–31. In contrast, Gustafson develops a theocentric theology and ethics.

10. Peter Berger, *The Heretical Imperative: Contemporary Possibilities of Religious Affirmation* (Garden City, N.Y.: Doubleday & Co., 1979), pp. 17–23.

11. Ibid., p. 11.

12. For a discussion of the gradual weakening of ascriptive ties to religion, see Wade Clark Roof and William McKinney, *American Mainline Religion: Its Changing Shape and Future* (New Brunswick, N.J.: Rutgers University Press, 1987), ch. 4.

13. See, for example, Hunter's comments on p. 131 of *American Evangelicalism*. He argues that his documentation of the compromising effects of modernization on contemporary evangelicalism is partial verification of the notion that it is inimical to religious belief. See also his *Evangelicalism: The Coming Generation* (Chicago: University of Chicago Press, 1987). Here the thesis is documented in terms of younger, better educated evangelicals.

14. I have found Peter Berger's essay "From the Crisis of Religion to the Crisis of Secularity" thought-provoking in this regard. See *Religion and America: Spirituality in a Secular Age*, ed. Stephen Tipton and Mary Douglas (Boston: Beacon Press, 1982), pp. 14–24.

15. Berger et al., *Homeless Mind*, pp. 72–77.

16. Roof and McKinney, *American Mainline Religion*, chs. 1–2.

17. Robert Bellah, Richard Madsen, William Sullivan, Ann Swidler, and Steven Tipton, *Habits of the Heart: Individualism and Commitment in American Life* (Berkeley, Calif.: University of California Press, 1985).

18. Ibid., p. 20.

19. John Locke, *Two Treatises of Government*, ed. Peter Laslett (London: Cambridge University Press, 1963).

20. See Jeremy Bentham, *An Introduction to the Principles of Morals and Legislation*, ed. J. H. Burns and H. L. A. Hart (London: Athlone Press, 1970); John Stuart Mill, *Utilitarianism: With Critical Essays*, ed. Samuel Gotovitz (Indianapolis: Bobbs-Merrill Co., 1971).

21. By making the criterion of the individual's self-interest operative, classical utilitarianism is transformed into the ethical stance of egoism.

22. Here I am relying on Daniel Bell, who traces the competing visions of the middle class and modern art more adequately than do Bellah and his coauthors; see *The Cultural Contradictions of Capitalism* (New York: Basic Books, 1976).

23. Ibid., Introduction, Part One. Bell provides an especially helpful analysis of the tensions between the entrepreneur and the independent artist that emerged with the breakdown of feudalism.

24. As Bell puts it, quoting Irving Howe, "Modernity consists in a revolt against the prevalent style, an unyielding rage against the official order"; ibid., p. 46. See also Richard Sennett, *The Fall of Public Man: On the Social Psychology of Capitalism* (New York: Random House, 1974), chs. 8–9.

25. Bellah et al., *Habits*, pp. 47–48 and ch. 4.

26. See, for example, two of the more influential writers during this period of time, Norman O. Brown and Herbert Marcuse, both of whom draw on psychoanalysis to critique present social conditions and project a utopian state: Norman O. Brown, *Life Against Death: The Psychoanalytical Meaning of History* (Middletown, Conn.: Wesleyan University Press, 1959) and *Love's Body* (New York: Vintage Books, 1966); Herbert Marcuse, *Eros and Civilization: A Philosophical Inquiry Into Freud* (New York: Vintage Books, 1955) and *Five Lectures: Psychoanalysis, Politics, and Utopia* (Boston: Beacon Press, 1970).

27. These are taken from Roof and McKinney, *American Mainline Religion*, pp. 48–50.

28. E. Brooks Holifield traces the influence of the therapeutic modalities on this movement in *A History of Pastoral Care in America: From Salvation to Self-Realization* (Nashville: Abingdon Press, 1983). For a somewhat different reading of this movement see

Allison Stoke's *Ministry After Freud* (New York: Pilgrim Press, 1985).

29. See Richard Sennett's discussion of this in *Authority* (New York: Alfred A. Knopf, 1980), ch. 1.

30. Holifield portrays the influence of this theme on the pastoral care and counseling movement in *A History of Pastoral Care in America,* pp. 276–288.

31. Roof and McKinney, *American Mainline Religion,* p. 56.

32. Ibid., p. 57.

33. Hunter's two books on evangelicalism have already been cited (in notes 6 and 13), as has Berger's fine article discussing evangelical Christianity as a form of counter-pluralism and counter-secularity (note 14). Berger gives a more extensive treatment of these themes in *Homeless Mind,* Part 3.

34. While drawing on Hunter's work on evangelicalism, I have chosen *not* to follow him in using the term "evangelicalism" to refer to conservative Protestantism. Evangelicals are a highly diverse group at present. Some clearly are not counter-modernizers in a sociological sense. Moreover, there are important differences between evangelicals and fundamentalists. I use the term "conservative Protestantism" instead. This is closer to Roof and McKinney's topology of religion than Hunter's terminology.

35. Hunter, *American Evangelicalism,* p. 7.

36. The doctrinal and behavioral norms that follow are found in Hunter, *American Evangelicalism,* ch. 5.

37. Hunter, *American Evangelicalism,* pp. 62–63. See also Roof and McKinney, *American Mainline Religion,* pp. 83–84. The difference in indicators focusing on belief in the afterlife reveals less disparity in this area, although conservative Christians are higher than members of other branches.

38. Hunter has excellent chapters on each of these in *Evangelicalism: The Coming Generation,* chs. 3–4. While he bewails the "modernizing" trends among the younger, better educated generation of evangelicals, this group still remains far more traditional in their attitude toward these issues than the younger members of other branches of Christianity.

39. See Roof and McKinney, *American Mainline Religion,* ch. 6, especially the chart on pp. 211–212.

40. Hunter, *Evangelicalism: The Coming Generation,* p. 158.

41. Ibid., pp. 158–159.

42. Hunter, *American Evangelicalism,* pp. 23–27; George Marsden, *Fundamentalism and American Culture* (New York: Oxford University Press, 1980).

43. As Hunter points out in *American Evangelicalism* (p. 59), "In virtually all ways, evangelicalism is located furthest from the institu-

tional structures and processes of modernity." See his excellent discussion of this throughout ch. 4.

44. Ibid., ch. 6.

45. Anton C. Zijderveld, *The Abstract Society* (Garden City, N.Y.: Doubleday & Co., 1970), p. 80.

46. See Roof and McKinney's discussion of this in *American Mainline Religion*, ch. 6.

Chapter 3: A Teachable Spirit

1. Lawrence Cremin, *Traditions of American Education* (New York: Basic Books, 1977), p. 136.

2. In his widely influential book *Will Our Children Have Faith?* (New York: Seabury Press, 1976), John Westerhoff recognizes that the educational ecology of nineteenth-century Protestant education broke down during the first part of this century; see pp. 13–16. But his proposed alternative remains firmly locked into the *congregation* as the central focus of the church's teaching ministry.

3. "New voluntarism" is a phrase coined by Wade Clark Roof and William McKinney to describe the effects of the 1960s on American denominationalism. See *American Mainline Religion: Its Changing Shape and Future* (New Brunswick, N.J.: Rutgers University Press, 1987), ch. 2.

4. See James Gustafson, *Ethics from a Theocentric Perspective: Theology and Ethics*, vol. 1 (Chicago: University of Chicago Press, 1981), pp. 198–199.

5. John Calvin, *Institutes of the Christian Religion*, vol. 1, ed. John McNeill, Library of Christian Classics, vol. 20 (Philadelphia: Westminster Press, 1960), p. 41.

6. Gustafson, *Ethics from a Theocentric Perspective*, p. 164.

7. Perry Miller, *The New England Mind: The Seventeenth Century* (Boston: Beacon Press, 1939), ch. 1. My discussion of the Augustinian strain of piety is deeply influenced by Miller.

8. See Miller's comments on the peculiarly modern quality of Augustine in this regard, ibid., p. 22.

9. John Calvin, *Commentary on the Book of Psalms*, tr. J. Anderson (Grand Rapids: Wm. B. Eerdmans Publishing Co., 1949), p. xl, emphasis added.

10. These are discussed in some detail by Wilhelm H. Neuser in "Calvin's Conversion to Teachableness," in *Calvin and Christian Ethics*, ed. Peter De Kierk (Grand Rapids: Calvin Studies Society, 1987). My interpretation of this concept in Calvin's thought goes beyond Neuser's belief that teachability represents an "initial stage on the road to belief." In Brian Armstrong's response to this article in the same collection of papers he points out that such a time-

sequence understanding of faith is not consistent with the rest of Calvin's thought and that teachability is a characteristic of faith, not only at the beginning but throughout the Christian life. This assessment is substantiated by my work on this concept as it appears in the *Institutes* and not the commentaries on which Neuser focused his attention. Neuser's discussion is based in part on Paul Sprenger's *Das Rätsel um die Bekehrung Calvins*, Beiträge zur Geschichte und Lehre der Reformierten Kirche, 11 (Neukirchen Kreis Moers: Neukirchener Verlag der Buchhandlung des Erziehungsvereins, 1960).

11. John Calvin, *A Commentary on a Harmony of the Evangelists, Matthew, Mark, and Luke*, vol. 1, tr. William Pringle (Grand Rapids: Wm. B. Eerdmans Publishing Co., 1949), p. 244.

12. John Calvin, *Commentary Upon the Acts of the Apostles*, ed. Henry Beveridge, tr. Christopher Fetherstone, vol. 1 (Edinburgh: Calvin Translation Society, 1844), p. 354.

13. For my disagreement with Neuser's interpretation of this concept as a first step toward faith see note 10 above.

14. Calvin, *Institutes*, vol. 2, p. 1017.

15. Ibid., vol. 1, p. 81.

16. Ibid., p. 237. For other references in which teachableness is related to the authority of scripture, see vol. 1, pp. 72, 81, 146, 656; vol. 2, p. 1392.

17. Of persons identifying themselves as evangelicals, 35.5 percent read it on a daily basis, 35.8 percent read it 1 to 3 times a week, 10.1 percent read it 1 to 3 times a month, and 18.6 percent read it less than monthly. See James Davison Hunter, *American Evangelicalism: Conservative Religion and the Quandary of Modernity* (New Brunswick, N.J.: Rutgers University Press, 1983), p. 67.

18. Ibid.

19. Calvin, *Institutes*, vol. 1, p. 72.

20. Ibid., vol. 2, p. 1021. Other instances can be found in vol. 1, p. 77, and vol. 2, pp. 1017, 1156.

21. Ibid., vol 2, p. 1054.

22. Calvin is willing to grant the highest power and authority to ministers, but only in that they are bound to scripture: "That is that they may dare boldly to do all things by God's Word; may compel all worldly power, glory, wisdom, and exaltation to yield to and obey his majesty; supported by his power, may command all from the highest even to the last; may build up Christ's household and cast down Satan's; may feed the sheep and drive away the wolves; may instruct and exhort the teachable; may accuse, rebuke, and subdue the rebellious and stubborn; may bind and loose; finally, if need be, may launch thunderbolts and lightnings; but do all things in God's Word." Ibid., pp. 1156–1157.

23. Ibid., vol. 1, p. 146.

24. Ibid., vol. 1, pp. 434, 961; vol. 2, pp. 1285, 1448, 1480.

Chapter 4: Structure and Spirit

1. Jaroslav Pelikan, *The Vindication of Tradition* (New Haven, Conn.: Yale University Press, 1984), ch. 1.

2. Ibid., p. 3.

3. For a helpful introduction to the Sunday school movement, see Robert Lynn and Elliott Wright, *The Big Little School—200 Years of the Sunday School* (Birmingham, Ala.: Religious Education Press, 1971).

4. C. Ellis Nelson, *Where Faith Begins* (Atlanta: John Knox Press, 1967); John Westerhoff, *Will Our Children Have Faith?* (New York: Seabury Press, 1976).

5. These criticisms are offered respectively by Sara Little and Thomas Groome in the following books: Sara Little, *To Set One's Heart* (Atlanta: John Knox Press, 1983); Thomas Groome, *Christian Religious Education* (San Francisco: Harper & Row, 1980).

6. See Ruth Doyle and Sheila Kelly, "Comparison of Trends in Ten Denominations, 1950–1975," in *Understanding Church Growth and Decline, 1950–1978,* ed. Dean Hoge and David Roozen (New York: Pilgrim Press, 1979), ch. 6.

7. See, for example, C. H. Dodd, *Apostolic Preaching and Its Developments* (New York: Harper & Brothers, 1936), ch. 2.

8. Dodd's thesis seems to presuppose a clear-cut distinction between the gospel and the law, something that becomes more apparent in his later writings. Charles Melchert makes this point in his Yale Ph.D. dissertation (cited in ch. 1, note 25). In contrast to Dodd's position, various scholars have argued that kerygma and didache are interrelated and virtually indistinguishable; see Robert Worley, *Preaching and Teaching in the Earliest Church* (Philadelphia: Westminster Press, 1967).

9. Raymond Brown raises this question in *The Churches the Apostles Left Behind* (New York: Paulist Press, 1984). I am largely following Brown's interpretation of the Pastoral epistles and the Johannine literature in this chapter. See also his *The Gospel According to John,* vols. 1–2 (Garden City, N.Y.: Doubleday & Co., 1966) and, with John Meier, *Antioch and Rome: New Testament Cradles of Catholic Christianity* (London: Geoffrey Chapman, 1983).

10. After Timothy is told to "guard the truth that has been entrusted to you" (2 Tim. 1:14), he is told in 3:14 to "continue in what you have learned and have firmly believed, knowing from whom you learned it."

11. Brown, *Churches Left Behind*, ch. 6.

12. Ibid., ch. 7.

Chapter 5: *Magisterium:* The Roman Catholic Tradition

1. Francis Sullivan, *Magisterium: Teaching Authority in the Catholic Church* (Mahwah, N.J.: Paulist Press, 1983), pp. 4–11.

2. Yves Congar, O.P., "A Semantic History of the Term 'Magisterium,'" *Moral Theology No. 3: The Magisterium and Morality*, ed. Charles Curran and Richard McCormick (New York: Paulist Press, 1982), p. 298. See also Congar's "A Brief History of the Forms of the Magisterium" in the same volume.

3. I am following Jaroslav Pelikan's account here as presented in *The Riddle of Roman Catholicism* (Nashville: Abingdon Press, 1959).

4. Ibid., p. 22.

5. Ibid.

6. See James McCue, "The Beginnings Through Nicaea," in *Papal Primacy and the Universal Church: Lutherans and Catholics in Dialogue V,* ed. Paul C. Empie and T. Austin Murphy (Minneapolis: Augsburg Publishing House, 1974), p. 59.

7. Ibid., p. 60.

8. Arthur Piepkorn, "From Nicea to Leo the Great," in *Papal Primacy,* p. 74.

9. Pelikan, *Riddle,* p. 19.

10. Avery Dulles, *A Church to Believe In: Discipleship and the Dynamics of Freedom* (New York: Crossroad Publishing Co., 1984), pp. 105–109.

11. John Riggs, *Studies of Political Thought from Gerson to Grotius, 1414–1625* (Cambridge: The University Press, 1956), chs. 1–3.

12. Dulles, *A Church to Believe In,* p. 109; see also Congar, "Brief History," p. 318.

13. Congar, "Brief History," p. 319.

14. Dulles, *A Church to Believe In,* pp. 111–115.

15. Howland Sanks, *Authority in the Church: A Study in Changing Paradigms,* American Academy of Religion Dissertation Series no. 2 (Missoula, Mont.: Scholars Press, 1974), ch. 4.

16. Ibid., p. 112.

17. In the last part of this chapter I am drawing on a distinction between "fallibilism" and "moderate infallibilism" made by George Lindbeck. See "The Reformation and the Infallibility Debate," *Teaching Authority and Infallibility in the Church,* ed. Paul Empie, T. Austin Murphy, and Joseph Burgess (Minneapolis: Augsburg Publishing House, 1980), p. 101.

18. Hans Kung, *The Church Maintained in Truth,* tr. Edward Quinn

(New York: Vintage Books, 1980), and *Infallible? An Inquiry*, tr. Edward Quinn (Garden City, N.Y.: Doubleday & Co., 1983).

19. While it is not possible to list all the influential literature representing this theological position, those which have been most helpful to me are: *Frontiers of Theology in Latin America*, ed. R. Gibellini, tr. John Drury (Maryknoll, N.Y.: Orbis Books, 1979); Gustavo Gutiérrez, *A Theology of Liberation*, ed. and tr. Sr. Caridad Inda and John Eagleson (Maryknoll, N.Y.: Orbis Books, 1973), and *The Power of the Poor in History*, ed. and tr. Robert Barr (Maryknoll, N.Y.: Orbis Books, 1983); José Miguez Bonino, *Christians and Marxists* (Grand Rapids: Wm. B. Eerdmans Publishing Co., 1976) and *Doing Theology in a Revolutionary Situation* (Philadelphia: Fortress Press, 1975); Juan Luis Segundo, *The Liberation of Theology* (Maryknoll, N.Y.: Orbis Books, 1976); *The Emergent Gospel: Theology from the Underside of History*, ed. Sergio Torres and Virginia Fabella (Maryknoll, N.Y.: Orbis Books, 1978); *Theology in the Americas*, ed. Sergio Torres and John Eagleson (Maryknoll, N.Y.: Orbis Books, 1976); and *The Challenge of Basic Christian Communities*, ed. Sergio Torres and John Eagleson, tr. John Drury (Maryknoll, N.Y.: Orbis Books, 1981).

20. The term "struggling poor" is Assmann's. See his brief essay in *Theology in the Americas*, p. 300. He discusses this in terms of the "epistemological privilege" of the poor.

21. Lindbeck, "The Reformation," in *Teaching Authority*, p. 101.

22. Dulles explicitly adopts Lindbeck's terminology to refer to his approach in his essay, "Moderate Infallibilism," in *Teaching Authority*, pp. 81–100. See also his essay "Infallibility: The Terminology" in the same volume. Among the many books and articles that Dulles has written on this topic, the following are particularly helpful: *A Church to Believe In* (cited in note 10); *The Survival of Dogma* (New York: Crossroad Publishing Co., 1971); "Teaching Authority and the Pastoral Office," *Dialog*, vol. 20 (summer 1981), pp. 212–216; and "Doctrinal Authority for a Pilgrim Church," *Moral Theology No. 3* (cited in note 2), pp. 247–270. Of the many books and articles by Karl Rahner, see the following: "The Dispute Concerning the Teaching Office of the Church" and "Open Questions in Dogma Considered by the Institutional Church as Definitively Answered,' in *Moral Theology No. 3*, pp. 113–150; "On the Relationship Between the Pope and the College of Bishops," in *Theological Investigations*, vol. 10, tr. David Bourke (London: Darton, Longman & Todd, 1973), pp. 50–70; "Theology and the Church's Teaching Authority after the Council," in *Theological Investigations*, vol. 9, tr. Graham Harrison (London: Darton, Longman & Todd, 1973), pp. 83–100; "A Critique of Hans Kung," in *Homiletic and Pastoral Review*, vol. 71 (May 1971), pp. 10–26; and "Magisterium," in *Sacra-*

mentum Mundi: An Encyclopedia of Theology, ed. Karl Rahner III (New York: Herder & Herder, 1969), pp. 351–358.

23. Sullivan, *Magisterium*, pp. 14–15, 80–81.

Chapter 6: Martin Luther's Break with *Magisterium*

1. Quoted in Paul Althaus, *The Theology of Martin Luther*, tr. R. Schultz (Philadelphia: Fortress Press, 1966), p. 335.

2. Scott Hendrix, *Luther and the Papacy: Stages in a Reformation Conflict* (Philadelphia: Fortress Press, 1981), p. 147.

3. Ibid., p. 133.

4. Ibid., p. 63.

5. Krister Stendahl, *The Bible and the Role of Women* (Philadelphia: Fortress Press, 1966), pp. 11–12.

6. Pelikan, *Spirit Versus Structure: Luther and the Institutions of the Church* (New York: Harper & Row, 1968), ch. 1.

7. Hendrix, *Luther*, p. xi.

8. Ibid., p. 9.

9. Ibid., p. 41.

10. John McNeill, *Unitive Protestantism: The Ecumenical Spirit and Its Persistent Expression* (Richmond: John Knox Press, 1964), pp. 96ff.

11. Ibid., p. 88.

12. Quoted in Gerhard Forde, "Infallibility Language and the Early Lutheran Tradition," in *Teaching Authority and Infallibility in the Church*, ed. Paul Empie, T. Austin Murphy, and Joseph Burgess (Minneapolis: Augsburg Publishing House, 1980), p. 125.

13. Eric W. Gritsch, "Lutheran Teaching Authority: Past and Present," in *Teaching Authority*, p. 141. See also Gritsch's "Lutheran Teaching Authority: Historical Dimensions and Ecumenical Implications," in *Lutheran Quarterly*, vol. 25 (Nov. 1973), p. 385, where he writes, "But essentially the teaching office *(Lehramt)* is a preaching office *(Predigtamt)*."

14. Quoted in Forde, "Infallibility Language," p. 124.

15. Gritsch, "Lutheran Teaching Authority: Past and Present," p. 138.

16. Warren Quanbeck points this out in "The *Magisterium* in the Lutheran Church with Special Reference to Infallibility," in *Teaching Authority*, pp. 149–158.

17. Gritsch, "Lutheran Teaching Authority, Past and Present," p. 138.

18. Quanbeck, "The *Magisterium*," p. 153.

19. Althaus, *Theology of Luther*, p. 5.

20. Carl Braaten, *Principles of Lutheran Theology* (Philadelphia: Fortress Press, 1983), p. 2.

21. Ibid., p. 5.

22. Ibid., p. 2.

23. Ibid., p. 3.

24. For a discussion of these issues in contemporary Lutheranism see: Richard Jungkuntz, "The Church in Tension in Teaching the Truth," *Concordia Theological Monthly,* vol. 37 (Dec. 1966), pp. 693–702; C. F. W. Walther, "Authority in the Church," *Concordia Theological Monthly,* vol. 44 (Nov. 1973), pp. 375–378; George Forell, "Luther and Conscience," *Encounter with Luther,* ed. Eric Gritsch (Gettysburg, Pa.: Institute for Luther Studies, 1980), vol. 1, pp. 218–235.

25. Jaroslav Pelikan, *The Riddle of Roman Catholicism* (Nashville: Abingdon Press, 1959), p. 223.

26. McNeill, *Unitive Protestantism,* ch. 3.

27. Braaten, *Principles,* p. 10.

28. Quoted in Althaus, *Theology of Luther,* p. 359.

29. Ibid., pp. 6–7.

30. *Teaching Authority,* p. 63.

31. At the heart of Luther's conception of the church is his affirmation of the priesthood of all believers. Christ alone is the high priest, whose intercession and sacrifice make possible the forgiveness of sins. All Christians receive a share in this priestly office, praying and interceding for one another, taking up their crosses in sacrifice to God, and, most importantly, proclaiming the gospel to one another. Luther never understood the priesthood of all believers as implying merely the believer's freedom to stand in a direct relationship to God without a human mediator. As priests, all Christians are bound to one another and to their neighbor in carrying out their ministries.

32. For an excellent discussion of the various shifts in Luther's thought see Gert Haendler, *Luther: On Ministerial Office and Congregational Function,* ed. Eric Gritsch, tr. Ruth Gritsch (Philadelphia: Fortress Press, 1981).

33. Quoted in Haendler, *Luther,* p. 59.

34. Ibid.

35. See Haendler's discussion in Luther, chs. 6–8.

36. Brian Gerrish, "Priesthood and Ministry in the Theology of Luther," *Church History,* vol. 34, no. 4 (Dec. 1965), pp. 404–422.

37. Gerrish, "Priesthood," p. 413.

38. Ibid., p. 415.

39. At various points in Luther's writing, these two lines of thought exist together in a single sentence, as they do in *On the Councils and the Church,* in which Luther tells us that we must have preachers and teachers to minister "for the sake, and in the name of, the Church, but still more because of the institution of Christ"; Gerrish, "Priesthood," p. 414.

40. Ibid., p. 416.

41. Carl Braaten, "Where Is the Magisterium?" *Dialog,* no. 22 (spring 1983), pp. 4–5.

42. See George Lindbeck, "The Reformation and the Infallibility Debate," *Teaching Authority,* p. 104, and *The Infallibility Debate,* ed. J. Kirvan (New York: Paulist Press, 1971), p. 117.

43. Gritsch, "Lutheran Teaching Authority: Historical Dimensions," p. 394.

Chapter 7: The Thought and Practice of John Calvin

1. Robert Clyde Johnson, *Authority in Protestant Theology* (Philadelphia: Westminster Press, 1959), p. 42.

2. Calvin's emphasis on the "Godness of God" and his attempt to protect God's right and dignity in every facet of his thought do not lead him to view God as "wholly other," along the lines of more recent neo-orthodoxy, but as ruling and ordering life even in the present. While Calvin himself did not frequently use the term, it is not inaccurate to describe his thought as emphasizing above all else the sovereignty of God.

3. For an excellent discussion of the differences between Luther and Calvin on the use of the law see Edward Dowey, *The Knowledge of God in Calvin's Theology* (New York: Columbia University Press, 1952), pp. 222ff.

4. See François Wendel's discussion of the three uses of the law in *Calvin: The Origins and Development of His Religious Thought,* tr. P. Mairet (New York: Harper & Row, 1950), pp. 196–208.

5. Calvin's doctrine of sanctification follows this same line of thought, focusing on the restoration of the *imago dei.* Regeneration and justification are placed on an equal footing. Indeed, regeneration is discussed *before* justification in the *Institutes.* The revivification of the Christian's life and the forgiveness of sins are benefits given simultaneously to those whom Christ has claimed. See Wilhelm Niesel, *The Gospel and the Churches: A Comparison of Catholicism, Orthodoxy, and Protestantism,* tr. D. Lewis (Philadelphia: Westminster Press, 1958), p. 191.

6. As Dowey points out, Calvin views the law in its various forms (conscience, the moral and ceremonial law given to Israel, and the teachings of Jesus) as standing in a kind of continuity. See Dowey, *Knowledge of God,* p. 228.

7. John Calvin, *Institutes of the Christian Religion,* vol. 2, ed. John McNeill, Library of Christian Classics, vol. 21 (Philadelphia: Westminster Press, 1960), p. 1155.

8. Ibid., p. 1152.

9. Ibid., p. 1158.

10. Ibid., p. 1162, emphasis mine.

11. Johnson has an excellent discussion of these two points. See *Authority*, pp. 54–56.

12. Jaroslav Pelikan, *The Christian Tradition: A History of the Development of Doctrine*, vol. 4, *Reformation of Church and Dogma 1300–1700* (Chicago: University of Chicago Press, 1984), p. 187.

13. See Niesel's discussion of the difference between the Lutheran and Reformed traditions in this regard, a discussion that focuses primarily on the similarities and differences between Luther and Calvin, in *The Gospel and the Churches*, pp. 225–231. See also Dowey, *Knowledge of God*, p. 104, where he writes, "[Calvin] does not, like Luther, hold some other theological criterion higher than the canon itself."

14. Dowey, *Knowledge of God*, pp. 90–105; A. D. R. Polman, "Calvin on the Inspiration of Scripture," in *John Calvin: Contemporary Prophet*, ed. J. Hoogstra (Grand Rapids: Baker Book House, 1959), pp. 97–112.

15. François Wendel, *Calvin*, p. 160; Donald McKim, "Calvin's View of Scripture," in *Readings in Calvin's Theology*, ed. Donald McKim (Grand Rapids: Baker Book House, 1984), pp. 43–68; see also Jack Rogers and Donald McKim, *The Authority and Interpretation of Scripture: An Historical Approach* (San Francisco: Harper & Row, 1979), pp. 89–116.

16. In contrast, Dowey argues that Calvin the exegete and Calvin the theologian are simply not consistent on this point, employing the critical methods of humanism while maintaining a dictation theory of biblical inspiration. See *Knowledge of God*, pp. 86–131.

17. As Polman puts it, "From the above it is evident that for Calvin, in contrast to much of subsequent orthodoxy, belief in the divine inspiration of Scripture is not merely a matter of the recognition of a formal truth. Rather it has a religious orientation and existential import. Calvin is not concerned with the analysis of a medicine, but with its use." See *John Calvin*, ed. J. Hoogstra, p. 105; see also Dowey's excellent discussion of this matter in *Knowledge of God*, pp. 89–90.

18. Calvin, *Institutes*, vol. 2, p. 1149. He discusses each of these in Book IV, chs. 8–12.

19. Ibid., p. 1150.

20. Quoted in G. S. M. Walker's article, "Calvin and the Church," in *Readings*, ed. D. McKim, p. 212.

21. See Ford Lewis Battles's excellent article on this: "God Was Accommodating Himself to Human Capacity," ibid., ch. 2.

22. Calvin, *Institutes*, vol. 2, p. 1019.

23. Ibid., p. 1110.

24. Ibid., p. 1065.

25. Ibid., p. 1018.

26. Ibid., p. 1150.

27. The law, for example, is described as the very "school" of God's children. It serves as a "tutor" in its first and second uses, and, even more importantly, in its third use, its "daily instruction" allows the Christian to make "fresh progress" toward a purer knowledge of the divine will. For the law as "school," see *Institutes,* vol. 1, p. 73; as "tutor" and as providing "daily instruction," p. 360. Elsewhere, Calvin writes that at no point has "the law become superfluous for believers, since it does not stop teaching and exhorting and urging them to good," vol. 1, pp. 834–835. As we have seen, the Holy Spirit is frequently described as a teacher of the heart of those whom God has elected.

28. Calvin, *Institutes,* vol. 2, p. 1016.

29. Ibid.

30. Ibid.

31. Ibid., p. 1017.

32. Nourishment and education are linked in many places in the *Institutes.* For example, Calvin writes that "we are indeed his children, whom he has received into his faithful protection to nourish and educate"; see vol. 1, p. 182.

33. Ibid., vol. 2, pp. 1011–1012

34. Ibid., p. 1017.

35. Ibid., pp. 1017–1018.

36. Ibid., p. 1018

37. Ibid.

38. Ibid., pp. 1150–1151. In the preceding paragraph he writes, in a similar manner, "Now the only way to build up the church is for the ministers themselves to endeavor to preserve Christ's authority for himself; this can only be secured if what he has received from his Father be left to him, namely that he alone is the schoolmaster of the church."

39. Ibid., p. 1153. Calvin also argues that only if ministers bind themselves to the teachings they have received will their natural disposition toward tyranny be overcome. "For if we simply grant to men such power as they are disposed to take, it is plain to all how abrupt is the fall into tyranny, which ought to be far from Christ's church" (p. 1150).

40. Ibid., p. 1175. Calvin makes this comment within the context of a critique of Roman Catholic claims to infallibility.

41. Ibid., p. 1176. Similarly, Calvin writes that "we are warned by examples from almost every age that the truth is not always nurtured in the bosom of the pastors, and the wholeness of the church does not depend upon their condition. . . . I am only warning that discrimination is to be made among these pastors themselves, lest we

also immediately regard as pastors those who are so called" (p. 1169).

42. In both the *Ecclesiastical Ordinances* of 1541 and the *Institutes,* Calvin described a variety structures by which the doctrine and conduct of ministers were checked by others. New ministers were to be examined by their peers, recommended to the Magistracy, and presented to the people, that they "be received by the common consent of the company of the faithful." *Calvin: Theological Treatises,* tr. J. K. S. Reid, Library of Christian Classics, vol. XXII (Philadelphia: Westminster Press, 1954), p. 59. Every week the ministers were to meet "for discussion of the Scriptures; and none are to be exempt from this without legitimate excuse" (p. 60). If differences in doctrine arose among them they were to adjust them in this assembly, if possible. If this could not be done, they should appeal to the elders of the church and finally to the Magistracy.

43. See Calvin, *Institutes,* vol. 2, pp. 1166–1179.

44. Ibid., pp. 1171–1176.

45. Ibid., p. 1166.

46. Ibid., p. 1176.

47. Ibid., p. 1171. Elsewhere (p. 1166), Calvin puts it as follows: "Now it is Christ's right to preside over all councils and to have no man share his dignity. But I say that he presides only when the holy assembly is governed by his word and Spirit."

48. Ibid., p. 1171. Similarly, he writes (p. 1176), "Accordingly, no names of councils, pastors, bishops . . . can prevent our being taught by the evidence of words and things to test all spirits of all men by the standard of God's Word in order to determine whether or not they are from God."

49. It is an unfortunate fact that many scholars who do an excellent job of explicating Calvin's educational interests in terms of his theology make little or no mention of the influence of humanism on his thought. It is almost as if his humanistic education were of no continuing importance after his conversion. This omission is seen in a number of articles that are otherwise quite good. See Peter de Jong, "Calvin's Contribution to Christian Education," *Calvin Theological Journal,* vol. 2 (Nov. 1967), pp. 162–201; J. H. Koekemoer, "Catechesis in the Light of Calvin's *Institutes,*" in *John Calvin's Institutes: His Opus Magnum* (Potchefstroom: Potchefstroom University for Christian Higher Education, 1986), pp. 375–383; Donald Kocher, "Calvinism and Confirmation," *Princeton Seminary Bulletin,* vol. 54 (Nov. 1960), pp. 28–31; Arie Brouwer, "Calvin's Doctrine of Children in the Covenant: Foundation for Christian Education," *Reformed Review,* vol. 18 (May 1965), pp. 17–29; and G. Aiken Taylor, "Calvin and Religious Education," *Christianity Today,* vol. 1 (July 22, 1957), pp. 16–17. For a more balanced discussion of this

topic, see: Charles Raynal, "The Place of the Academy in John Calvin's Polity," *Calvin Studies II: Papers presented at a Colloquium on Calvin Studies at Davidson College*, ed. J. Leith and C. Raynal, vol. 2, unpublished manuscript, library of Union Theological Seminary in Virginia (1984), pp. 92–103, and W. Stanford Reid, "Calvin and the Founding of the Academy of Geneva," *Westminster Theological Journal*, vol. 18 (Nov. 1955), pp. 1–33.

50. During the early Middle Ages, the university was based on the organization of knowledge into the seven liberal arts found in late classical culture. The first division was called the *trivium* and focused on the use of language (including grammar), logic, and rhetoric. The second division, the *quadrivium*, focused on the mathematical arts: arithmetic, geometry, astronomy, and music. See Rashdall Hastings, *The Universities of Europe in the Middle Ages*, ed. F. M. Powicke and A. B. Emden (Oxford: Clarendon Press, 1936), pp. 33–39. With the changes in education that began to take place during the twelfth century, grammar came to be considered primarily as a preparatory discipline for children; literary studies were reduced in importance. Rhetoric was viewed as suspect, at best dealing with decorative devices of communication and, at worst, appealing to the passions rather than the intellect. It was precisely these things that Renaissance humanism sought to restore.

51. Renaissance humanism first appeared in Italy during the mid-fourteenth century; see G. H. Bantock's excellent discussion of this period, *Studies in the History of Educational Theory: Artifice and Nature 1350–1765*, vol. 1 (London: George Allen & Unwin, 1980). The humanists' disdain for medieval thought and life led them to reach behind it to the classical periods of Greece and Rome. In general, they evaluated tradition negatively, for it seemed to represent the hold of the immediate past on the present. The appeal of Greece and Rome, in large part, lay in the way that they combined learning and active civic participation, something that seemed appropriate to the needs of a more cosmopolitan urban culture. See Irene Quenzler Brown, "Renaissance and Humanism," in *Encyclopedia of Education*, vol. 7, ed. Leigh C. Deighton (New York: Macmillan Co., 1971), p. 498.

52. As Lawrence Stone points out, it was not uncommon during the Middle Ages for the nobility to be far less educated than the clergy and other persons working for the church. Changes in the nature of warfare and the functions of the city-state demanded a changing role for the aristocracy. Part of the appeal of humanistic education was to meet the needs of this situation. See Lawrence Stone, "Foreword," in William Woodward's *Studies in Education During the Age of the Renaissance, 1400–1600*, Classics in Education no. 32 (New York: Teachers College Press, 1967), p. xi.

53. Ibid., p. 13.

54. Bantock, *Studies*, p. 19.

55. J. Charles Coetzee, "Calvin and the School," in *John Calvin: Contemporary Prophet* (cited in note 14), p. 197. His father procured a chaplaincy for him in Noyon Cathedral, serving as a kind of scholarship that enabled him to pursue his studies beyond the elementary level. Calvin held this position, a sinecure, until 1527, when he resigned it, only to resume it in 1531. It was not infrequent for this sort of arrangement to serve as a kind of scholarship for students.

56. Cordier was an extremely influential proponent of humanistic education and is generally considered one of the founders of modern pedagogy. See Quirinus Breen, *John Calvin: A Study in French Humanism* (Grand Rapids: Wm. B. Eerdmans Publishing Co., 1931), pp. 15–17.

57. In this dedication, Calvin writes that "under your auspices . . . I made proficiency at least so far as to be prepared to profit in some degree the Church of God. . . . Providence so ordered it that I had, for a short time, the privilege of having you as my instructor . . . to me it was a singular kindness on the part of God that I happened to have an auspicious commencement of such a course of training, and although I was permitted to have the use of it only for a short time . . . yet I derived so much assistance afterwards from your training, that it is with good reason that I acknowledge myself indebted to you for such progress as has since been made." John Calvin, *Commentaries on the Epistles to the Philippians, Colossians, and Thessalonians with Four Homilies or Sermons on Idolatry and an Exposition of Psalm LXXXVII*, tr. John Pringle (Edinburgh: Calvin Translation Society, 1951), p. 234.

58. The college was founded by John Standonck, who introduced something of the spirit of the Brothers of the Common Life into the school. The school was notorious for its strictness, attempting to foster a cloisterlike atmosphere. Even the smallest child was forbidden to run and jump, and corporal punishment was used generously. The head of the school was Noel Beda, who was well known for his efforts to wipe out the teachings of the Reformers and humanists as they made their way into Paris.

59. Wendel points out in *Calvin* (cited in note 4), p. 21, that Calvin's father had run into difficulties with the church in Noyon for which he had been settling estates. Perhaps he was no longer assured of the support of the church in the advancement of his son.

60. Legal codes were examined in their historical context and not interpreted exclusively on the basis of traditional authoritative commentaries and textbooks. This contextual and historical mode of investigation was to influence Calvin's practice of scriptural exegesis,

leading him to examine a biblical passage in terms of its broader biblical and cultural context. See McKim, ed., *Readings* (cited in note 15), p. 48.

61. At some point, Calvin interrupted his studies at the Royal College and returned to Orleans to finish his education in law and receive his degree.

62. See Breen's discussion of this book in *Calvin*, chs. 4–5. The book offers only three quotations from the Bible, while drawing extensively from Roman and Greek literature, contemporary humanists, and the church fathers. Calvin's methods are typically humanistic, focusing heavily on philological, historical, and rhetorical analysis. Breen is surely correct, when he writes, p. 146: "It may be said that at twenty-four he was a seasoned humanist, as a study of the *Seneca Commentaries* abundantly testifies."

63. Wendel argues that Calvin retained four things from his humanistic background: (1) a notion of natural law from the stoics, (2) an admiration for the ancient writers, (3) a scientific-historical method of investigation, and (4) a negative attitude toward tradition, especially the tradition of scholasticism. As will become apparent, I am arguing that Calvin also retained an appreciation for the educational ideals spawned by humanism, something that is clearly evident in the Genevan Academy. See *Calvin*, pp. 27–37.

64. W. Stanford Reid, "Calvin" (cited in note 49), p. 2.

65. Ibid., p. 7.

66. Unfortunately this document has never been translated into English and was not included in the *Opera Omnia*, the collected works of Calvin. It has been reprinted by A. L. Heminjard in his *Correspondences des réformateurs* (Geneva, 1866–1897). Coetzee provides a partial summary of it in "Calvin and the School" (cited in note 14), p. 201.

67. As Coetzee puts it (p. 201), "Calvin was convinced that the Reformation could grow and increase only through a study of the arts and sciences as well as that of theology."

68. See ibid. The proposed course of study also included a place for teaching the vernacular and for practical arithmetic.

69. W. Stanford Reid, "Calvin," p. 5.

70. Ibid., p. 6.

71. Ibid., p. 63.

72. Calvin, *Ecclesiastical Ordinances*, in *Theological Treatises* (cited in note 42), p. 62.

73. John McNeill, *The History and Character of Calvinism* (New York: Oxford University Press, 1954), p. 193.

74. See Reid's translation of this appended to his article, "Calvin" (cited in note 49), pp. 22–33.

75. Ibid., p. 23.

76. John Calvin, *Commentary on the Epistles of Paul the Apostle to the Corinthians*, vol. 1, tr. J. Pringle (Edinburgh: Calvin Translation Society, 1848), p. 75.

77. Ibid.

78. McKim, ed., *Readings*, chs. 2–3.

79. Dowey, *Knowledge*, p. 140.

80. Conservative Protestants in the Reformed tradition have been far more willing to address this issue than their more centrist counterparts. Frank Gaebelein, for example, wrote of the need for American Protestantism to support schools explicitly based on the knowledge of God given in Jesus Christ as early as the late 1940s; see his *Christian Education in a Democracy* (New York: Oxford University Press, 1951). A more recent conservative perspective is offered by Rockne McCarthy, Donald Oppewal, Walfred Peterson, and Gordon Spykman in *Society, State, and Schools: A Case for Structural and Confessional Pluralism* (Grand Rapids: Wm. B. Eerdmans Publishing Co., 1981). For a perspective that views the contemporary church's task as the renewal and support of public education, see Jack Seymour, Robert O'Gorman, and Charles Foster, *The Church in the Education of the Public: Refocusing the Task of Religious Education* (Nashville: Abingdon Press, 1984). An excellent book on the church's stake in public life in general is Parker J. Palmer's *The Company of Strangers: Christians and the Renewal of America's Public Life* (New York: Crossroad Publishing Co., 1981).

81. John Calvin, *Commentary on the Book of Psalms*, tr. J. Anderson (Edinburgh: Calvin Translation Society, 1845), vol. 1, p. xli.

82. Calvin, *Institutes*, vol. 1, p. 9.

83. John Calvin, "Articles concerning the Organization of the Church and of Worship at Geneva 1537," *Theological Treatises*, tr. J. K. S. Reid, Library of Christian Classics, vol. 22 (Philadelphia: Westminster Press, 1954), p. 54.

84. Ibid.

85. His argument is typically humanistic in this regard. The practices of the "near" tradition are criticized in light of a recovery of those of antiquity.

86. See Ronald Wallace's discussion of this in *Calvin's Doctrine of the Word and Sacrament* (Grand Rapids: Wm. B. Eerdmans Publishing Co., 1957), pp. 191–195.

87. Brouwer provides this quote from Calvin and those that follow in his excellent article, "Calvin's Doctrine of Children in the Covenant: Foundation for Christian Education" (cited in note 49). He is quoting from Calvin's "Second Defense of the Pious and Orthodox Faith Concerning the Sacraments, in answer to the Calumnies of Joachim Westphal," *Tracts*, vol. 2, tr. H. Beveridge (Edinburgh: 1844).

88. Calvin, *Commentary on a Harmony of the Evangelists, Matthew, Mark, and Luke*, vol. 2 (Edinburgh: Calvin Translation Society, 1946). See his commentary on Matthew 19:4, pp. 378–379.

89. Calvin, "Articles," p. 48.

90. Ibid.

91. Oddly enough, this catechism—*Instruction in Faith* (1537)—soon disappeared from circulation and was lost for 340 years until it was rediscovered in Paris in 1877 by H. Bordier. Paul T. Fuhrmann has provided the only English translation (Philadelphia: Westminster Press, 1949).

92. De Jong, "Calvin's Contribution to Christian Education" (cited in note 49), p. 175.

93. The passages are 1 Peter 2:2 ("Like newborn babes, long for the pure spiritual milk"), 3:15 ("Be prepared to make a defense to any one who calls you to account for the hope that is in you"), and 4:11 ("Whoever speaks, as one who utters oracles of God").

94. Wendel, *Calvin*, p. 61.

95. John Calvin, "Draft Ecclesiastical Ordinances," in *Theological Treatises*, p. 66 (cited in note 42).

96. Ibid., p. 69.

97. For example, the law in *Instruction in Faith* was presented with more of a Lutheran flavor, focusing primarily on how it convinces us of our iniquity; see p. 34. Now its positive, ordering functions are emphasized. It serves as the "rule of life." T. E. Torrance provides an excellent translation with questions and answers numbered in *The School of Faith: The Catechisms of the Reformed Churches* (London: Clarke & Co., 1959), p. 107.

98. Calvin, *Theological Treatises*, p. 90.

99. Ibid., p. 88.

100. Calvin goes on to acknowledge the fact that a common catechism among all the Protestant churches is unlikely, although this remains the ideal; ibid., pp. 88–89.

101. Ibid., p. 89.

102. Calvin, *Institutes*, vol. 2, p. 1461.

103. Koekemoer provides a helpful analysis of this passage in "Catechesis" (cited in note 49), pp. 376ff.

Chapter 8: A New Theological Paradigm

1. This contrast is developed by Jaroslav Pelikan in *Vindication of Tradition* (New Haven, Conn.: Yale University Press, 1984), pp. 23ff.

2. For an interesting account of Calvin's influence on the Consistory, see François Wendel's *Calvin: The Origins and Development of His Religious Thought*, tr. P. Mairet (New York: Harper & Row, 1950), ch. 3.

3. Thomas Kuhn, *The Structure of Scientific Revolutions* (Chicago: University of Chicago Press, 1962).

4. Thomas Kuhn, "Second Thoughts on Paradigms," in *The Structure of Scientific Theories*, ed. F. Suppe (Urbana, Ill.: University of Illinois Press, 1977), pp. 459–482.

5. Every paradigm has anomalies that it cannot resolve at any given time. It is only when these anomalies are viewed as particularly pressing and a promising alternative emerges that a paradigm shift takes place.

6. Ian Barbour, *Myths, Models, and Paradigms: A Comparative Study in Science and Religion* (New York: Harper & Row, 1974); Sallie McFague, *Metaphorical Theology: Models of God in Religious Language* (Philadelphia: Fortress Press, 1982); Howland Sanks, *Authority in the Church: A Study in Changing Paradigms* (Missoula, Mont.: Scholars Press, 1974). See also George Lindbeck's interesting comments in "Spiritual Formation and Theological Education," *Theological Education*, suppl. 1, vol. 24 (1988), pp. 25–27.

7. It is quite possible for a community to shift from one paradigm to another or for several paradigms to exist simultaneously in a community. Howland Sanks, for example, in *Authority in the Church*, argues that the Roman Catholic Church is currently in the midst of a conflict between a hierarchical, authoritarian paradigm of the *magisterium* and one that is more participatory, collegial, open to the sense of the faithful, and tolerant of dissent.

8. Edward Farley, *Theologia: The Fragmentation and Unity of Theological Education* (Philadelphia: Fortress Press, 1983).

9. Edward Farley, "Theology and Practice Outside the Clerical Paradigm," in *Practical Theology: The Emerging Field in Theology, Church, and World*, ed. D. Browning (San Francisco: Harper & Row, 1983), pp. 21–41.

10. Farley, *Theologia*, ch. 2.

11. Ibid., p. 31.

12. Ibid., ch. 7.

13. Edward Farley has traced the history of practical theology in conjunction with his work on the theological encyclopedia, and I will be following the basic movements he outlines in this section and adding my own understanding of the recent history of practical theology that Farley omits. See "Interpreting Situations: An Inquiry Into the Nature of Practical Theology," *Formation and Reflection: The Promise of Practical Theology*, ed. Lewis Mudge and James Poling (Philadelphia: Fortress Press, 1987), pp. 1–26.

14. H. Richard Niebuhr, *Radical Monotheism and Western Culture* (New York: Harper & Row, 1943), pp. 115–116.

15. See John Leith's introduction to *The Christian Life*, which is

composed of excerpts of Calvin's *Institutes* (San Francisco: Harper & Row, 1984), p. vii.

16. For example, contrast the way that practical theology is used in these two books: Dennis McCann and Charles Strain, *Polity and Praxis: A Program for American Practical Theology* (Minneapolis: Winston Press, 1985), and Charles Gerkin, *Widening the Horizons: Pastoral Responses to a Fragmented Society* (Philadelphia: Westminster Press, 1986).

17. In administering the sacrament of penance the priest needed to employ some sort of criteria by which he could categorize the various sinful acts he was hearing in confession. Manuals began to appear that assisted in judging the seriousness of particular sins and the kind of penitential acts that should be undertaken. See James Gustafson, *Protestant and Roman Catholic Ethics: Prospects for Rapprochement* (Chicago: University of Chicago Press, 1978), ch. 1. This is indicative of a much broader function of moral theology in Roman Catholicism. It is closely related to the church's magisterial teaching authority by which the hierarchy formulates official moral teachings to guide congregations and individuals.

18. The emphasis of the English Puritans on praxis grows out of the work of Peter Ramus, who defines theology as a form of praxis that can lead persons toward eternal fellowship with God. See Richard Muller, *Post-Reformation Reformed Dogmatics*, vol. 1 (Grand Rapids: Baker Book House, 1987), p. 78.

19. William Ames, *The Marrow of Theology*, tr. John Eusden (Philadelphia: United Church Press, 1968), p. 77.

20. Ibid., p. 78.

21. Ibid., p. 77.

22. William Perkins, *A Discourse of Conscience*, first published 1596. This text is from the second edition, published in 1608, reprinted in *William Perkins, 1558–1602: English Puritanist*, ed. Thomas Merrill (Nieuwkoop, Netherlands: B. DeGraaf, 1966), p. 5.

23. Ibid.

24. Ibid., p. 6.

25. Farley, "Interpreting Situations" (cited in note 13), p. 2.

26. This is translated in part in *Reformed Dogmatics: Seventeenth-Century Reformed Theology Through the Writings of Wollebius, Voetius, and Turretin*, ed. and tr. John Beardslee (Grand Rapids: Baker Book House, 1965), pp. 265–334.

27. Ibid., pp. 266–267.

28. Ibid., p. 265.

29. Ibid.

30. See Farley's brief discussion of this in "Interpreting Situations," p. 19, note 5.

31. Friedrich Schleiermacher, *Brief Outline on the Study of Theol-*

ogy, tr. T. Tice (Richmond: John Knox Press, 1966); *Christian Caring: Selections from Practical Theology*, ed. J. Duke and H. Stone, tr. J. Duke (Philadelphia: Fortress Press, 1988).

32. This quote comes from *Christian Caring*, p. 86.

33. Ibid., p. 98.

34. Ibid., p. 106. At one point he describes his understanding of practical theology in terms of the contrast between the fine arts and the mechanical arts, drawing on the former to describe the artistry of ministry that is guided by practical theology.

35. Schleiermacher uses the term "rules of art" in a variety of places. See, for example, *Brief Outline*, p. 93, paragraph 265.

36. Schleiermacher, *Christian Caring*, p. 106.

37. Ibid., p. 113.

38. Edward Farley's view that Schleiermacher is the father of the "clerical paradigm" is only partially correct. Throughout his lectures on practical theology, Schleiermacher defined it in terms of the "principle of inequality" that has existed in the church from the beginning between those who are more active and lead and those who are more passive and are led. It is the leadership function, not clergy per se, that undergirds his understanding of practical theology; see "Interpreting Situations," pp. 92ff. In the course of history, however, Schleiermacher's defense of theology's place in the university, in terms of its role in the education of clergy, did contribute to the clerical paradigm as Farley suggests. See Farley, "Theology and Practice Outside the Clerical Paradigm" (cited in note 9), pp. 21–41.

39. As Schleiermacher puts it in *Christian Caring*, p. 66, "As Protestant ministers we should assume that members of the congregation are spiritually free and independent. Yet we should seek to promote their freedom and independence as we seek to meet the demands that each of them places upon us. The rule, then, would be that whenever such demands are made, the occasion should be used to increase the spiritual freedom of the member of the congregation and to lead him or her to such clarity that the demand will no longer arise."

40. Ibid., p. 110; *Brief Outline*, pp. 92–93.

41. Karl Hagenbach, who taught at Basel in the mid 1800s, defines practical theology as follows: "Practical theology embraces the theory of Church activities or functions, whether they be exercised by the Church as a whole or by individual members and representative persons acting for the church. . . . Its immediate sphere of action, however, is that of art—that is, of action emanating from known laws." Quoted in George Crooks and John Hurst, *Theological Encyclopedia and Methodology on the Basis of Hagenbach* (New York: Phillips & Hunt, 1884), p. 472. He goes on to describe it as

the sort of theoretical reflection which serves as a "guide to practice." It "transmutes" the findings of the other theological disciplines into action. It is scientific in that "it will not rest satisfied with mere routine, but demands, and makes possible, a regulated action in behalf of the Church and in harmony with its spirit." It is a "theory of art," however, in that it informs the practice of ministry in its particularity.

42. Philip Schaff, *Theological Propaedeutic: A General Introduction to the Study of Theology—Exegetical, Historical, Systematic, and Practical, Including Encyclopedia, Methodology, and Bibliography: A Manual for Students* (New York: Charles Scribner's Sons, 1893), p. 448.

43. Ibid.

44. Ibid., p. 449.

45. In a sense, Schaff's importation of a more Germanic understanding of practical theology (and theology as a whole) was indicative of a much broader movement among theologians that was taking place during the mid-1800s. See Robert Wood Lynn, "Notes Toward a History: Theological Encyclopedia and the Evolution of Protestant Seminary Curriculum, 1808–1968," *Theological Education*, vol. 17, no. 2 (spring 1981), pp. 118–144. As the most promising young American theologians began to study in Halle and Berlin, they would come back highly critical of American theological schools. They pressed for the adoption of the fourfold pattern of the theological encyclopedia that was in ascendancy in Germany, in hopes that greater specialization in the theological faculty would allow American theologians to make more important contributions to an international exchange of ideas in each of the theological sciences. It is during this period that "practical theology" began to appear in the seminary curricula for the first time. When it did appear, it was along the lines of Schaff's definition, which was indebted to Schleiermacher's work in many important ways.

46. Hagenbach, for example, focuses pastoral theology on the cure of souls; see Crooks and Hurst, *Theological Encyclopedia*, pp. 544–545. Alexandre Vinet substitutes pastoral theology for practical theology in *Pastoral Theology; or the Theory of the Evangelical Ministry*, ed. and tr. T. Skinner (New York: Harper & Brothers, 1853). Alfred Cave does the same thing; see *An Introduction to Theology: Its Principles, Its Branches, Its Results, and Its Literature*, 2nd ed. (Edinburgh: T. & T. Clark, 1896).

47. Schleiermacher, *Brief Outline*, p. 92.

48. Ibid., p. 93. On this page and the one preceding it, Schleiermacher distinguishes the knowledge that the first two branches of theology generate from the rules of art of practical theology by which they are applied. Also see pp. 96–98.

49. Of seminal importance in the pastoral care and counseling movement and the redefinition of pastoral theology is Seward Hiltner's book *Preface to Pastoral Theology* (Nashville: Abingdon Press, 1958). Hiltner raises the question of the distinctive nature of pastoral theology and the unique contribution it has to make to the other theological disciplines. For other perspectives on this movement, see: Allison Stokes, *Ministry After Freud* (New York: Pilgrim Press, 1985); Edward Thornton, *Professional Education for Ministry* (Nashville: Abingdon Press, 1970); E. Brooks Holifield, *A History of Pastoral Care in America: From Salvation to Self-Realization* (Nashville: Abingdon Press, 1983); Charles Gerkin, *The Living Human Document: Revisioning Pastoral Counseling in a Hermeneutical Mode* (Nashville: Abingdon Press, 1984); and *The New Shape of Pastoral Theology: Essays in Honor of Seward Hiltner*, ed. W. Oglesby (Nashville: Abingdon Press, 1969).

50. I have discussed the entirety of Coe's thought in much greater detail in my dissertation, "Practical Theology and Christian Education," vol. 1, ch. 2, in *Christian Education in Crisis: An Historical Examination of John Dewey, George Albert Coe, H. Shelton Smith, and James Smart*, Emory University, 1985, unpublished.

51. Coe was one of a number of brilliant young scholars who had the opportunity to study in Germany during the early part of his career, so he would have had ample opportunity to be exposed to the fourfold pattern of theological education.

52. This is clear in Coe's use of the norm "the democracy of God" in *A Social Theory of Religious Education* (New York: Charles Scribner's Sons, 1927). This norm grew out of his appropriation of the social gospel movement's understanding of the kingdom of God and John Dewey's understanding of democracy and education.

53. The following interpretation of Smart is spelled out in greater detail in ch. 3 of my dissertation (see note 50, above).

54. Barth sets forth the basic divisions of theology as biblical or exegetical theology, ecclesiastical and dogmatic history, systematic theology or dogmatics, and practical theology; see *Church Dogmatics* IV/3, II, tr. G. W. Bromiley (Edinburgh: T. & T. Clark, 1962), pp. 879–880. Thurneysen sets forth these basic divisions: historical theology (including exegesis and church history), systematic theology, and practical theology; see *A Theology of Pastoral Care*, tr. J. Worthington and T. Wiser (Richmond: John Knox Press, 1962), pp. 11–12.

55. James Smart, *The Rebirth of Ministry* (Philadelphia: Westminster Press, 1960), p. 135.

56. Ibid.

57. James Smart, *The Teaching Ministry of the Church: An Examination of the Basic Principles of Christian Education* (Philadelphia: Westminster Press, 1954), p. 38.

58. Clearly, this deductive style of reflection in Smart's practical theology is in part a function of the Barthian suspicion of experience he has internalized. It is by no means clear, however, that higher-level theological norms could not interact with ongoing experience in a more dialectical fashion within a Barthian framework. Experience would not serve as a source of theology or a substitute for revelation, but it would be granted a place in the living dialogue of word and context. Barth's own ethics seems to point in this contextualist direction.

59. See chapter 3.

60. This discussion of professions is influenced by James Luther Adams. See "The Social Import of the Professions" in *Voluntary Associations: Sociocultural Analyses and Theological Interpretation*, ed. Ronald Engel (Chicago: Exploration Press, 1986), pp. 261–277.

61. Here I am drawing on the thought of H. Richard Niebuhr and James Fowler. Both men describe faith as a universal that is an inherent dimension of human life. See Niebuhr's *Radical Monotheism in Western Culture* (New York: Harper & Row, 1960), chs. 1 and 2 and ch. 3 of the supplementary essays. Also see Fowler's *Stages of Faith: The Psychology of Human Development and the Quest for Meaning* (San Francisco: Harper & Row, 1981), Part 1.

62. Niebuhr's essay "The Center of Value" in *Radical Monotheism* explores this issue.

63. John Dewey, *Experience and Nature* (Chicago: Open Court, 1925), chs. 2–3.

64. What I have in mind here is closely related to John Dewey's understanding of what it is to have *an* experience. See Dewey, *Art as Experience* (New York: Minton Balch & Co., 1934; reprint, G. P. Putnam's Sons, 1958), ch. 3. We have *an* experience only when "it is integrated with and demarcated in the general stream of experience from other experiences," p. 35. That is, it stands out from the flow of everyday life, with "its own plot, its own inception and movement toward its close," pp. 35–36.

65. Michael Polanyi, *The Tacit Dimension* (Garden City, N.Y.: Doubleday & Co., 1967). In a similar fashion, Alfred Schutz has described the knowing involved in our participation in everyday reality; see *On Phenomenology and Social Relations*, ed. H. Wagner (Chicago: University of Chicago Press, 1970), and *The Phenomenology of the Social World*, tr. George Walsh and Frederick Lehnert (Chicago: Northwestern University Press, 1967). More than Polanyi, however, Schutz called attention to the social basis of our tacit knowing. The communities of which we are members prestructure our experience by offering us patterns of language that are linked to routinized forms of action.

66. Schön describes this sort of process as a "reflective conversa-

tion" in which thought is seen as speaking to and hearing the "talk back" of the situation as it develops. See Donald A. Schön, *The Reflective Practitioner: How Professionals Think in Action* (New York: Basic Books, 1983), ch. 3.

67. Dewey referred to this as problem-definition.

68. E. Wanner, *On Remembering, Forgetting, and Understanding Sentences* (The Hague: Mouton, 1974); J. R. Barclay, J. D. Bransford, and J. J. Franks, "Sentence Memory: A Constructive vs. Interpretive Approach," *Cognitive Psychology*, vol. 3 (1972), pp. 193–209.

69. E. Rosch, "Human Categorization," in *Advances in Cross-Cultural Psychology*, ed. N. Warren, vol. 1 (London: Academic Press, 1977); "On the Internal Structure of Perceptual and Semantic Categories," in *Cognitive Development and the Acquisition of Language*, ed. Timothy E. Moore (New York: Academic Press, 1973).

70. See this facet of moral discernment as described by James Gustafson in *Ethics from a Theocentric Perspective: Ethics and Theology*, vol. 1 (Chicago: University of Chicago Press, 1984), ch. 7.

71. Schön, *Reflective Practitioner*, pp. 307–325.

72. I am drawing on James Gustafson at this point. See *Theocentric Ethics*, vol. 2, pp. 12–21.

73. See Donald Browning, *Religious Ethics and Pastoral Care* (Philadelphia: Fortress Press, 1983); "Pastoral Theology in a Pluralistic Age," in *Practical Theology*, pp. 187–202; and "Practical Theology and Religious Education," in *Formation and Reflection*.

74. In *Religious Ethics*, ch. 6, Browning identifies five levels that are at stake in all practical moral reasoning. The last two of these levels, in particular, are sensitive to the situationality inherent in practical theological reflection.

75. See Gerkin's writings cited in chapter 1, note 2.

76. Gerkin, *Widening the Horizons*, pp. 20, 54–58. Gerkin notes that "my understanding is that humans tend to make what may be seen externally as moral decisions more on the basis of characteristic modes of interpretation of what is going on in their narratively constructed world than on grounds of what can legitimately be called 'moral reasoning,' even though moral reasoning may at times be involved" (p. 130).

77. Many of James Gustafson's writings have already been cited in this book. See, particularly, *Ethics from a Theocentric Perspective*, vols. 1 and 2 (cited in note 70). See also *Can Ethics Be Christian?* (Chicago: University of Chicago Press, 1975), *Christ and the Moral Life* (Chicago: University of Chicago Press, 1968), and *Theology and Christian Ethics* (Philadelphia: Pilgrim Press, 1974).

78. Gustafson, *Can Ethics Be Christian?*, pp. 148–149, 154.

79. Gustafson, *Theocentric Ethics*, vol. 2, p. 13.

80. Ibid., p. 1.

81. Ibid., p. 17.

82. John Dewey, *How We Think: A Restatement of the Relation of Reflective Thinking to the Educative Process* (Lexington, Mass.: D. C. Heath & Co., 1933), Part 2, and *Reconstruction in Philosophy* (Boston: Beacon Press, 1920), chs. 4 and 6.

83. Schön, *Reflective Practitioner* (cited in note 66), pp. 151, 163–164.

Chapter 9: Centers of Authority: A Contemporary Proposal

1. In recent Roman Catholic thought, this has been defined as the supernatural gift of the Holy Spirit by which the faithful are able to discern and cling to the truth that has been delivered to the church and maintained by its leaders. Within the Catholic Church the authority granted this dimension of church life has been a matter of debate. At various points, it has been viewed primarily in passive terms as the activity by which the faithful give assent to official church teaching. If they truly have faith, they will recognize the truth of the teachings of the *magisterium* and give assent to them. At other points, it has been granted a stronger role in the development of the normative beliefs and practices of the church and in the reception of official teaching. The latter was given classic expression by Cardinal John H. Newman's *On Consulting the Faithful in Matters of Doctrine*, ed. J. Coulson (Kansas City, Mo.: Sheed & Ward, 1961; originally published in the *Rambler*, July 1859). Newman argues that the leaders of the church cannot isolate themselves from the faithful in the definition of doctrine. The faithful also have a role in the "reception" of doctrine, its universal acceptance throughout the church. Yves Congar's work in this area has been especially important; see "Reception as an Ecclesiological Reality," *Concilium* 7/8 (Sept. 1972), pp. 43–68.

2. Luther frequently uses the expression "communion of saints" to describe the church in order to call attention to the important role that the concrete fellowship of believers plays in the life of faith.

3. James Hopewell, *Congregation: Stories and Structures*, ed. B. Wheeler (Philadelphia: Fortress Press, 1987); *Handbook of Congregational Studies*, ed. J. Carroll, C. Dudley, and W. McKinney (Nashville: Abingdon Press, 1986); Denham Grierson, *Transforming a People of God* (Melbourne, Australia: Joint Board of Christian Education of Australia and New Zealand, 1984).

4. Grierson's work just cited makes extensive use of these categories.

5. Hopewell, *Congregation*, part 1; Charles Gerkin, *Widening the*

Horizons: Pastoral Responses to a Fragmented Society (Philadelphia: Westminster Press, 1986), chs. 2–3.

6. Here I am recalling the seed imagery of Calvin as discussed earlier. The phrase "living dialogue" is from Thomas Torrance. See the Introduction of *The School of Faith: The Catechisms of the Reformed Churches* (London: Clarke & Co., 1959).

7. See the work of C. Ellis Nelson and John Westerhoff (cited in chapter 4, note 4), and Denham Grierson (cited in this chapter in note 3).

8. It is important to point out that I am assuming a difference here between education, teaching, and socialization.

9. For a review of some of these Bible study programs, see my article "The Study of Scripture in the Congregation: Old Problems and New Programs," *Interpretation*, vol. 62 (July 1988), pp. 254–267.

10. As Gerhard Forde points out, the one possible exception to this is the use of infallibility to refer to scripture. See "Infallibility Language and the Early Lutheran Tradition," in *Teaching Authority and Infallibility in the Church*, ed. Paul Empie, T. Austin Murphy, and Joseph Burgess (Minneapolis: Augsburg Publishing House, 1980).

11. *The Constitution of the Presbyterian Church (U.S.A.); Part II, Book of Order*, G-2.0100.

12. See the Preface to *The Book of Concord: The Confessions of the Evangelical Lutheran Church*, ed. and tr. T. Tappert (Philadelphia: Muhlenberg Press, 1959).

13. Thomas Oden, *Doctrinal Standards in the Wesleyan Tradition* (Grand Rapids: Francis Asbury Press, 1988).

14. *The Book of Discipline of the United Methodist Church, 1984* (Nashville: United Methodist Publishing House), p. 25.

15. Ibid., p. 41.

16. *Book of Order*, G-18.0200.

17. *UMC Discipline*, p. 41.

18. *Book of Order*, G-14.0305.

19. Ibid., G-14.0207, G-14.0405.

20. *UMC Discipline*, p. 212.

21. John Cobb has made a proposal that is similar to this in "Authority and Theology in Ecumenical Protestantism," *Theological Education*, vol. 19 (spring 1983), pp. 23–24.

22. Glenn Olsen, "The Theologian and the *Magisterium:* The Ancient and Medieval Background of a Contemporary Controversy," *Communio*, vol. 7 (winter 1980), pp. 292–319; Yves Congar, "Theologians and the *Magisterium* in the West: From the Gregorian Reform to the Council of Trent," *Chicago Studies*, vol. 17, no. 2 (summer 1978), pp. 210–223.

23. For insight into recent discussion of this debate, see Raymond Brown, "The Dilemma of the *Magisterium* vs. the Theologians—Debunking Some Fictions," *Chicago Studies*, vol. 17, no. 2 (summer 1978), pp. 290–307; *Moral Theology No. 3: The Magisterium and Morality*, ed. Charles Curran and Richard McCormick (New York: Paulist Press, 1982); Avery Dulles, *The Survival of Dogma* (New York: Crossroad Publishing Co., 1971).

24. Throughout this section I have been using the term "professional theologians" to refer to those who teach or write theology with a scholarly competence that is based on extensive specialized education. I am unwilling, however, to view only this group as carrying out the theological task. Hence the qualifier "professional" is added when referring to those carrying out scholarly theological inquiry.

25. H. Richard Niebuhr, *The Purpose of the Church and Its Ministry: Reflections on the Aims of Theological Education* (New York: Harper & Row, 1956), p. 110.

26. Niebuhr puts this as follows (ibid., p. 108): "Of course, the theological school is not the Church in its wholeness. It is not even the intellect of the Church; as an intellectual center it is a member of the body. While intellectual activity is as widely diffused throughout the whole Church as are activities of worship and of compassion, there are also centers or occasions of special intellectual activity in it as there are centers or occasions of special adoration and charity."

27. Ibid., p. 114.

28. Throughout his description of these two functions, Niebuhr uses the *analogy* of the differences between "pure" and "applied" science to explain what he means. This is a somewhat problematic distinction if taken literally, as Niebuhr did not. The point he is making is essentially valid. In the first function, truth is pursued for truth's sake. In the second function, it is pursued for the sake of some practical effect in the life of the church. Niebuhr was quite clear that this does not mean that theology is speculative in the medieval sense. His thinking is basically Calvinist in this regard: All knowledge of God is knowledge of God in relation to self and humanity. See ibid., p. 113.

29. It is unclear, thus, that the role of seminaries and professional theologians in the teaching office can be distinguished as sharply as they frequently are in contemporary Roman Catholic thought, in which a contrast between the "conservative" function of the pastoral *magisterium* and the reinterpretive, scholarly function of theologians is posited. In the absence of centralized offices and agencies like the pope and bishops with a high degree of teaching authority, seminaries and theologians must hand on and conserve the faith just as much as they must reinterpret it.

30. Donald A. Schön, *The Reflective Practitioner: How Profession-als Think in Action* (New York: Basic Books, 1983), chs. 1–2.

31. One of the best examples is John Cobb and Joseph Hough's book, *Christian Identity and Theological Education* (Chico, Calif.: Scholars Press, 1985).

32. As Farley puts it, "The most general feature of church leader-ship is the facilitation of *theologia* itself"; see his *Theologia: The Fragmentation and Unity of Theological Education* (Philadelphia: Fortress Press, 1983), p. 170. Robert Lynn provides an excellent overview of the way that the fourfold pattern of the theological encyclopedia has structured theological education in this country. See Robert Wood Lynn, "Notes Toward a History: Theological En-cyclopedia and the Evolution of Protestant Seminary Curriculum, 1808–1968," *Theological Education*, vol. 17, no. 2 (spring 1981), pp. 118–144.

33. Cobb and Hough say that "it is crucial that the seminaries organize themselves so as to make a maximum contribution to the development of practical theologians." See Cobb and Hough, *Chris-tian Identity*, p. 95.

Chapter 10: Congregational Education and Nurture

1. In recent years, the term "Christian education" has been virtu-ally synonymous with congregational education. Even persons with markedly different approaches to Christian education have focused their attention on the local church and its teaching ministry. While John Westerhoff and Sara Little, for example, differ in their evalua-tion of intentional contexts of teaching and learning, both view Christian education in terms of the congregation.

2. Frequently, this is an ideal community, which will be realized only partially in reality. John Dewey's theory of education, for ex-ample, was predicated on his concept of a democratic society; *see Democracy and Education* (New York: Free Press, 1916). In a similar fashion, the church projects understandings of ideal communal life that characterize the congregation, the wider social order, and ulti-mately the kingdom of God.

3. The role of the imagination is addressed, for example, in the following two books: Craig Dykstra, *Vision and Character: A Chris-tian Educator's Alternative to Kohlberg* (New York: Paulist Press, 1981), and Maria Harris, *Teaching and Religious Imagination: An Essay in the Theology of Teaching* (San Francisco: Harper & Row, 1987). The role of justice and liberation is found in a number of books: Brian Wren, *Education for Justice: Pedagogical Principles* (Maryknoll, N.Y.: Orbis Books, 1977); *Education for Peace and Jus-tice*, ed. Padric O'Hare (San Francisco: Harper & Row, 1983); Die-

ter Hessel, *A Social Action Primer* (Philadelphia: Westminster Press, 1972); and Kenneth Barker, *Religious Education, Catechesis, and Freedom* (Birmingham, Ala.: Religious Education Press, 1981). The role of the religious affections has not been addressed as directly, but see Don Saliers's two books: *The Soul in Paraphrase: Prayer and the Religious Affections* (New York: Seabury Press, 1980) and *Worship and Spirituality* (Philadelphia: Westminster Press, 1984).

4. Ian Barbour's *Myths, Models, and Paradigms: A Comparative Study in Science and Religion* (New York: Harper & Row, 1974) provides an excellent introduction to this literature.

5. See, for example, Maria Harris's excellent essay, "Completion and Faith Development," in *Faith Development and Fowler*, ed. Craig Dykstra and Sharon Parks (Birmingham, Ala.: Religious Education Press, 1986).

6. Thomas Groome's book, *Christian Religious Education: Sharing Our Story and Vision* (San Francisco: Harper & Row, 1980), is an excellent example of the new focus on praxis epistemologies in Christian education.

7. See my article "Appraising Fowler's Work: Natural Piety and the Pattern of Grace," forthcoming in *Religious Education*.

8. John Westerhoff, for example, in *Will Our Children Have Faith?* (New York: Seabury Press, 1976), draws the contrast in an overly strong manner.

9. James Fowler, *Faith Development and Pastoral Care* (Philadelphia: Fortress Press, 1987), p. 81. Elsewhere in the same book (p. 95), he writes in a similar fashion, "I also cautioned against making development an end in itself or seeing movement from one stage to another as something that can be accelerated or pushed."

10. In the realm of education, David Elkind has been particularly critical of recent attempts to accelerate children's reading skills by pushing them down to an earlier and earlier age; see *The Hurried Child: Growing Up Too Fast, Too Soon* (Reading, Mass.: Addison-Wesley, 1981) and *All Grown Up and No Place to Go: Teenagers in Crisis* (Reading, Mass.: Addison-Wesley, 1984). Kieran Egan also points out the need to develop the capacities of a stage in its fullness and not to push children to move to the next stage as quickly as possible, in *Educational Development* (New York: Oxford University Press, 1979).

11. Among the many books dealing with education from a moral development perspective, the following are especially good overviews: *Readings in Moral Education*, ed. Peter Scharf (Minneapolis: Winston Press, 1978), and *Moral Development, Moral Education, and Kohlberg: Basic Issues in Philosophy, Psychology, Religion, and Education*, ed. Brenda Munsey (Birmingham, Ala.: Religious Education Press, 1980).

12. Fowler, *Faith Development,* p. 96.

13. An example of the growth/anxiety nature of these moments of separation and individuation is the phenomenon commonly referred to as "stranger anxiety." Sometime between six and nine months, many infants suddenly become very anxious in the presence of strangers.

14. Margaret S. Mahler, Fred Pine, and Annie Bergman, *The Psychological Birth of the Human Infant* (New York: Basic Books, 1975).

15. Attachment is the feeling of security and closeness that an infant invests in the caretaker. A wide range of research has shown a direct relationship between strength of attachment and later independence. To the extent that the infant internalizes the sense of security that healthy attachment provides, he or she will have more confidence to explore the world, peer relations, and so forth. As Ainsworth and Bell discovered, mothers who are responsive in their feeding during the first three months are far more likely to have a one-year-old who is securely attached; see Mary Ainsworth and S. M. Bell, "Some Contemporary Patterns of Mother-Infant Interaction in the Feeding Situation," in *Stimulation in Early Infancy,* ed. A. Amrose (New York: Academic Press, 1969). Other research has shown the close relationship between attachment and independence. Toddlers who were strongly attached at fifteen months were far more likely to interact well with their peers during their nursery school years; see E. Water, J. Wippman, and L. A. Stroufe, "Attachment, Positive Affect, and Competence in the Peer Group," *Child Development,* vol. 50 (1979), pp. 821–830.

16. Working out of an object-relations psychoanalytic framework, Anna Maria Rizzuto has done fascinating research in this area; see *Birth of the Living God* (Chicago: University of Chicago Press, 1979).

17. Thomas Lickona, *Raising Good Children: Helping Your Child Through the Stages of Moral Development—From Birth Through the Teenage Years* (New York: Bantam Books, 1983), pp. 46–52.

18. In describing the stages, I will give rough estimates of the ages at which they typically appear in American culture. The stages are not age-specific, however. Unlike some developmental theories that link age and stage closely (e.g., that of Daniel Levinson), the structural developmental tradition does not do so. Cross-cultural research in cognitive and moral development, moreover, has indicated that the shift from one stage to another varies in different cultural settings.

19. Robert Selman, *The Growth of Interpersonal Understanding* (New York: Academic Press, 1980).

20. The deep and long-lasting importance of the metaphorical images of God that are formed during this stage of faith is under-

scored by research conducted by Andrew Greeley on Roman Catholics who left the church for a period of time. The single most important variable in differentiating those who eventually returned to the church from those who did not was the kind of image formed during their childhood stage of faith. Those who had "warm" images of God—images of God as nurturing, accepting, close, loving— were likely to return. Those whose images were "cold"—distant, harsh, judgmental, moralistic—were not. In light of the mainline Protestant churches' difficulty in holding on to their youth and young adults, this should provide strong encouragement for them to pay more attention to the sorts of images that are being formed in their children during this stage of faith. See Andrew Greeley, *The Religious Imagination* (New York: W. H. Sadlier, 1981).

21. There are exceptions to this general statement, of course. Some children find their way to church in spite of their parents' complete lack of faith and begin to form an understanding of God through their experiences there. This is quite rare during the preschool years, however.

22. Dorothy Jean Furnish's book, *Living the Bible with Children* (Nashville: Abingdon Press, 1979), for example, provides many helpful illustrations of the ways that experientially oriented methods of drama, storytelling, and dance can be used to present biblical material.

23. Egan, *Educational Development*, pp. 11–16.

24. Patricia Griggs, *Using Storytelling in Christian Education* (Nashville: Abingdon Press, 1981).

25. David and Elizabeth Gray describe a number of different ways that the flow of everyday life and the changing seasons of the Christian year can be ritualized for children, in *Children of Joy: Raising Your Own Home-Grown Christians: A Parent's Guide to the First Dozen Years* (Branford, Conn.: Readers Press, 1975). The examples that follow are taken from this book.

26. Lickona offers a helpful list in *Raising Good Children*, Appendix D.

27. Ibid., ch. 1.

28. Ibid., pp. 124–125.

29. Ibid., p. 126.

30. Egan's discussion of this is particularly helpful; see *Educational Development*, pp. 28–30.

31. Lawrence Kohlberg, "Moral Stages and Moralization," in *Moral Development and Behavior*, ed. T. Lickona (New York: Holt, Rinehart & Winston, 1976).

32. Mircea Eliade, *The Sacred and the Profane: The Nature of Religion*, tr. W. Trask (New York: Harvest Books, 1959); *Myth and Reality*, tr. W. Trask (New York: Harper & Row, 1963); *Cosmos and*

History: The Myth of the Eternal Return, tr. W. Trask (New York: Harper & Row, 1959). See also Victor Turner, *The Ritual Process: Structure and Anti-Structure* (Ithaca, N.Y.: Cornell University Press, 1969).

33. While there are real differences between how myths function in relatively closed societies with little sense of historical time and those in which life events are seen as unique and irreversible, there are mythic dimensions to virtually every community. Even highly secularized communities still need an overarching narrative by which they hold up their highest ideals and define social reality, as Durkheim, MacIntyre, and others have pointed out. In the absence of such a community-forming myth, some secularized version typically emerges to fill this function—often of a totalitarian nature. See Emile Durkheim, *On Morality and Society*, ed. Robert Bellah (Chicago: University of Chicago Press, 1973), and *The Elementary Forms of the Religious Life* (New York: Free Press, 1965); and Alasdair MacIntyre, *After Virtue: A Study in Moral Theory* (Notre Dame, Ind.: University of Notre Dame Press, 1981).

34. In a very real sense, much contemporary religion has fallen behind so-called "primitive" societies in its ability to articulate the story by which the religious community is bound together and the external world is named.

35. One especially helpful book in this regard is John Westerhoff and William Willimon's *Liturgy and Learning Through the Life Cycle* (New York: Seabury Press, 1980).

36. Lewis and Helen Sherrill wrote a remarkable manual for communicant classes that illustrates the combination of narrative and beliefs that could be worked toward: *Becoming a Christian: A Manual for Communicant Classes* (Richmond: John Knox Press, 1943). The first chapter, for example, tells the story of Jesus in a manner ideally suited for mythic literal faith: a clear story line set in the real world that is filled with persons with whom the reader can identify. The reader is explicitly asked to identify with the story and grapple personally with what it means to be a follower of Jesus. The chapter concludes with summary statements of what Jesus expected of his followers that approach a definitional statement of what faith is. The manual uses the story form throughout, focusing most of its attention on contemporary settings. A modern-day catechism would do well to stay close to the biblical story and the basic beliefs that emerge out of it.

37. Lickona's discussion of this is an insightful beginning point for parents to reflect on the special role of religious values in parenting; see *Raising Good Children*, p. 152.

38. See Sharon Parks's book *The Critical Years: The Young Adult Search for a Faith to Live By* (San Francisco: Harper & Row, 1986)

39. "Significant others" are persons with whom an individual identifies to the point that those persons influence the values and beliefs the individual holds. "Primary reference groups" are groups whose generalized others (social norms) are internalized by the individual, who looks to the group in making decisions. Obviously, every individual is not a significant other, nor is every group with which the person interacts a primary reference group.

40. This runs against the conventional wisdom that emerged out of the 1960s, in which youth was seen as a time of major individuation and rebellion. A faith development perspective, in contrast, views this period as a time that is conformist in the sense that authority is still external. As Carol Gilligan and Lawrence Kohlberg pointed out many years ago in a joint article, most adolescents cannot be said to experience an identity crisis in the sense of genuine individuation; see their "The Adolescent as a Philosopher: The Discovery of the Self in a Post-Conventional World," *Daedalus*, vol. 100 (1971), pp. 1051–1086.

41. This is not easy to achieve, but there are concrete steps that youth group leaders can undertake to teach young people how to accept one another in spite of their differences. Barbara Varenhorst's *Real Friends*, for example, outlines a program for peer counseling that could easily be adapted to church youth groups; see Barbara Varenhorst, *Real Friends: Becoming the Friend You'd Like to Have* (San Francisco: Harper & Row, 1983). It teaches young people how to reach out to those who do not fit in easily at school or are having special difficulties. In a congregational context, the program could be modified to focus on teaching the older members of the group to reach out to and include the younger or newer members. The communication and interpersonal skills involved in this kind of program could be taught to every member of the youth group when he or she reached a certain age: the second semester of the junior year, for example. An explicit vision of the congregation as a caring community could be taught as a part of the program, with special emphasis on the ways that Christ breaks down barriers between Greek and Jew, slave and free, male and female, and continues to break down barriers today.

42. Charles Shelton, S.J., *Adolescent Spirituality: Pastoral Ministry for High School and College Youth* (Chicago: Loyola University Press, 1983).

43. Roberta Hestenes provides many helpful methods and an overview of the general dynamics of small-group life; see *Using the Bible in Groups* (Philadelphia: Westminster Press, 1983).

44. The term "politicization" is Michael Warren's. He advocates a form of youth ministry that is both relational and political; see *Youth and the Future of the Church* (New York: Seabury Press, 1982), ch. 9,

and *Youth, Gospel, Liberation* (San Francisco: Harper & Row, 1987). Thomas Groome's widely influential shared praxis approach is designed to assist persons in critically appropriating the Christian faith and bringing it into dialogue with contemporary human experience; see his *Christian Religious Education* (cited in note 6)

45. Warren, for example, describes an educational process which he has used to help young people become more aware of the messages that their music is communicating to them about human sexuality, the role of women, and male-female relationships; see Warren, *Youth and the Future of the Church*, ch. 7 Young people are supported in their ability to "speak to the songs,' self-consciously choosing what they will accept and reject in the music that they listen to.

46. Groome gives explicit attention to this in the third step of his shared praxis approach.

47. Jaroslav Pelikan, *The Vindication of Tradition* (New Haven, Conn.: Yale University Press, 1984), p. 65.

48. Egan, *Educational Development*, ch. 4 (cited in note 10)

Index

adiaphora, 93–95, 104
Ames, Wilham, 149
Aquinas, Thomas, 79

Barth, Karl, 45, 159
Baxter, Richard, 149
Bellah, Robert, 31
Berger, Peter, 28, 38
Braaten, Carl, 105
Brown, Raymond, 69, 71
Browning, Don, 170–171
Bucer, Martin, 124

Calvin, John
  Academy of Geneva,
    123–128
  as basis of contemporary
    teaching office, 128–134
  catechetical instruction,
    128–134
  church authority, 112–114
  church as teacher, 115–116
  conversion, 52–53
  on councils, 118–119
  divine accommodation, 111,
    112–114
  education, 120–123
  and humanism, 120–128
  ordained ministers, 116–118
  and piety, 50

and sin, 108
and teachable spirit, 52–58
word and Spirit, 108–112
catholic, defined, 74–75
Coe, Albert, 157–158
commanding authority, 22
congregation
  in Calvin, 182
  as center of practical
    theology, 181–192
  and education, 212–216
  in Luther, 101–102,
    181–182
conscience, 85–86, 103–104
consensus fidelium, 46, 143–144
Cordier, Mathurin, 121, 124
councils
  in Calvin, 118–119
  in Luther, 98–99
counter-modern
  authoritarianism, 38–40
  and conservative
    Protestantism, 40–45
  and teaching office, 43–44,
    140
Cremin, Lawrence, 48

Dewey, John, 158, 173
Dodd, C. H., 14–15
Dowey, Edward, 111

Dulles, Avery, 80, 82
Durkheim, Emile, 24

education
  in congregations, 187–192,
    212–216
  definition, 19, 188
  developmental principles of,
    219–224
  dimensions of, 213
  ecology of, 48–49
  political nature of, 20
  in representative bodies and
    leaders, 200–201
  role of ordained ministers in,
    210–211
  in seminaries, 206–207
  as task of teaching office,
    18–19
Egan, Kieran, 221, 229–230,
  232, 249
Elkind, David, 221
Erickson, Erik, 219

faith development, 213–218
  modal level of, 219
Farel, Guillaume, 123–124, 131
Farley, Edward, 145–147, 206
Fowler, James, 169, 213–215,
  221–222, 226, 242

Geertz, Clifford, 25
Gerkin, Charles, 170–171, 183
Gerson, Jean, 87
gospel, 91–93, 177
Gritsch, Eric, 105
Groome, Thomas, 241
Gustafson, James, 171

Hoffman, Martin, 231
Hofmann, Georg, 90
Holy Spirit, 68–70, 85–86
Hopewell, James, 183
Hunt, R. N., 112
Hunter, James Davison, 38, 40

individualism
  expressive, 33
  and modernization, 30,
    36–37
  and teaching office, 31, 140,
    198
  utilitarian, 32–33

Johnson, Robert, 107

Kohlberg, Lawrence, 219, 232
Kuhn, Thomas, 143, 144
Kung, Hans, 81, 82

Lindbeck, George, 82, 105
Little, Sara, 159
Luther, Martin
  as basis of contemporary
    teaching office, 176–178
  as doctor of church, 88
  and papacy, 87–90
  on scripture, 94–96, 110
  and sin, 107–108
  teaching authority, 84–86
  theology of cross, 92–93

magisterium, 73–74, 84, 93–94,
  109, 120, 177, 201
Mahler, Margaret, 224
mainline Protestanism
  and civic faith, 10–11
  declining influence of, 9–10
  disestablishment, 3–4
  membership decline, 6–9
Marsden, George, 41
McKim, Donald, 111
McNeill, John, 97, 98
Mead, George Herbert, 237
Miller, Perry, 50
modernization
  and counter-modern
    authoritarianism, 38–45
  and cultural pluralism, 28–29
  definition, 25–26
  and individualism, 30–31

and rapid social change, 27
and religion, 29–30
and structural pluralism,
    27–28
and teaching office, 141

neo-orthodoxy, 45
Niebuhr, H. Richard, 12, 45,
    147–148, 163, 202–203,
    205, 207, 219
normative beliefs and practices,
    15–17
  in congregations, 184–186
  ordained ministry and,
    208–209
  in representative bodies and
    leaders, 193–197
  in scholarly inquiry, 205

ordained ministers
  in Calvin, 116–118
  in Luther, 102–103
  in teaching office, 207–211,
    253–254

paideia, 16
Parks, Sharon, 237
Pelikan, Jaroslav, 61, 78, 97,
    248
Perkins, William, 149, 150
Piaget, Jean, 219, 220, 226
piety
  Augustianian, 50–52
  definition, 49–50
  and teachability, 52–58
Polanyi, Michael, 165–166
practical theology
  and the Christian life,
    216–218
  and clergy education,
    206–207
  in congregations, 181–192
  definition, 162–163
  history of, 148–161
  parents' role, 230, 236

and situations, 165–167
and social practices, 163–166
stages of, 167–174

Rahner, Karl, 82
reinterpreting beliefs and
    practices, 17–18
  in congregations, 186–187
  in ordained ministry,
    209–210
  in representative bodies and
    leaders, 197–200
  in scholarly inquiry, 204–205
religious education movement,
    63, 157–158

Sanks, Howland, 80
Schaff, Philip, 154–155
Schleiermacher, Friedrich, 149,
    152–155, 156, 159
Schön, Donald, 173
Selman, Robert, 226–227
Smart, James, 14–15, 159–161
social practices, 24–25,
    163–166
stages of faith
  conjunctive, 214, 247–251
  individuative reflective,
    242–247
  intuitive projective, 226–232
  mythic literal, 232–236
  primal, 224–226
  synthetic conventional,
    236–242
  universalizing, 215–216
Stendahl, Krister, 86
Sturm, Johannes, 124
Sunday school movement, 62,
    188
switching, 7–8, 29

teachable spirit, 52–58
teaching, defined, 21, 188
teaching authority, 21–22,
    47–48

teaching authority *(cont.)*
  of apostles, 66–67
  of bishops, 75
  centers of, 178–181
  of Christian congregations,
    181–184
  in Luther, 48–86
  of ordained ministers,
    207–208
  of professional theologians,
    201–202
  of representative bodies and
    leaders, 192–193, 195–196
  theology, 63, 64–65, 135,
    144–147, 159–160,
    202–205
teaching office
  conciliar model, 78–79,
    97–98
  and congregations, 63,
    181–192, 212–216
  definition, 13–14
  and denominationalism,
    142–143, 178
  and early church, 66–67
  and emerging catholicism,
    75–76
  and established pattern of
    church life, 141–142, 178
  fallibilist model, 81

  in Johannine literature,
    68–71
  liberationist model, 81–82
  in Luther, 91–94
  moderate infallibilist model,
    82–83
  monarchical model, 80–81
  in pastoral epistles, 67–68
  and professional theologians,
    201–207
  and Reformers, 176–178
  and representative bodies and
    leaders, 192–201
  and Rome, 76–77
  tasks, 15, 46–47, 63, 115,
    139–140, 181
  twofold model, 79–80, 201
Thomas Aquinas, 79
Thurneysen, Eduard, 159
tradition
  guardians of, 247–248
  in Luther, 99

Voetius, Gisbert, 151–152

Warren, Michael, 241
Weber, Max, 24–26, 39
Wendel, François, 111, 122
Wesley, John, 194
Westerhoff, John 48

LINCOLN CHRISTIAN COLLEGE AND SEMINARY